THE COUNTRY LIFE COLLECTOR'S
POCKET BOOK
OF FURNITURE

THE COUNTRY LIFE COLLECTOR'S
POCKET BOOK
OF FURNITURE

Written and illustrated by

THERLE HUGHES

COUNTRY LIFE
LONDON · NEW YORK · SYDNEY · TORONTO

Published by Country Life Books
and distributed for them by
The Hamlyn Publishing Group Limited
London · New York · Sydney · Toronto
Astronaut House, Feltham, Middlesex, England

First published 1968
Sixth impression 1979

ISBN 0 600 43067 7

Printed in England by
Hazell Watson & Viney Limited,
Aylesbury

Contents

Introduction

The most important aspects of antique English furniture—which make it such a joy to collect—are its design (closely allied to function, while at the same time reflecting passing fashions), and the skilful handling of fine materials, which give lasting pleasure in use. However, there are no hallmarks, no makers' cyphers, scarcely ever even as much as a printed paper label, to offer clues to origin or date. Collectors must rely on their own skill to determine the style of design and ornament, the materials and manufacturing methods involved, and the quality of the workmanship. Only from knowledge and experience can they deduce the likely period of its making and its original situation, and hence some idea as to whether it was an early trend-setting piece or a more humble creation trailing in the wake of high fashion, but often for this very reason showing homely modifications of design that make it the more acceptable in contemporary interiors.

A piece that shows a confusion of styles, materials and manufacturing methods is almost always attributable to Victorian eclecticism, though occasionally to present day fake. The Victorians had an insatiable desire to reproduce the massive flamboyance of Gothic and Elizabethan furniture, and the suave grace of George III's day, randomly acclaimed as Louis Quinze and Louis Seize. Some direct copies are hard to detect, but frequently detail of proportion, ornament or manufacturing technique betrays the 19th-century origin.

The aim of this book is to give beginners a simple outline of the changing periods and their products, to make them familiar with the terms in common use in museums and

1. Victorian delight in earlier styles that may confuse the beginner-collector. TOP: 'Louis XV' desk showing detail of typical ormolu-mounted foot; stool, 'Louis XVI'; 'Louis XV' stand (detail above of its keyhole). BOTTOM: 'Louis XV' and 'Louis XVI' chairs from the 1851 exhibition; 1880s imitation of Hepplewhite chair (Victoria and Albert Museum).

salerooms, to indicate the factors governing design and orna-ment and the techniques applied. In this way the book will not only be valuable to the beginner-collector but also a handy guide to the contents of museums and country houses.

It is current practice to classify furniture by periods, and monarchs' names tend to be applied to periods considerably outlasting their actual reigns. Even so, there was a conspicuous time-lag between the period of fashion that produced the costly museum piece and the moment when provincial furniture makers repeated the style in a form modified to meet the requirements of conservative-minded clients. As already pointed out, monarchs' names were reintroduced indiscriminately by the Victorians. Many terms commonly used to describe furniture details are explained briefly in Part II; the crafts involved in Part XVII; the main types of wood in Part XVIII.

THE 17TH CENTURY

The development of furniture making. Before the end of the 16th century English furniture was strongly and handsomely made by the joiner using more refined techniques than the early carpenter, and much lesser furniture came from the turner. Ornament was provided by carving or paint. The last years of the period saw the development of the entirely different skills required of the cabinet maker (*see* Part XVII).

Few collectors can take more than a theoretical interest in authentic pieces of Gothic and Elizabethan furniture, but it is important to realise that Gothic 'church window' motifs never entirely disappeared from sight, but kept reappearing, particularly around 1750 and in the first half of the 19th century (Fig. 9).

What has remained from Elizabethan days is mainly massive furniture, heavily panelled and boldly carved. In the early 17th century (early Stuart) years the furniture was still heavy, but plainer in style, with much comparatively lifeless repetitive carving. The gradual development of more family privacy in the big self-contained home produced an increasing range

9

of smaller furnishings—lighter chairs, folding tables for games and family meals. There was cupboarding in the modern sense of the word to augment the storage chest and the display shelves of 'court cupboards': this included the hall or parlour cupboard and livery cupboard that served as forerunners to the compartmented sideboard. But collectors today tend to underestimate the amount of built-in seating and cupboarding and also the wealth of cushions and covers and painted hangings that contributed to the splendour and comfort of these houses.

This period saw a change to more consciously planned, less haphazard, homes whose rooms required increasingly specific purpose-planned furniture such as sets of dining chairs. But the most conspicuous change in style and thought came with the influx of Continental retainers accompanying Charles II and his court on the restoration of the monarchy in 1660. English craftsmen had to adapt themselves to entirely new materials and methods, and the rich luxury of those in power meant a vast widening of the gap between fashionable display furniture and homely comfort: this was a basic difference in purpose rather than a time-lag.

Materials: Wainscot oak was widely imported and furniture was made in solid walnut, as well as beech, ash, elm and fruitwoods. At the end of the period the use of surface veneers meant that fine graining—such as the knotty effects of burr woods—could be exploited irrespective of their constructional strength. Some oak was used as carcase wood under the early veneers, but there was soon a general preference for yellow deal.

Construction: The early, simple boarded construction was largely ousted by the joiner's construction using mortise-and-tenon joints to link the framework around loose panels which could respond to atmospheric changes (*see* Part XVII and Fig. 121). This was particularly suitable for oak, which case hardens rather than fully weathering. In the last years of the period glued-on veneers tended to mask constructional detail in cabinet work.

When furniture was no longer coloured with paint, the wood required polishing to bring out its natural grain. The process consisted of rubbing with boiled oil—linseed, nut or poppy. An early alternative or supplementary finish was a rubbing of beeswax dissolved in turpentine. John Evelyn (1620–1706) refers to the preparation of black walnut warmed and polished with its own oil. The alternative was a brushed-on varnish finish composed of a resinous substance such as seed-lac, shell-lac or copal with an oil or spirit base, finally polished with tripoli powder (*see* Japanning Part XVII).

Ornament: Early chip carving (Fig. 58) and heads in roundels and the panel-strengthening corrugations known as linenfold (Fig. 58) are most usually found in later reproductions. Elizabethan carving included much bold strapwork, caryatid figures in deep relief and borders of heavy gadrooning, but there was a change to lozenge and lunette patterns in lower relief in the early 17th century (for explanations of such terms *see* Part II). Bulbous pillars deeply carved in cup-and-cover outlines date mainly from the late 16th century, being elongated and often reduced to spindle turnings in 17th-century work. In the later 17th century, carved work was very popular—in walnut on chairs and in gilded soft woods for cabinet stands.

Turned ornament—on table legs, for example—includes repetitive bead-and-reel swellings around the mid-17th century, followed by extremely handsome baluster shapings. The barley sugar twist or swash turning was mainly fashionable in the late 17th century. Post-1660 carving is dominated by crestings on such items of furniture as chairs and clocks displaying amorini supporting crowns among leafy scrolls, but towards the end of the century more formal scrolling is conspicuous in both ornament and constructional features.

Elizabethan surface ornament includes simple inlay in contrasting woods or bone. 17th-century chest furniture frequently has split turnings glued to the framework, and heavy mouldings glued on to suggest mitred panel framing.

Veneering technique at the end of the period is seen at its most decorative in the interlacing veneer patterns known as marquetry, and the squared patterns of parquetry. Some marquetry of this period shows strong Dutch influence with patterns of naturalistic flowers, but more colour was introduced by the technique known as japanning, inspired by imports of Oriental lacquer cabinets and boards. Gilded and silvered surfaces expressed the flamboyance of post-Restoration display furniture, and a particularly delightful notion is the silvered or gilded side table or mirror frame textured with a pattern in low relief, of gesso composition.

Other details: English ironwork of the highest quality was available even to medieval furniture makers, and it is interesting to compare the hinges, hasps and key escutcheons of the 15th and 16th centuries with the products of the early 19th century romantics and later craft movement enthusiasts. The later 17th-century cabinet maker introduced the refinement of brass furniture mounts. Iron screw pins were used for fixing hinges—among other things—as early as 1594, but it was only in the second half of the 17th century that brass screws began to replace nails. This in turn influenced hingeing, and thus the whole design and development of folding and falling tables.

Fixed upholstery, as distinct from cushions, was limited to a small amount of luxury furniture with fabric glued on over the wood in the Continental manner, and to simple seats and chair backs covered in cloth, serge, turkey work or the cofferers' close-nailed leather. This was based on webbing and horse hair, but lighter, resilient seating is found in the popular

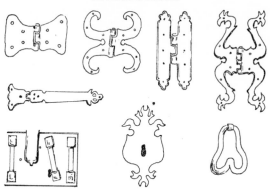

2. Iron mounts. TOP, hinges: 16th-century butterfly; 16th-century forerunner of cockshead; 'H' hinge; 17th-century cockshead, thinning to extremities. CENTRE: strap hinge. BOTTOM: chest lock with movable keyhole cover, 15th–17th centuries; keyhole escutcheon, 17th century; early drawer handle.

high-backed walnut chair of the later 17th century with seat and back panel of caning.

Articles to collect: are rare and generally costly, but there are some magnificent museum pieces of oak furniture such as carved beds and cradles, panelled chairs and stools, cupboards, table desks and so-called Bible boxes. There is also a large range of tables—long and draw tables for dining, folding and gate-leg or falling tables that are early examples of occasional furniture. But this period shows also the beginnings of more specialised cabinet and bureau pieces with drawers and pigeon holes; the wide use of walnut in solid and veneer for chairs, tables and cabinet work; the beginnings of a new era in home comfort with caned day beds, for example, and fringed velvet stools, that all became assimilated as the style now generally called Queen Anne.

QUEEN ANNE (1700–1720s)

The dating is somewhat arbitrary as Anne reigned 1702–14, but this covers the period characterised by the development of gracious, accommodating furniture with conspicuous emphasis on curved outlines—pediments and cupboard doors, mirror cresting and chair backs and epitomised in the cabriole leg.

Materials: The most fashionable wood was walnut, with yellow deal carcases for veneer and marquetry work. Cabinets, clock cases and such minor furniture as dressing mirrors may be found in colourful japannning, sometimes in association with magnificent Oriental work imported as lacquer boards. Costly imported marbles were introduced on carved and gilded table and console frames. The frequent appearance of plain but fine quality cupboard furniture in oak with 18th-century fielded panels testifies to the fact that oak and cheaper native woods never went out of demand.

Constructional methods show greater mastery of veneer techniques, with lap dovetails instead of through dovetails for drawers, and several successive ideas for edging the veneer around the drawer openings. Quality in a cabriole leg may be judged by the original girth of the wood that has been sacrificed in obtaining the desirable springy outline of knee and foot; quality of finish in the cabinet work of this period may be judged by the superb fitting of the arched and rounded pigeon holes and small, curved drawers.

Ornament: covers the flat patterns of balanced veneers with cross-banded borders and lines of slanting or herringbone grain to satisfy the eye accustomed to panel outlines. Magnificent burr wood veneers—walnut, yew, mulberry and others—are found more frequently than marquetry, which is mainly restricted to two-tone effects in arabesque and sea-weed patterns. Carving is dominated by the scallop shell motif in low relief on chair cresting, mirror and cabriole knee. Even

3. Brass handles and keyhole escutcheons. TOP: late 17th century to Queen Anne. SECOND ROW: early 18th-century development of bail handle, from incised plate and insecure attachment to early Georgian cut-out backplate securely bolted. THIRD ROW: mid-18th-century detail in rococo mount; two-part backplate for curved surface; 'Chinese' piercing. BOTTOM: two late 18th-century handles flanking keyholes of 1750s, 1770s, 1790s.

15

the most flamboyant furniture, such as console tables and the stands for Oriental cabinets, lacks the uninhibited carving of the previous decades.

Other details: include the development of winged key escutcheons, matched by the back plates of the simple but stronger bail handles of cabinet furniture, which show interesting constructional developments (Fig. 3). Furniture upholstery includes some fine tent-stitch and cross-stitch embroidery covering wing armchairs.

Articles to collect: The beds of the time are usually vast, but the rest of the bedroom furniture is charming: dressing tables with arched kneeholes flanked by small drawers, and dressing glasses—sometimes with a base of fitted compartments, and resting on a matching stand originally flanked by candlestands. Other items are firescreens in both pole and horse (cheval) shapes; long case clocks becoming increasingly tall and massive; chairs—wing, arm, single and some with comfortable, figure-fitting bended backs—tables for cards, writing, dining and a full range of cupboarded furniture from the bookcase-bureau of high fashion to the farmhouse style of dresser then evolving from the serving table.

EARLY GEORGIAN (1720–1760)

Collectors of English furniture accept this time-span—covering roughly the reigns of George I (1714–27) and George II (1727–60)—as early Georgian, but certain changes in taste appeared towards the mid-century. Furniture remaining from the early years includes heavy pieces of architectural style associated with the Palladian ideals of William Kent and others, but for the collector the important feature of the period is the appearance of mahogany furniture. Mahogany was first introduced in the Queen Anne period, but it was only in the 1730s and 1740s that furniture makers really began to exploit its width of plank, immense strength and close grain.

Furniture remaining from the mid-century years shows the passing vogues for rococo asymmetry and various Gothic and Chinese whims of ornament now perhaps regarded with exaggerated importance. Such furniture tends to be referred to as 'Chippendale' because 1754 saw the first edition of Thomas Chippendale's influential *Gentleman and Cabinet Maker's Director* (reissued 1755, 1762). It may be compared in some respects with Louis Quinze furniture in France and provided the furniture trade with a wide mixture of rococo, Chinese and Gothic patterns. The period's uninhibited gaiety is illustrated also by Chippendale's lesser rivals such as Ince and Mayhew, whose *Universal System of Household Furniture* was published 1759–62.

Materials: include not only the early Spanish or San Domingo mahogany, but a great amount of walnut, japanned soft woods and, for more humble homes, oak and more easily worked local woods. Cane was out of fashion again, but for country chairs rush seats were plentiful.

Construction expresses the furniture maker's delight in the bolder outlines and sharp indentations made possible by mahogany. Table tops consist of single widths of plank cut from trees of huge girth and often have no stretchers. It is interesting to compare the gate-leg table in oak or walnut with the gate table in Spanish mahogany (*see* Part IV). Chair splats are adventurously pierced and cabinet furniture is conceived on a grand scale, with broken and swan-neck pediments and heavy dentil mouldings. This was in keeping with the architectural design of the period, but it can also be argued that the substantial ornament was prompted by the early mahogany's lack of spectacular graining.

There was, too, a return to panel construction on cupboard doors. Glazed cabinets in the 1750s began to show a new elegance with thin, shapely glazing bars. The wood lent itself to gracious drawing room pieces such as pillar-and-claw tables, some with pierced 'cut-work' galleries, some with rims of the eccentric cyma turning known as piecrust. Only at the end of this period was there much use of the more richly patterned Cuban mahogany with its characteristic flame grain, frequently veneered onto more easily worked wood, including the cheaper Honduras mahogany or baywood popular in the succeeding period. Brilliant veneering technique was required for the double curves of the mid-century's fashionable, bombé-shaped commodes and smaller-scale tea chests. Costly furniture was finished by prolonged rubbing with oil and tripoli powder, while cheaper woods received linseed oil or beeswax polish.

Ornament: includes not only architectural treatments but the clear-cut carving that is the supreme distinction of this early mahogany—lions' and eagles' heads on chair arms, ball-and-claw and lion paw to foot the cabriole leg, altogether too exuberant to remain in fashion for very long. The more slender, modified cabriole, known as the French leg, has a simpler knurl or scroll foot. Carved detail may be laid over the chair's pierced splat, as in the most elaborate ribband-back designs favoured by Chippendale, since such ornament had to be cut all ways of the grain and could only be handled freely in this way. The most spectacular ornament is found in the mid-century rococo carvings on less vulnerable mirrors and wall brackets.

Other details: include the brasswork of drawer handles, showing similarly flamboyant rococo treatment, and the application of protective mounts to drawing room commodes with gleaming scrolls of ormolu or gilded brass. Handles passed through several phases, which may help to date a piece, with fretted piercing and asymmetrical scrolling, and finally the use of a separate back plate for each end of the bail loop (Fig. 3). Small low castors are found on items such as breakfast tables, the wheels built up of leather rollers held by low brass arms.

Articles to collect: cover the full range of furniture mentioned above, with the addition of such lavish pieces as drawing room commodes and decorative hanging shelves. On a smaller scale there are the early pillar-and-claw tables, never more lively in shape and finish, hanging corner cupboards, wash-basin stands (now sometimes mistakenly called wig stands), knife boxes and wine cisterns.

Chairs tend to be large, but their design was never bettered. Favourite collector's items are the reading chair for straddling to display silken coat tails, the corner chair for desk or card table and the angular frets of mid-century 'Chinese' whimsy.

1760s–1800s

This later 18th-century period is particularly important and covers a succession of styles dominated by the neo-classic mood. These are illustrated to a considerable extent by the pattern books issued by men whose names are now applied indiscriminately to a vast amount of furniture which they neither designed nor made.

The architect Robert Adam (1728–92) is thought to have anticipated the French in giving impetus and direction from 1758 to European neo-classicism, with exquisite designs which some regard as effeminate. George Hepplewhite is associated with a more homely interpretation of the mood and a certain amount of originality. But his *Cabinet-Maker and Upholsterer's Guide* was first published in 1788—two years after his death—and new designs appeared in the third (and much revised) edition of 1794, so that his personal responsibility is in doubt. In any case it seems highly improbable that any furniture actually made by him or his firm—continued by his widow, Alice—will ever come to light.

Another important influence was *The Cabinet-Maker's London Book of Prices*, a trade manual containing 20 plates in the first edition, 17 of them signed by Thomas Shearer. An enlarged edition appeared in 1794 and *The Union Book of Prices* based upon it was issued in 1811, 1824, 1836 and 1866.

Even more furniture tends to be credited to Thomas Sheraton (1751–1806), but it seems improbable that he made any at all after coming to London in about 1790. His fame

4. Looking glasses in chronological sequence. TOP: late 17th-century, wide-bevelled glass in nearly flat frame, japanned; elaborate carving of 1700s; architectural style, the glass cut straight, walnut and gilding, George II; mid-18th-century glass showing pagoda, pillar and waterfall motifs. BOTTOM, all gilded: rich rococo design with (below) detail of popular flame motif; contrasting neo-classic glass of 1770s; Hepplewhite design (1788) showing early eagle motif.

more properly rests on his books, especially his *Cabinet-Maker's and Upholsterer's Drawing Book* (published in parts, 1791–4, to over 600 subscribers). His *Cabinet Dictionary* (1803) was followed by his still less successful *Encylopaedia*, of which he saw only the first volume published, A–C, in 1805. These show further recognisable changes which can be identified in delightful furniture from the end of the century such as chairs and light cabinet work. His work may be regarded as a link between Adam's free 'modern' application of classic ornament and the more exacting formal classicism of the later Regency years. Some pieces, such as the Carlton House table (Fig. 88) have been in intermittent production ever since.

Design throughout this period combined grace of line with formality and restraint, with sweeping, uninterrupted curves and much use of elliptical outline. Serpentine shapes to table and cupboard furniture gradually lost favour to more severe bow and square fronts. Legs for the first time were straight and tapering on neat symmetrical feet; chair back construction was basically altered and the cupid's bow cresting disappeared in favour of less expansive lines.

Materials: include much magnificent mahogany, but also the lighter tones of satinwood, in solid and veneer, contrasted with borders and bandings of the more exotic tulipwood and kingwood. Light tones were also introduced with greenish-stained sycamore (known as harewood) and other native woods such as birch and chestnut. Chairs and tables and cabinets for a cheaper market may be in pine covered with light tones of paint. One finds much gilded furniture, and on minor pieces—mirrors, for example (Figs. 4, 5)—the ornament may be gilded. Flame grain Cuban mahogany may be found veneered on cheaper mahogany, or the cheaper baywood, suitably stained, on carcases of red pine. Oak is found in provincial production, but even here there may be bandings of mahogany in an attempt to associate it with fashionable work.

5. Later looking glasses. TOP: wall or chimney mirrors. BOTTOM: circular designs: glass by Smith, 1808; glass showing eagle with two suspended balls, c. 1810 (V. and A. Museum): more elaborate development of eagle motif.

Construction: shows great use of veneers and, when panel effects are suggested, they frequently depend upon applied mouldings in sinuous curves with low relief carving. Even cabinet glass shows some use of purely ornamental glued-on bars, whilst a change took place in drawer construction. Previously the base boards ran from front to back, but this was changed to a side-to-side arrangement with a central support. Swan neck pediments may show pierced ornament through wood strengthened in the plywood manner. Dining chairs in the more easily worked Honduras mahogany are often strengthened with stretchers, usually in H shape, the chair legs themselves slightly tapering and wave moulded.

It may be mentioned here that the entirely different technique of the Windsor chair became important at this period, with all the members strongly dowelled into the solid saddle seat. This was a countryman's technique for using native woods, with simple turning on the pole lathe and a minimum of joiners' work to produce arm and single chairs, stools, rocking chairs and children's chairs that would bounce rather than break under rough usage in the garden and on stone-flagged floors. This Windsor work has been dated to as early as the 1720s, but the fashion time-lag makes it probable that even the 'early' specimens found today with cabriole legs date mainly to the second half of the century.

Ornament: was expressed in a small range of classical motifs such as urns, swags of drapery, the anthemion or formalised honeysuckle, husk, bell-flower and acanthus leaf. Carving was scarcely more ambitious than such motifs in low relief, simple paterae and the flutings characteristic of the tapering legs in square section (thermed) which preceded the tapering, turned leg of round section. Extensive use of veneers encouraged a renewed interest in marquetry which, like inlay in the solid wood, displays the same neo-classical themes, often contained within round, elliptical or fan-shaped panels.

Classical figures were introduced in low relief plaques and medallions of Wedgwood jasper ware, or painted directly upon the wood. Late in the period there was much minor flower painting. Even furniture with no pretensions to high fashion, such as simple long case clocks, dressers and oak corner cupboards, may show small ornamental motifs, most often composed by specialist marquetry men and set into the veneer or solid wood. These include a popular conch shell, conventional flower and fan and the lines of dark and light checker work known as stringing (Fig. 125).

Other details to note include the changes in handle design to conform with current liking for round and elliptical outlines (Fig. 3). From the 1770s these could be shaped and ornamented in low relief by machine-stamping. Castors are more conspicuous, often projecting from brass sockets. Fashionable fabrics include colourful haircloths as well as rich silks, which at this period were often protected by linen covers. During the last few years of the century there was a renewed liking for cane.

Articles to collect: include a wide range of dining room furniture. Fitted sideboards were first illustrated by Thomas Shearer in 1788 in his guide to costing for furniture makers commissioned by the Cabinet Makers' Society. Other articles range from plate pails, trays and the folding table and tray known as a butler's tray to the ubiquitous pillar-and-claw dumb waiter.

There is purpose-concealing furniture for the visitor-thronged dressing room, including fitted dressing tables and washbasin stands. For the library-study one finds barometers, globes and a range of substantial desks, the Carlton House type of fitted table and the reading desk with tilting top now usually called an architect's table. Library steps include the design patented by Robert Campbell in 1774. But some of the most charming pieces of furniture still available to the collector are effeminate little pieces for 'ladies'—worktables, urn stands, small bonheur-du-jour desks, Pembroke tables with richly patterned flaps supported by small fly brackets. Again there are many delightful chairs, and collectors, confused by later reproductions, may study the measurements and proportions advised by the pattern designers and often ruined by enterprising Victorians.

REGENCY (1800s–1830s)

This period takes its name from the Regency (1811–20), but covers also the last days of George III (1760–1820) and the reign of George IV (1820–30), a decade sometimes called late Georgian. The period is familiar as being the last with a coherent style—though more varied, diverse and confused than the Continental style it rivalled and imitated. In France the transitional Directoire style may be dated 1790–1800. The Empire style with its extreme classicism dates 1800–15,

6. Late 18th-century worktables. TOP: basic pattern with fitted drawer and rising firescreen; elaborate design with rising firescreen, slide on left, fabric-hung workbox drawer opening to the right, and wide front drawer with rising top containing book rest; table with rising lid to serve as firescreen, fitted top section and, below, a spindle-rimmed shelf around the central well. BOTTOM: two ladies' worktable designs by Sheraton.

followed by the florid, degenerate version associated with Louis XVIII, 1815–24.

By 1810 there was a heavier, archeological approach to classical ornament and an attempt, too, at imitating rather than creating classical shapes in couches, stools and scimitar-

legged chairs, based on Graeco-Roman discoveries and with colour schemes taken from Etruscan vases. Serious excavation at Pompeii began in 1799. Sphinxes had been introduced as ornament as early as the 1770s, but there was more widespread enjoyment of Egyptian motifs such as sheathed caryatid figures, lotus buds and winged lions, prompted by Napoleon's campaigns in Syria and Egypt (1798–1801) and the writings of V. Denon. Influential furniture design in this mood came in 1807 from Thomas Hope (1768–1831), whose book notably covered 'interior decoration' and in 1808 and 1826 from George Smith, whose approach was more personal and popular.

Hope was among those who welcomed the more rigid, uncompromising classicism governing the second phase of Regency furniture. Regency design stressed severe simplicity with broad, uninterrupted surfaces, low, horizontal lines and much emphatic, vertical reeding. The rounded X form of two opposing curves is noted on many Regency chairs; so, also, is the loss of the simple tapering leg in favour of the scimitar curve and the late Regency 'Greek' leg with massive swelling at knee height and tapering quickly, often heavily fluted or reeded and sometimes spirally cabled.

At the same time there was an escapist interest in the Orient shared by the Prince Regent, prompting cheap furnishings in beechwood, turned and painted to suggest bamboo, or

---

7. Early 19th-century chairs with Regency characteristics. TOP: Sheraton conversation chair 'extraordinary long between back and front for the ... fashionable posture'; three late Sheraton backs. SECOND ROW: style of Hope, c. 1807; lyre splat, 1800s; 'Trafalgar' rope twist in back rails; hall chair, Sheraton design (V. and A. Museum) and (below) an alternative shape for such a seat. BOTTOM Smith parlour chair, 1808; Morgan & Sanders chair with scimitar leg from Ackermann's *Repository of Arts*, January, 1810; 'Grecian' style in the *Repository*.

japanned and gilded to resemble lacquer. Already, too, there was some renewed interest in pinnacled, turreted Gothic design, carved in light oak or painted light stone colour.

Thomas Chippendale and his successors had developed factory methods for making high quality furniture on a considerable scale in the second half of the previous century—the firm of George Seddon in 1768 suffered a loss of £20,000 through a fire—but it was during the Regency that factory mass production made more conspicuous progress. Mechanisation of planes and saws and veneering knives eventually altered techniques and cut costs, but inevitably meant a loss of individualistic craftsmanship and the beginnings of cheap, shoddy substitutes for proven methods and materials. Design included a considerable amount of compact, multi-purpose furniture required by army officers, ships' captains, emigrants and others, patent in name rather than in fact and associated with such innovators as the firm of Morgan and Sanders.

Materials: show a return to dark lustrous surfaces, typically mahogany and widely available Brazilian rosewood, brown burr amboyna and such streaked and stripy woods as calamander, zebra and kingwood, together with cheap woods variously painted, blacked and gilded. A none-too-welcome detail from 1821 was the surface finish known as French polishing: the several applications of shellac dissolved in spirit were intended to protect veneer from effects of damp, but the result lacks the glow of oiled and dust-polished grain and is easily spoilt by heat. On new furniture the treatment was applied in the course of construction, the polish being composed of shellac dissolved in methylated spirits. The treatment involved filling the grain, usually with a dyed whiting composition now often faded and unsightly.

Construction: reflects the use of more efficient tools. Machines for planing, moulding, grooving, rebating, sawing and shaping all kinds of wood in all kinds of outline had been patented in 1793 by Samuel Bentham. These could be worked by steam, water or other power, and steam was in use before the end of this period. In 1806 Brunel patented a horizontal compound knife for cutting veneers, although more wasteful saws were still needed for some difficult grains. The Newbury band or ribbon saw dates from 1808, and soon afterwards a machine was evolved for cutting dovetails. In 1818 the Society of Arts made an award to the originator of a method for steaming unseasoned small furniture work to reduce warping. Brass inlay machinery was developed, too.

The other obvious 'need' for mechanical aid was met by the Jordan and Irving wood-carving machines in 1848. But many of these developments were slow to gain acceptance. It must be noted, too, that 1813 saw the repeal of the apprenticeship laws, with an inevitable relaxation of quality control.

Ornament: Work in brass is typified in the Sheraton design for a lady's secretary 'finished in black rosewood and tulip cross banding, together with brass moulding ... The upper shelf is intended to be of marble supported with brass pillars and a brass ornamental rim round the top'. Ornamental motifs include those listed by Hope as 'trophies ... terms, caryatides, griffins, chimaeras, scenic masks, sacrificial implements, civil and military emblems ...'; but even Hope was distressed at the way cabinet makers produced merely 'extravagant caricatures'. Other favourites are the Greek anthemion or honeysuckle, palm and acanthus leaves, the spavin leg and hocked animal hooves. The lion monopodium, a leg composed of lion head, leg and paw foot is found in varying quality.

In addition to the wealth of ornament in brass there was use of cast iron, but still usually masked by gilding or even wood graining. The japanned finish to cheap wood, often mentioned

8. Worktables. TOP: two adapted from Sheraton designs, 1800s; design from Ackermann's *Repository*, 1811. SECOND ROW: table with lyre-shaped supports, brass galleries to rounded ends, c. 1810; typical detail of small pivoting drawer; heavier design with reversible top for chess. BOTTOM: late Regency table; typical fringe often recorded on these worktables and illustrated, for example, by Henry Moses (above, on chair); table with round pouch, c. 1820s.

at this period, consisted merely in the use of a varnish base to colour instead of oil paint. A common ornamental detail that may be derived from Trafalgar enthusiasm is the close cable twist found in chair backs and on the corner pilasters of much case furniture. Penwork was a late Regency fashion consisting of black line patterns on such items as small cabinets. This often shows a combination of poor material and laborious workmanship, suggesting that it may have been one of the many crafts now generally classed as French prisoners-of-war work (*see* Part XVII).

Other details: include lion head and ring handles on desks, wine cisterns; brass lion paws for the projecting castors on pillar tables, sofas and couches. Stamped drawer handles included lion heads with rings, and by 1800 rosettes were added to them. Glass knobs were becoming popular by 1815 and, when fancy glass suffered from heavy taxing in 1822, wooden knobs were adopted in attractive turnery, and china knobs with painted ornament. Such changes—as Smith admitted in 1826—had by then rendered his earlier *Designs for Household Furniture* wholly obsolete. Caning is found again on chairs and swinging cots.

Articles to collect: include gracious sofa tables and sofas, including the meridienne, games tables with reversible tops to serve a number of games (and often also to house the pieces and counters), small tables fitted with portable bookshelves and known as sheverets, work-tables with fabric bags and adjustable firescreens, the banner firescreen on a solid plinth and the low lyre screen, canterbury sheet-music stands and davenport desks. Tea caddies on stands became popular under the name of teapoys; floor mirrors were called horse dressing glasses or, more appealingly, psyches. Light, hanging book-shelves remain, reminding one of the popularity of wire trellis, and there are small 'sociable' tables, as well as the increasingly massive dining tables.

VICTORIAN (1830s–1900)

Victoria's reign (1837–1901) offers endless confusion to the beginner. All earlier styles were copied, shamelessly 'improved' and mingled until often the original purpose of a feature was lost. Even at the time the period's critics endlessly deplored the fact that designers, makers and users were out of touch with each other. With a rapidly expanding population there was more concern over comfort for the many than elegance for the few. Thomas Hope had complained of a lack of skilled craftsmen, but for ever-increasing numbers with money in their pockets and no inhibiting traditions of cultured taste, the price-cutting mass production methods meant that a middling family home could have more rooms packed with furnishings than ever before.

Those new to wealth, like those newly escaped from poverty, gladly accepted current tastes, which meant that the many small manufacturers could continue far into mid-Victorian days the same range of style-corruptions that quickly transformed furniture design after the Regency. This, indeed, was a wide range. There could be no greater contrast than typical 'Gothic' furniture with church-window tracery, tall angular outlines, heavy, dark carving and the concurrent bright 'Louis Quinze' or 'rococo' revival almost entirely lacking straight lines and sharp angles and informally decorated with flowers and arabesques. Between these extremes was the so-called 'Renaissance' and 'Elizabethan' work which, in fact, laboriously copied much Jacobean furnishing for the massive dining room it was most usually expected to serve, eventually producing original designs in the same mood.

In general, having rejected the Regency's pedantic classicism, these heavy-handed attempts to give each stylistic notion a safe historical attribution reflect the same escapist romanticism that had brought fantastic success to Scott's novels;

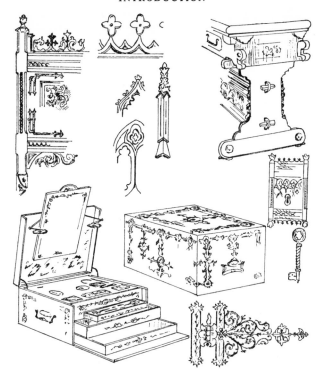

9. Early Victorian Romanticism. TOP: detail from cabinet of Pugin design; typical 'Medieval' or 'Gothic' detail, machine carved, 1851; table detail from the Medieval Court, 1851 exhibition, showing pegged stretcher and end support and complex linking of side and end frieze. BOTTOM: inside and outside of 'Medieval' dressing box, walnut with pierced silver mounts showing elaborate metalwork which may suggest greater antiquity; 'Gothic' lock and key and (at bottom) 'Gothic' hinge. All shown in 1851.

Morland's scenes of rural peace; narrative paintings and the celebrity figures of the mantelshelf.

Mid-Victorian furniture may be regarded as generally more assertive, shaking free of the all-enfolding upholstery in favour of the bold, angular lines of Louis Seize design and a wealth of surface ornament in marquetry, ormolu, china plaques and embossed leather. Furniture at the 1851 exhibition can hardly be accepted as a foretaste, but at least a set of doors shown by William Holland may illustrate what became a mid-Victorian mood. For dining room or library there was a painted imitation of oak inlaid with ebony and pearl; for the drawing room polished white enamel with gold mouldings; for the more imposing saloon painted figures in Pompeiian style; for the lady's boudoir a painted imitation of walnut inlaid with flowers to go with marquetry furniture; for either drawing room, saloon or boudoir a door with plate glass panels embossed with gold and silver. One is reminded of the Balmoral drawing room with tartans patterning the chairs and settee covers, table cloth, curtains and pelmets.

So-called art in furniture design consisted largely of extreme elaboration of ornament, defying cheap imitation. All this produced inevitable reactions in favour of simplicity in design and rugged craftsmanship. Among the pioneers was William Morris (1834–96) who founded the firm of Morris, Marshall, Faulkner and Company in 1861, making, among other things, simple cupboard furniture as a basis for painting by Morris and his fellow Pre-Raphaelites. The Morris firm produced some attractively forthright furniture, including, from the 1860s, the familiar rush-seated chairs and settees derived from traditional Sussex country design; but Morris, personally, was not involved in furniture design. It may be mentioned that, even by 1862, this firm of 'fine art workmen in painting, carving, furniture and the metals' had been awarded two gold medals by those striving to improve public taste.

In a similar mood of revolt against such 'objectionable and pretentious deceit' as wood graining, machine carving and the parodies of old carving then being produced, 'smeared thickly over with dark varnish to give an appearance of age', Charles Eastlake brought out his *Hints on Household Taste in Furniture, etc*, in 1868, sufficiently popular to reappear, revised, in 1878. He illustrates massive joiner constructions of his own design with pegged shelving and showing every pin of the mortise-and-tenon joints. He stresses the need for simplicity of form and shows it in a library bookcase and a square-ended sofa, but deplores the Victorian uncritical conviction that every new fancy is the finest yet.

Late Victorian furniture includes more copying of earlier centuries, and especially of the 18th century's graceful chairs and tables. The drawing room, especially, was filled with fragile pieces, the spindly shapes attempting to reflect the 1870s' 'discovery' of Japan led by Bruce Talbert and others. Even at the time, this period was mocked for its aestheticism, Bohemianism, its delight in ragged tapestries, antique furniture—'an incoherent style that the period dubbed Queen Anne although,' as Lady Marian Alford pointed out in 1886, 'the style of her reign is looked upon with suspicion and never admitted for imitation. The 19th century would be a better name for it as it has formed itself only within the last 30 years, in the very heart of the century . . . It combines simplicity, roominess and comfort, colour, light and shade'.

In the final decades of the century, numerous arts and crafts societies came into being. Their effect on commercial furniture-making was somewhat limited, but prompted the creation of furniture that is straight and simple in line, but richly and imaginatively ornamented in a wide range of materials. Important names towards the end of the century include C. R. Ashbee, who launched the Guild of Handicrafts in 1888, Ernest Gimson (1864–1920), C. F. A. Voysey (1857–1941)

10. Later Victorian chairs, c. 1870–1900. TOP: dining chair with typical shallow leg turning; 'imitation Hepplewhite'; design recommended, 1874, as a boudoir chair in white and gilt; Eaton Hall chair. SECOND ROW: design by Owen Jones, 1872; wicker chair shown in *The Queen*, 1874, the detail showing the braid, twine fringe and wool pompoms that covered it; wicker chair, 1880s. BOTTOM: two cane chairs; towards *art nouveau* style in working chair at Slade School of Art, 1881; design by C. R. Mackintosh, 1897.

and C. R. Mackintosh (1868–1928). To modern eyes the prevailing lines sometimes appear over-elongated, the ornament pinched and thin. This country, however, never became so deeply involved as the Continent in the short-lived style dominated by light rosewood, inlaid and highly polished, in quaint spindly forms that originated in Belgium and was known as *art nouveau*.

Even this summary inadequately conveys the confusion and overlapping of styles and the contrasts of ungainly design with much superb workmanship.

Materials: include continuing use of mahogany, such as the cheap Honduras variety, still in logs of huge girth but responsible for the eventual disparagement of veneers. Much of this was stained red with a solution of bichromate of potash and now shows blotchy fading.

To the early Victorian, mahogany was the dining room wood, with rosewood in the drawing room, but these were displaced in the 1860s and 1870s by oak for dining and walnut for the drawing room. The late years of the century showed great use of ebonised woods; light oak, when used, was stained a green tone. The early Victorian liked his wood plain and solid—not necessarily excessively heavy: the return to marquetry and such elaborations as Victorian buhl belong to the second half of the century. After long banishment of satinwood there was a conspicuous return, too, to golden tones, especially in walnut but also in cheap furniture in yellow-tinged ash and such details as picture frames in the popular bird's eye maple. Imports in 1850 included 417 planks of this wood, but 7,807 planks of rosewood and 6,812 tons of mahogany.

By the 1840s iron—cast and wrought—was becoming acceptable on its own merits, finished in black, bronze or a japanned imitation of oak. Furnishings included Coalbrookdale's hall stands, even velvet-covered iron chairs, and much conservatory furniture. In the conservatory, however, rustic chairs might be of less enduring terracotta (Fig. 33). As early as the 1830s J. C. Loudon in his *Encyclopaedia of Cottage, Farm and Villa Architecture and Furniture* was praising the use of iron furniture including beds 'to be found in the houses of people of wealth and fashion in London'. Brass beds, too, were made from the end of the Regency period

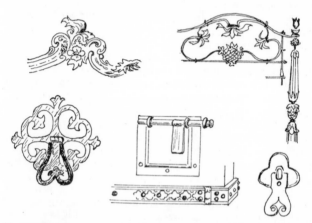

11. Metalwork. TOP: cast brass cot ornament, 1851; detail from iron bedstead 1851. SECOND ROW: iron 'Gothic' handle; lock and metal band on a Philip Webb piece, 1862, showing the casual placing of the big, unmasked screws; handle design by Ernest Gimson, early 1900s.

onwards, but only became popular in the 1850s: these were of iron tubing thinly covered with sheet brass.

Papier mâché soon proved too brittle, and few chairs have survived, but the small, slender cane-seated chairs are still to be found made of papier mâché combined with black japanned wood similarly enriched with bright japan colours and encrusted with glinting shell or, after 1847, 'gem inlay'. Papier mâché tables, firescreens, workboxes and trays are found. Much bamboo and cane dates to the last quarter of the century, and from the 1860s there was a vogue for black bentwood furniture such as light chairs in the manner first exhibited by the Thonet brothers of Austria in 1851. When their patent expired the method was developed by the London firm of Hewlett and Company.

Construction: ranges from the chair-a-minute boast of Wycombe factory manufacture to the revival of pegged and tenoned hand joinery. In general the furniture makers sought only a superficial resemblance to the historical styles they copied, and betrayed themselves even in such obvious details as their use of twist-turned pillars with opposing twists.

Ornament: defies analysis, but the eventual profusion of indifferent carving that has remained may be explained to some extent by carving machinery. Victorian origin is often revealed, too, by the weak, repetitive and quite distinctive turning of pillars and legs. Amateur craftsmanship is abundant, with poker work, painted plaques, encrustations of beads and shells. Fret carving machines delighted amateurs. Even japanned coal scuttles were painted with flowers or covered with pasted-on photographs.

Mid-Victorians also admired flamboyant gilding, often in contrasts of matt and burnished surfaces. The English ormolu of gilded bronze might be derided by the aesthetes, but electro-gilding and silvering was a feature of furniture ornament early in the reign, and the notion of buhl was revived in veneers of metal and tortoise-shell, as well as an abundance of marquetry. Several methods of applying photographs to furniture were patented in the 1870s. Sunflowers dominated ornament of the 1880s. Much inlay of pewter and mother of pearl dates to the last years of the century, replacing carving. Glowing copper often replaced mirror glass.

12. Victorian 'Elizabethan' furniture. TOP: two chairs of 1851 flanking detail from a piano showing caryatids, arches, gadroon borders, etc. BOTTOM: chair of 1851 and another noted as late as 1870, flanking a triangular stool, a piano leg and (below) a typical detail of Victorian-Elizabethan strapwork carving.

40

Other details: include the important role of fabrics. Every sofa had its draped shawl, every table its cloth, every dressing table its draperies (as it had a century earlier) with fly-defying mirror curtains. Fabric details are given at the end of this book; also consideration of pictorial embroideries in cross stitch worked on squared canvas in soft merino wools. Known as Berlin wool work, it became very popular in the 1830s. Reference has already been made to the popularity of brass-collared glass and china knob handles: white china castor rollers may be mentioned too. Wooden knob handles, finely turned, were fashionable in early Victorian days when metal details such as hinges were often considered unsightly. But by the last quarter of the century the knobs were often clumsy and confined to less than elegant work.

Articles to collect: include minor pieces in well-preserved papier mâché and in enduring cast iron and wire. There are many attractively spindled whatnots and étagères, and a range of chairs from the back-hugging Eaton Hall and the tough kitchen Wycombe to the round-seated black bentwood and even the various balloon-backs that were established as early as William IV's reign.

PART II

Terms Used by Collectors

Abbotsford: popular term for Victorian-Jacobean carved oak furniture, stimulated in the 1830s and 1840s by such illustrated works as Joseph Nash's *Mansions of England*. George Augustus Sala in 1868 shrewdly attributed the revival to Walter Scott's novels and declared: 'the library of Abbotsford was the precursor of innumerable picturesquely furnished English houses'.

Acanthus (Fig. 14): much indented, stylised leaf from the acanthus plant found on Corinthian and Composite capitals (*see* ORDERS), and widely applied in carved ornament.

Adzed surface: irregularity of surface on wood faced with an adze, dating from medieval or Tudor days. The tool, with hatchet-like blade at right angles to the shaft, left slight ridges and saucer-shaped hollows.

Alkanet: plant juice used with linseed oil to enrich the colour of 18th-century mahogany, as distinct from the later staining with bichromate of potash.

Amorini: 'boys' popular in carving, especially in late 17th century, when amorini supporting a crown among foliage appeared on such items as walnut chair crestings.

Anthemion (Fig. 13, *top left*): stylised honeysuckle popular in neo-classical ornament.

Apron: shaped piece under table underframing or chair seat rail.

Arabesque: ornament of interlaced lines, sometimes foliated.

Arcaded moulding: *see* Peardrop moulding.

Arcading: arching ornaments applied on panels such as Elizabethan chest fronts.

Ball-and-claw (Fig. 21): foot design from Oriental dragon holding pearl. Popular in early 18th century, sometimes with the claw shaped as eagle's talons.

Baluster (Fig. 49): turned pillar used widely for chair and table legs, the term applied especially to those in vase outline. Split lengthwise, such turnings were applied as ornament on chests, etc., in the 17th century.

Banding (Fig. 62): ornamental borders such as the checkers edging 17th-century oak. Also veneered borders around veneered panels. The banding may be diagonal—that is, cut with the grain at a slant, popular in walnut, 1680–1705. Cross banding has the grain at right angles to the line of the band—popular from about 1695 to 1715, together with a narrower, inner line of herringbone or feather banding composed of two very narrow lines of opposing diagonal grains; cross banding alone was much used after 1710. Banding cut with the grain of the wood is known as straight banding. Wide bandings of exotic woods were popular late in the 18th century.

13. Regency brasswork. Seven specimens of inlay and ten frets or galleries from writing tables, bookshelves, etc.

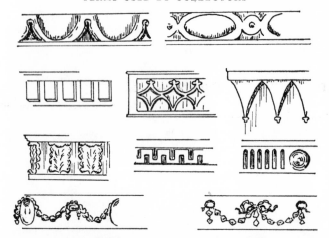

14. Ornamental mouldings. TOP: egg-and-dart and egg-and-tongue. SECOND ROW: dentil moulding; *bas-relief* fret; peardrop. THIRD ROW: acanthus foliage; key pattern; vertical pales and corner patera. BOTTOM: carved neo-classic paterae and swags; inlaid swags with ribbon.

Banker: early term for bench and for a seat cushion or bench cloth.

Barley sugar twist: *see* SWASH TURNING.

Baroque: heavy style of classical architecture expressed in elaborate furnishings of the late 17th and early 18th centuries.

Base: the lower valance on a draped bed.

Bas relief: low relief work in carving, gesso, etc.

Batten: thin strip of wood.

Beading: small half-round moulding popular in later 18th century. Also known as astragal.

Bead-and-reel: form of turning with round motifs interspersed with spool shapes.

44

Bevel: sloping edge to a flat surface such as mirror glass.

Birdcage (Fig. 53): device for securing top of pillar-and-claw table so that it could be tilted or lifted off when required.

Board: early name for table.

Bolection moulding: moulding that projects beyond the surface it decorates, as when it covers the joint between two surfaces.

Bombé (Fig. 64): French word for a swelling outline in the body of cabinet work.

Bow front: convex shaping to front of chest furniture.

Bracket foot (Fig. 65): foot for chest furniture extending vertically from the corner and projecting a short way horizontally under the bottom front and side rails.

Brass (Figs. 3, 13): group of yellow-toned alloys of copper and zinc. Used for handles from second half of 17th century and for small rails, galleries and ornamental inlays from the late 18th century. *See* ORMOLU.

Brocade: textile woven with contrasting pattern in gilded or silver thread or coloured silks. Used for costly upholstery.

Broken front, breakfront (Fig. 79): case furniture such as wardrobe with the central part of the front flanked by wings set a little forward or back to give an interrupted line.

Broken pediment (Fig. 81): arched or gabled pediment above the cornice on cabinet furniture or long case clocks, with a central break or gap frequently containing an ornament.

Buffet or niche: corner alcove built into a panelled room, decoratively shelved and associated especially with early 18th century; also a double corner cupboard.

Buffet furniture: upholstered furniture such as stools.

Buhl, boulle (Fig. 82): from Frenchman, André-Charles Boulle (1642–1732). A form of marquetry with tortoiseshell and brass. English imitations from mid-Regency days.

Bun foot (Fig. 59): flattened variant of the ball foot popular in later 17th century.

Butt hinge: door hinge that shows only a thin line of metal.

Butterfly hinge (Fig. 2): door hinge with expansive straps or leaves. Found in early iron, and in shaped and engraved brass. Replaced butt hinges on high quality walnut furniture.

Cable moulding (Fig. 115): closely twisted reeding on turned chair rails, legs, pilasters, etc., of Regency period, perhaps traceable to Trafalgar enthusiasm.

Cabochon (Fig. 45): convex oval suggesting jewel shape, ornamenting early furniture and revived, somewhat kidney-shaped, usually in a setting of asymmetrical scrolls, in mid-18th-century furniture in lavish French manner.

Cabriole bracket foot (Fig. 79): bracket foot with the corner vertical modified to a curved 'knee'.

Cabriole leg (Fig. 22): familiar leg form introduced on English chairs around 1700, the word being a French dancing term for a leap or caper, presumably originating in the Italian for a goat's leap, *capriole*. Found in a range of outlines becoming sturdier at the knee when chairs were made without stretchers. It was much modified in the mid-century 'French' leg and lost all importance when legs became straight and tapering in the neo-classical style.

Candleslide: *see* SLIDE.

Canted: *see* CHAMFERED.

Canterbury (Figs 94, 98): Sheraton applied the term to both a small stand for sheet-music and a partitioned supper tray (*see* Parts XI, XII).

Capital: head of column or pilaster, a different design being used for each of the five Orders. *See* ORDERS.

Carcase: foundation structure of a piece of furniture; this usually applied to a piece of case furniture which was intended for covering with veneer. Such construction had to ensure that the veneer could be glued to smooth unbroken surfaces, and thus avoid the end grain that would not hold the glue: panel techniques had to be modified and even the common dovetail replaced by the lap dovetail (Fig. 62).

Card-cut (Fig. 23): Fret-cut lattice glued against the face of a piece of furniture, or for the difficult relief carving that achieved the same effect. The term is also used in silver.

Carolean: usually refers to Charles II's reign (1660–85).

Carpets: until the end of the 17th century the term included table and wall covers irrespective of material or weave.

Cartouche: tablet usually decoratively shaped, as in the many rococo ornaments, with scrolls or curled-over edges.

Carver: sometimes applied to an armchair in a set of dining chairs.

Caryatid (Figs 12, 93): carved female figure introduced on furniture as the leg of a cabinet stand, etc., and as a pilaster on case furniture or early beds. The male counterparts are Atlantes. Taken from the architectural figures used as columns to support entablatures.

Castors (Fig. 98, etc.): small, solid wheels attached to furniture legs. The rare early 18th-century specimen might be of hard wood. Around the mid-century it was constructed of a number of leather discs between arms of brass, but by the last quarter of the century the castor was entirely of brass. The plate castor could be attached with screws to the bottom face of a leg; the socket castor included a square or round socket to fit over the end of the leg; the chair castor had a similar socket, but projecting to the side of the wheel for the style of projecting leg typical of pillar-and-claw furniture. Projecting swivel jaws or horns were variously developed for the legs of Regency furniture such as sofas; some had brass sockets shaped as lion paws. Castors with glazed eathernware wheels date from 1851.

Cat: wood or metal rest for plates, etc., to stand in the hearth. The shape is a double tripod approximately resembling three straight turned legs joined together at the centre and projecting in different directions. It could thus be made to stand steadily on the uneven hearth stones on any three legs—like a cat falling always on its feet, and hence its unusual name.

Cavetto moulding (Fig. 80): hollow quarter-circle moulding often found on cabinet cornices of Queen Anne's reign.

Centre hinge (Fig. 125): Dutch introduction used from late 17th century onwards but seldom on high quality English work after the mid-18th century. Small metal horns attached to top and bottom of a door pivoted on pins fixed above and below.

Chamber horse: armchair with leather-covered seat containing springs, used for exercising in the second half of the 18th century and illustrated by Sheraton.

Chamfer (Fig. 125): surface produced by cutting or bevelling off a corner or angle; also canted, splayed. Frequent in early Georgian case furniture.

Channel moulding: groove or flute often found on framing of oak chests, etc.

Checkers: pattern suggesting chessboard squares in dark and light wood, often used as inlay in 16th and 17th centuries.

Cheval (Fig. 130 etc.): in the 18th century the term was 'horse'. Sometimes thought to refer to the pulley for adjusting the piece but more probably from the shape, consisting of vertical end-supports on projecting feet. This was an extremely popular form of construction in Regency years, as for example in the sofa table where the legs at each end of the table form a trestle unit on out-jutting feet and are linked along the length of the table by an ornamental stretcher.

Chinoiserie (Fig. 60): decoration using Chinese motifs, as on mid-18th-century so-called Chinese-Chippendale furniture and usually implying a Western interpretation.

Chintz: cotton or cotton-linen fabric painted or printed with colours or dyes. Such 'painted calicoes' were imported by the East India Co. from the 17th century onwards and were in great demand for bed hangings and upholstery in the early 18th century, but their use was restricted in deference to the woollen industry. Highly glazed from the 1850s.

Claw tables: 18th-century name for the pillar-and-claw or tripod table; sometimes called a snap table when the top could be tilted by releasing a spring catch.

Club or pad foot (Fig. 21): simple protruding rounded foot resting on a turned circular base suggesting the head of a club. Frequent on cabriole leg.

Cluster column (Fig. 23): often on 18th-century 'Gothic' furniture as a table or chair leg composed of three or four separate or partially joined shafts.

Coaster or slider: small, round tray with vertical rim to hold a decanter or one or more bottles, the bottom usually covered with baize to protect the dining table when it was pushed around after the cloth was removed. Inside, the base frequently shows low relief ringing to facilitate removing the decanter.

Cockbead (Fig. 62): small projecting mould round the edges of a drawer front in walnut or mahogany. Used from about 1730.

Cock's head hinge (Fig. 2): most decorative iron hinge in scrolling shape used in 16th and 17th centuries.

Coffered panel: sunk panel; the reverse of a fielded panel.

Colonette (Fig. 98): small column.

Column: architectural term comprising capital, pillar or shaft and base. This supported the entablature (q.v.) In cabinet furniture a column or pilaster may show a debased version of a column belonging to one of the five classical Orders.

Composition, compo: usually a mixture of whiting, resin and size or glue for mould-shaped ornaments imitating carved wood, especially in the late 18th century.

Console: this is a type of bracket usually scroll shaped, and called a 'shouldering piece' in Bailey's dictionary, 1730. Often used to support the front of a table which was fixed to the wall, at the back (*see* Part IV).

Corbel (Fig. 59): projecting bracket found on the frieze of cabinet furniture.

Cornice (Fig. 80): in architecture the top horizontal moulding of an entablature (q.v.), hence the projecting top mouldings in cabinet furniture. The cabinet maker, using small moulding

planes, constructed the decorative top of his furniture piece by piece, in contrast to the power-driven tooling that can produce the requisite shapings in a single operation. The term was also applied to the supports for festoons of bed valances and curtains.

Counter: table or chest marked out for use in calculating; often with locked compartments below.

Counter-sunk: term used to describe the depression around a screw hole in a hinge, etc., permitting the screw head to be sunk flush; not found on early hinges.

Country Chippendale: modern name for country-made chairs of the later 18th century onwards in simplified versions of the patterns approved by Chippendale and his contemporaries.

Credence: long obsolete in domestic furniture but originally a side or serving table. Now ecclesiastical.

Cresting: carved decoration surmounting the top rail of chairs, mirrors and cabinet furniture.

Cretonne: strong, unglazed cotton cloth, dyed or printed or woven with a shadow pattern.

Crown glass (Fig. 83): glass for cabinets, etc., made by the early process of blowing and then flattening by spinning. The distorted centre of the disc was known as a bull's eye. Crown glass was made thinner and lighter in the 1740s.

Cross banding: common finish to veneered drawer front, invariably mitred at the corners in good quality English work. *See* BANDING.

15. Chairs of around 1810. TOP: two from Hope's *Household Furniture and Interior Decoration*, 1807, and detail of a leg from his drawing room at Deepdene; 'Gothic' drawing room chair by George Smith and detail of a Smith arm rest. SECOND ROW: dominant wide cresting and bolder reeded legs typical of the time; detail of side rail and back leg, sometimes a point of weak construction; japanned, by T. & G. Seddon (V. and A. Museum). BOTTOM: chair of stained beech; chair for drawing room (Ackermann's *Repository*); heavy rounded cresting and goat-head arm terminals.

Cupid's bow (Fig. 21): waved cresting on mid-18th-century chairbacks which meets the verticals at a pronounced angle.

Damask: furnishing fabric woven with rich figurings.

Dentil moulding (Fig. 14): small, rectangular blocks regularly spaced and protruding downwards like teeth; usually found as cornice ornament.

Dished (Fig. 38): term for a shallow depression as in candle slides and in card tables for holding counters.

Dovetails (Fig. 62): method of joining end grain into side grain at right angles, as in drawer corners, by fitting shaped projections into corresponding cuts.

Drawer runners: two strips of oak fixed inside the carcase to carry a drawer which was correspondingly grooved; a 17th-century method.

Drawer slip: *see* RUNNER.

Dust boards: introduced between drawers as part of the carcase in a chest of drawers and customary in antique specimens.

Echinus: *see* EGG-AND-TONGUE.

Egg-and-tongue (Fig. 14): also known as 'egg-and-dart', 'egg-and-anchor' and echinus. Rounded ovals alternating with more or less pointed arrow-head shapes. Popular as a line of carved ornament on cabinet furniture in classical style.

Empire style (Fig. 15 etc.): term widely used in England, but originating in the French style of the early 19th century when Napoleon became Emperor (1804–15). Also 'English Empire', although the war interrupted communications and prevented much direct copying.

Engraving: process of enriching marquetry by lines filled with black composition.

Entablature (Figs 80, 81): architectural term for the cornice (uppermost), frieze (central) and architrave (lowest) which rested upon the columns: hence the use of these terms in cabinet furniture. The entablature might be surmounted by a gabled or segmented pediment.

Escutcheon (Figs 2, 3, 125 etc.): shield shape for coat of arms, etc., but applied to the plate around a keyhole, irrespective of shape.

Fiddle back (Fig. 20): applied to early 18th-century chairs but variously interpreted. It has been taken to indicate a splat in violin outline or a waisted shaping to the side rails.

Fiddle back veneer: rippled grain as on high quality violins.

Fielded panel (Fig. 16): panel with a flat central field projecting slightly above the frame and with bevelled—that is, downward sloping—edges.

Filigree paper ornament: usually composed of narrow strips of coloured, gilt-edged paper, so stiffened, rolled, assembled and glued, with the gilded edge protruding, that they produce patterns suggesting gold filigree. Sometimes augmented with beads, shells, etc. This was in fashion between 1660 and 1720, and is found mounted as ornament on the sides of mirror frames, small cabinets, etc. Early work served as an alternative to the raised embroidery known as stump work, but it continued popular as an amateur handicraft on, for example, tea caddies through the 18th century. Much dates between about 1770 and 1810.

Fillet: a flat moulding.

Finial (Fig. 122 etc.): word widely applied to a decorative terminal such as was found on most kinds of furniture—chairs, cabinets, bed testers, etc.

Flutes, fluting (Fig. 14): concave channels cut to present a series of hollows, usually vertical, as ornament on pilasters, etc., in contrast to reedings, which are convex.

Fly bracket (Fig. 50): hinged side rail supporting a flap on a Pembroke or similar table.

French foot (Fig. 79): bracket foot for case furniture that curves outward instead of being vertical on the outer edge.

Frets, fretwork, lattice (Fig. 23): perforated ornament cut in wood, as for instance the Chinese and Gothic frets popular around the mid-18th century and often used on chair legs.

Frieze (Fig. 87): architectural term applied to cabinet furniture (*see* ENTABLATURE). The member immediately below the cornice. Often convex in flat-topped post-Restoration cabinets.

Gadrooning, knurling, nulling (Figs 16, 46): extremely popular form of carved moulding consisting of a series of convex knobs or knuckles, often separated by narrow flutes, either straight or slanting.

Gallery (Figs 48, 53 etc.): raised border to table, tray, etc., usually composed of miniature spindles or wood or metal fret.

Galloon, galon: furnishing braid.

Glazing bars (Figs 83, 88): narrow wooden bars supporting the glass in cabinets. In the mid-18th century these became slender and decoratively arranged.

Gothic (e.g. Figs 9, 15, 24, 77, 88): term used by collectors mainly for the romantic mock-Gothic fashion of the mid-18th century, which continued for some years after the general change to neo-classicism. Somewhat more correct Gothic forms appeared in a little Regency furniture, and there was a further important fashion in Victorian days.

Gouging: ornament composed of small depressions scooped out with a gouge.

Graining: the colour and grain of expensive, often exotic, woods, usually given to cheap woods with paint. Even in the 16th century oak and walnut were thus simulated, and the practice was still rife in Victorian days, involving a wide range of techniques.

Greek leg (Fig. 7): wide below the knee and tapering quickly, the surface frequently reeded or heavily fluted; a chair leg associated with William IV's reign.

Grille (Fig. 93): lattice or trellis of brass as filling for doors of cabinet furniture.

Guilloche (Fig. 16): Greek pattern of continuous plait or intertwining circles, sometimes containing conventional flowers. In use from the later 16th century onwards, most frequently carved.

Gutta foot, pl. guttae (Fig. 23): square-section foot, broadening slightly to the base and with an incision on each face. Used on thermed (*see* TERM, THERM) legs of neo-classical furniture.

Hardwood: term applied to timbers of broadleaved trees irrespective of their physical quality.

Herculaneum: excavations here and at Pompeii supplied much of the information concerning Roman and Graeco-Roman design and ornament that prompted neo-classical fashions.

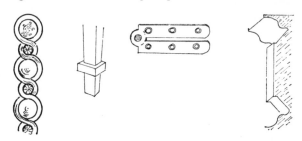

16. Guilloche pattern; Marlborough foot; rule hinge; silhouette of fielded panel (its proportions exaggerated).

Herringbone banding (Fig. 62): composed of two very narrow lines of veneer with opposing slanting grains.

Hock leg: cabriole (q.v.) leg with an interrupted line to the inner curve of the knee.

Hood (Fig. 123 etc.): semicircular top on some cabinets; also the framework around the upper part of a long case clock.

Hoof foot (Fig. 21): most often found in England as a goat's hoof on early cabriole (q.v.) leg chairs from about 1700 onwards.

Horse: the 18th-century term for the construction form now more familiar in its 19th-century form, the cheval (q.v.).

Horsehair: horse's mane and tail hair woven with linen or cotton warp. Popular from about 1775. Suitably crimped, the hair was combined with wool waste (flock) for stuffing upholstery.

Irish Chippendale: mahogany furniture of Irish origin in heavy-handed versions of early Georgian and mid-18th-century taste. Design appears to be based on imports from England, but conspicuous details include an excessively deep apron, often with a heavy, carved mask (q.v.), diapered (diamond) patterns against punched grounds for leaf and scroll carvings, and a hocked effect to the cabriole leg.

Jacobean: specifically should refer only to work of the reigns of James I and James II (1603–25 and 1685–88), but occasionally 'early Jacobean' and 'late Jacobean' are used to cover all but the Cromwellian years of the 17th century.

Knurled foot (Fig. 22): the opposite to a scroll foot, used around the mid-18th century, the scrolling curled in, under the foot, instead of outwards, and perhaps suggesting knuckles.

Loper: *see* RUNNER.

Lozenge (Fig. 59, *bottom left*): ornament in diamond outline, carved or inlaid.

Lunette (Fig. 59): design based on semicircles, usually filled with ornament: this included much low relief carving in the 17th century.

Marlborough foot (Fig. 16): square-cut collar projecting low on a thermed leg.

Mask: carved ornament in shape of face, human or animal.

Medallion (Fig. 128 etc.): ornamental plaque, round or oval.

Medullary rays: lines of dense non-cellular tissue radiating from the medulla or heart of a tree, cutting across the annual growth rings. Early carpenters found that they could split the newly felled oak along the rays, such riven timber showing the desirable 'silver grain'.

Mitre (Fig. 62): diagonal line of junction where two mouldings intersect at right angles.

Mohair: at first a fabric woven with Angora goat hair, but in 18th-century upholstery a closely woven silk.

Monopodium (Fig. 93): leg shaped and carved as an animal's head and leg, with paw foot; frequent in Regency as lion, leopard or chimaera.

Mother of pearl (Fig. 131): layer of iridescent nacre found in a number of different sea shells. Cut and polished, was applied as inlay from the 17th century. Ground wafer thin, it was cut with acid for application upon the surface of 19th-century papier mâché.

Mouldings: profiles in curved or faceted section, shaped with moulding planes to ornament cornices, plinths, panel framings, etc. In some work the mouldings were shaped separately and attached to a piece of furniture.

Muntin: the vertical framework between panels, the end pieces of the frame being stiles (q.v.).

Nulling: *see* GADROONING.

Ogee: name for the shape of a moulding which in section shows a double curve, concave above and convex below.

Orders: systems of architectural design which governed the proportions of the members. The five Orders are Doric, Ionic and Corinthian (Greek) and the Tuscan and Composite added by the Romans. In furniture debased versions may be found. *See* COLUMN and ENTABLATURE.

Ormolu (Fig. 1): originally *or moulu*—gold ground to a powder and used for gilding other metals: hence the gilded bronze that decorated fine furniture. The term came to mean a gold-coloured alloy of copper, zinc and tin, and was used by Matthew Boulton through the last quarter of the 18th century. Ure's *Dictionary of the Arts*, which was published in 1835, defined it as 'a brass in which there is less zinc and more copper than in ordinary brass'.

Ovolo: convex moulding used for mirror frames, etc., the section being a quarter-circle.

Pad foot: *see* CLUB FOOT.

Pagoda (Figs 82, 122): Oriental tower with projecting roofs introduced in the ornament of much mid-18th-century 'Chinese' furniture. A long case clock hood with an incurved slanting dome is known as a pagoda hood.

Panel (Fig. 127): a board within a framework of stiles (q.v.) and rails (q.v.) grooved to hold it.

Patera: circular or oval ornament, flattish but often decorated in low relief; widely used on neo-classical furniture.

Patina: the colour, texture and general appearance of the surface of a piece of wooden furniture resulting from age and the conditions it has experienced—hence an important quality in judging an antique.

Peardrop or arcaded moulding (Fig. 14): a series of arches separated by small swellings or drops, vaguely pear-shaped; often found below the cornice in cabinet furniture. The outline may suggest the Gothic work of the 1760s.

Pedestal: architectural term applied to furniture to indicate a solid support as contrasted with legs, as in a pedestal sideboard, desk, etc. Also the carved splat of an 18th-century chair (Figs 20, 21, 24).

Pegged furniture (Fig. 58): early chests, trestle tables, etc., which could be dismantled by withdrawing wooden pegs; popular with 19th-century medievalists.

Petit point: popular name for tent-stitch (q.v.).

Pigeon holes (Fig. 84 etc.): small compartments in a desk or bureau.

Piecrust (Fig. 53): this is a popular name for the pillar table with its circular rim shaped in cyma curves. It is especially popular in modern reproductions which of course are exactly round, whereas 18th-century specimens show shrinkage across the grain.

Pilasters (Figs 88, 93): columns attached along their length to the piece of furniture against which they are placed, such as the front corners of a chest of drawers.

Plinth: square member at base of column and hence the base of a piece of cabinet furniture not raised on feet.

Portuguese leg (Fig. 45): shapely leg with turned, swelling knee, sometimes gadrooned or cup-shaped above straight tapering leg with a smaller swelling to correspond at ankle height; popular on chairs and side tables of late 17th century.

Purdonium: Victorian name for coal scuttle when it became customary to keep supplies of coal in the living rooms.

Rebate, rabbet: continuous recess formed by reducing the thickness of the wood along its edge, as when cupboard doors or a cabinet-and-stand are thus fitted together.

Rail: horizontal piece of constructional framework above or below a panel, across the back of seat of a chair, etc.

Reeding (Figs 57, 88): two or more parallel mouldings in convex profile, usually placed vertically as low relief ornament, especially in neo-classical furniture; the opposite of fluting.

Restoration period: the years following 1660.

Riven wood: *see* MEDULLARY RAYS.

Rococo (Fig. 4 etc.): used in 19th century and now accepted as resembling the Rocaille popular in France between 1720 and 1755 and gradually adapted by the British through early Georgian days as a light-hearted escape from pseudo-classical or Baroque. It shows a sophisticated delight in well-balanced disorder, with fanciful introduction not only of rhythmic scrolling forms, cartouches, opposing C-scrolls, but of shells, rocks, waterfalls, foliage and flowers and other similar enthusiasms better suited to huge gilded mirror frames than to the Englishman's idea of serviceable furniture. It was still widely illustrated in the third edition of Chippendale's *Director* (1762). 'Revived rococo' dates from the 1820s.

Rule hinge (Fig. 16): hinge attached to the ends of the top and flap on a folding table, so that when closed the edges and not the faces of the hinge-halves are in contact.

Rule joint (Fig. 49): found on gate tables, folding screens, etc., where the edges of the adjoining parts are shaped in corresponding profile: in this way folding leaves no gap.

Run moulding: moulding consisting of continuous groovings made with the moulding plane along the solid wood of a member, such as a stile (q.v.) or muntin (q.v.) in a chest.

Runner (Fig. 84): rectangular-sectioned member fitting a slot or groove, to support a fall-flap desk, etc. Also known as slip or loper.

Rustic furniture (Fig. 33): dates from as early as the 18th century when Manwaring and others gave designs for furniture in the rustic taste for arbours, grottoes, etc. Manwaring's rustic seats were to be made 'with the limbs of yew and apple trees, as Nature produces them', but seasoned and de-barked. Probably Windsor chairs were the most widely used garden furniture. Great quantities of rustic furniture were made by the Victorians in iron; some in ceramic.

Sabre or scimitar leg (Fig. 15): chair leg with uninterrupted concave curve. Chairs with these forward and backward curving legs were copied from Graeco-Roman design popular in the Regency.

Saddle seat (Fig. 41): shaped with slight depressions separated by a low ridge towards the front to ensure comfort without cushions; customary on Windsor chairs.

Sand burning: wood dipped in hot sand to shade and mark its surface, such as the veins in marquetry leaves; described by Evelyn, 1664.

Scagliola: imitation marble; *see* Part XVII.

Screw: 'Skrewe pinnes' are listed in a bill for a 'cupboard of boxes' in the Chamberlain's Accounts of Stratford-on-Avon, 1594. The same item lists iron hinges, locks and keys. Brass pins, secured in the wood by screwing, came into wide use

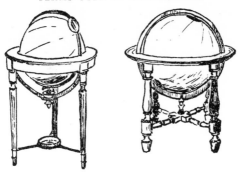

17. Globes. LEFT: design of early 1800s, with compass in base. RIGHT: globe c. 1810.

with the thinner wood and more delicate craftsmanship of the later 17th century. Early brass screws had slotted heads but irregular hand-filed thread. They were lathe-shaped by George III's day, but the machine-made, gimlet-pointed type are Victorian or later.

Scroll foot (Figs 23, 25, 53 etc.): projecting foot with scroll turning out and over itself; opposite of knurl (q.v.). (For other scroll forms, *see* Figs 19, 55 etc.)

Serpentine front (Fig. 61): two concave curves flanking a convex swell, a frequent shaping for chest furniture during the third quarter of the 18th century.

Setwork: inlay ornament in furniture.

Shagreen: untanned leather with a granular texture, usually dyed green or black and glued upon small jewel cabinets, desks, etc., in the 17th century. Later the skins of sharks and other fish were used as substitutes.

Sham drawer (Fig. 89): frequent in the later 18th century to avoid an undecorated area on the face of a piece such as a bureau dressing table containing a well with fitted compartments.

Shield back (Fig. 25): chair back outline associated with Hepplewhite and known at the time as vase shaped.

Shoe-piece (Fig. 20 etc.): shaped projection housing the base of a chair splat. In a late 17th-century chair this was attached to the chair's lower cross rail, not connected with the seat. During much of the 18th century it was attached to the back seat rail. Only in reproductions is it made in one with the cross rail or seat rail.

Slat (Fig. 37): narrow horizontal rail such as a cross bar in a simple ladder back chair.

Slide, slider (Fig. 56): flat rimless tray that can be pulled out like a drawer in a piece of cabinet furniture. A chest of drawers often has this fitting above the drawers for writing, etc., and smaller ones were fitted as candlestick rests.

Softwoods: term now applied by furniture makers to coniferous woods such as pine.

Spandrel (Fig. 124): triangular space between the curve of a circle or arch and the right angle of its surrounding frame, as on the dial of a long case clock.

Spavin leg (Fig. 15): Graeco-Roman line much used in Regency, adapted from crooked leg shape of a lion, but often modified into a meaningless jerky curve.

Spindle (Fig. 37, etc.): thin, lathe-turned rod, on country chair backs, for example, usually rendered ornamental by balanced variations of thickness. Split lengthways they were glued to the face of case furniture as ornament in the 17th century.

Spiral turning: *see* SWASH TURNING.

Splat (Fig. 20): central vertical piece in a chair back linking the top cresting rail with the shoe-piece (q.v.) on the back seat rail or a lower cross rail.

Squab: cushion tightly stuffed like seat upholstery that would fit within the low rim of a wooden-seated chair or serve as a substantial head rest upon a sofa.

Stile (Fig. 127): vertical member of a framework placed at the end or corner of a piece of panelled furniture. *See also* MUNTIN.

Strapwork (Fig. 12): ornament carved in low relief, usually in repetitive borders, etc., to suggest interlacing metal ornament.

Strawwork: flat ornament composed of short lengths of split straw glued to the surface of tea caddies, etc., usually also inside and on the drawer fronts of small cabinets. The design may be pictorial or conventional, the effect being achieved by slanting the straws at contrasting angles to catch the light and by surface colouring. This tedious work came to England from the Continent, probably in the 17th century, but little remains that can be dated earlier than the early 19th century. It was widely and expertly made for sale by some of the many thousands of prisoners-of-war held in this country between 1793 and 1815 and permitted to pursue a number of crafts for profit.

Stretcher (Figs 19, 37 etc.): rail or bar linking the legs of a chair or table, important for strength and rigidity. Often treated decoratively—shaped in flat curves (waved), perforated or turned in ornamental outlines.

Stringing (Figs 97, 125): generally applied to very narrow lines of contrasting wood separating areas and borders of veneer, but especially associated with the checker-patterned lines in dark and light wood, sometimes suggesting rope twist, that were extremely popular in the late 18th century. Regency stringing may be of brass.

Swag (Fig. 14): festoon of drapery, flowers, etc., carved or painted, usually on neo-classical furniture.

Swan neck pediment (Fig. 81): this is a broken pediment which is composed of a pair of opposing S-scrolls, their upper ends finished with paterae (q.v.).

Swash turning (Fig. 19 etc.): descriptively known as barley sugar twist, a clever feat of eccentric turning used for much late 17th-century furniture. This Eastern motif came from Holland, but the English version shows larger hollows than the Dutch, which is tightly twisted.

Tambour (Fig. 85): flexible table or cupboard fitting known as a reed top. Narrow convex mouldings were glued on strong canvas, side by side on their flat faces, the ends fitting into grooves so that they form, vertically, a sliding door and, horizontally, a lid to a desk. Hepplewhite found them 'convenient', but Sheraton in 1803 noted they were easily broken and almost out of use.

Tea board: tea tray.

Tent-stitch (Fig. 130): embroidery stitch, fine and very strong, worked over each single vertical and horizontal thread of the fabric so that each stitch is at a backward slant, giving additional strength to the back of the work.

Term, therm: as applied to furniture stands, the word was not generally differentiated from a pedestal; more strictly applied to the form of stand with a top resting on a human bust, without arms, this top often being a capital of one of the Orders (q.v.). Thermed legs are distinguished by their tapering shape, square on plan (Fig. 23 etc.).

Thumb mould (Fig. 46): Rounded projecting edge, to table top, etc. Also a repetitive pattern of small gouge cuts along the edge of a chest, etc.

Till: small drawer or box fitted into a chest.

Tongue-and-groove (Fig. 49): a method of joining the side edges of planks, as, for example, for carcase work under veneer. It preceded the rule joint for the flaps of some early gate-leg tables.

Tortoiseshell: used as a veneer, but more frequently on the Continent. The shell, semi-transparent, might be coloured on the underside to show its markings, or clear shell might be laid upon a ground of mottled colours. When heated the pieces of shell could be joined and moulded to any shape.

Trenail, treenail: old term for cylindrical pin of hardwood used for fastening timbers together.

Twist: *see* SWASH TURNING.

Verre églomisé: sometimes found on borders of mirrors around 1700. Such a border was of glass ornamented on the underside by a painted design backed by gold or silver leaf which was set against a background of black or red, sometimes green. The basis of the design could be taken from a print, as in the amateur hobby of making 'glass pictures'.

Vitruvian scroll: ornament composed of a series of S-scrolls, frequently on a frieze. Vitruvius was a Roman architect of the Augustan age.

Voyder: tray used for voiding or clearing a table after a meal.

Wave moulding (Fig. 72): undulating moulding usually composed of narrow, low relief reeding, flanking a wider central convexity. Found on front and sides of straight, very slightly tapering chair legs of late 18th-century medium quality.

PART III

Chairs

To the 16th-century Englishman a chair was something of a status symbol—a massive piece of joinery or turnery that was occasionally upholstered—whereas most of his household and staff were served by well-cushioned wall benches, settles and easily shifted stools. Needless to say, such armchairs are now extremely rare.

The flamboyant Continental style of the fabric-covered X chair and the limited range of delightful working chairs made by the turner (known as thrown chairs) must be mentioned separately, but the principal chair style from late medieval days was the joiner's chair. The design consisted of heavy framed-up panelling, the back stiles of the box seat being extended to support the solid panelling of the back, and this design was customary until the 1620s. Randle Holme, in 1649, described it as a 'settle-chair'. Occasionally, instead of panelling, the seat rested on four plain legs linked by low stretchers, and by the end of the 16th century the front legs were sometimes turned and fluted. Above the seat the flat arms rested on continuations of the front legs, being rounded out for comfort and finished with scrolled ends. By then the top rail extended across and beyond the somewhat raked back uprights with an 'ear-piece' effect emphasised by carving.

Such chairs continued to be made by country joiners through the 17th century, but a wider range then came into more general use, including such single chairs as the farthingale (q.v.). Here, as in many armchairs, weight was reduced by confining the back support to a panel at about shoulder height. This left space for a deep cushion, and the seat was

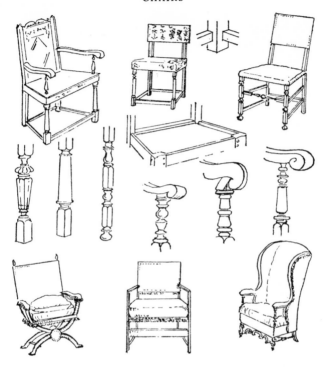

18. Seventeenth-century chairs. TOP: early design panelled back; mid-century (in turkey-work) with stretcher detail and (below) an alternative seat, rimmed for squab cushion; later design with more elaborate stretchers. SECOND ROW: three legs; three scroll arms—wide, narrow (seen from inner side) and rounded. BOTTOM, easy chairs: X-chair, wholly fabric-covered; Continental style of c. 1660s with braid and fringes; later wing chair.

67

often rimmed to hold it in position. But, as an alternative to carved wood, the panel was often of padded and fringed fabric, turkeywork or close-nailed leather.

19. Later 17th-century chairs. TOP: c. 1670, designed for deep cushion with coarse caning, stretcher at back (omitted in some Continental specimens); periwig type of last years, probably originally with fringe to mask heavy back legs; with trumpet legs and curved X-stretchers. SECOND ROW: three arms of 1670s–90s and two front views to show the elaborate curves. BOTTOM diagrams of leg and stretcher arrangement through the period.

Another alternative was the open-backed chair with broad cresting and cross rails, sometimes including a few spindles. The most elaborate of these included the chairs known as Derbyshire and Yorkshire (q.v.), though in fact they were not confined to this area. Arms around the mid-17th century were more or less flat, but the legs and stretchers showed the period's wide range of decorative turnery.

It may be noted that chairs of about the 1660s and later showed a change of stretcher arrangement, the legs being linked by two stretchers each side, one at the back and, at the front, an increasingly decorative member, sometimes turned, but often extensively carved, so that for hard wear it was supplemented by another between the lower side stretchers.

Charles II's court returned from the Continent with new ideas about comfort, and started a new fashion. Some chairs of this well-established pattern, but with back and seat panels of caning, may be regarded as humbler versions of the most magnificent, familiar—and widely reproduced—armchairs introduced in the 1670s. The walnut 'Charles II' chair needs little description. The decoratively turned side verticals supported wide top and cross rails which, with inner vertical members, framed a rectangle of caning. Elaborately carved cresting was echoed to the sides and base of the caning and again on a high, wide, front stretcher.

On the most elaborate specimens the arm and leg verticals, and even the seat framing, were carved, the dominant motif often being the familiar amorini supporting a crown among scrolling foliage. The general design came to England from France via Holland, the English swash turning being a deeply furrowed slender twist, and the English back panel rectangular rather than oval with leg construction including a high back stretcher. Typically the arms had a wide, welcoming dip and scrolled massively over their decorative supports, which were still extensions of the front legs.

Chairs were also made in oak, beech and other available woods, but the elaborate style is now most often found in walnut. Variants abound: late in the century the chair tended to acquire the more emphatic lines of the so-called periwig chair (q.v.). The increasingly fine mesh of cane work aids dating, as does the change of emphasis from square to scrolling lines. Before the end of the century the cresting again tended to ride over the side verticals, and the seat in a single chair might ride over the front legs, instead of being tenoned into them, which was a constructional fault.

The backs of some chairs of this period had carving instead of caning, and the seats were upholstered. Some were japanned, but the main change at the end of the century was to more disciplined, neatly vertical outlines. Elongated baluster shapes supported the open scrolls of the cresting and the dipping arms. Legs, front and back, tapered below swelling mushroom or pear-shaped knees, often gadrooned although still left square for stretchers. These sometimes included a deep-carved front stretcher somewhat set back under the seat and tenoned into the side stretchers in an H arrangement. Alternatively, they were placed diagonally as flattish mouldings, in waved outlines. Before the end of the 17th century, winged easy chairs were coming into use, their rich fabrics set off by carved and gilded or painted front legs and stretchers.

The first cabriole legs appeared in England soon after 1700. They were narrow at the knee, lacking the attached brackets that later became customary, and ending in scrolls or hoof feet. In Queen Anne's reign the style became fully established, first with straight side verticals rounded at the shoulder, and then with the full S curve at each side which flowed into the thickened section above the back of the seat and continued smoothly into the outcurving back leg. The central back was filled with a vase-shaped splat ending at seat level in an attached shoe-piece. This became known as the bended-back chair.

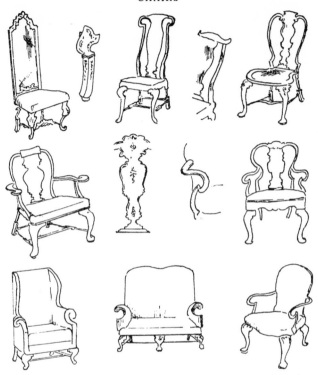

20. Early 18th-century chairs. TOP: late periwig; leg transition between S-scroll and cabriole; the new bended-back style (detail showing the double curve); transition to curves complete but retaining stretchers. SECOND ROW: heavy type of 1720s design; splat detail, sometimes now called fiddle back; detail of arm curve; typical 1720s–30s design, the side-rail shaping also sometimes called fiddleback. BOTTOM: chair c. 1710; so-called loveseat, c. 1710; upholstered variant of the spoon-back, c. 1720s–30s.

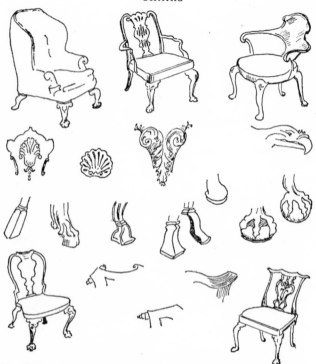

21. Chairs of 1730s–50s. TOP: easy chair; armchair; spoonback. SECOND ROW: knee details with shells and acanthus foliage; eagle-head arm terminal. THIRD ROW, feet: back foot on many early cabrioles; hoof and stylised hoof; two views of a foot found on many early cabrioles, perhaps derived from Spanish foot; two ball and claw, one webbed. BOTTOM: left and right show contrasts of the 1730s and the 1740s onwards; centre, cresting rail details of late 1740s when side and top-rail junction changed from rounded curve to sharp angle, including the Onslow scroll (left) and paper scroll (below).

When the cabriole leg in its various forms was broadened at the shoulder and integrated into the seat rails, stretchers became unnecessary. The swelling knee called for carved enrichment such as the typical Dutch scallop shell, often with a husk, and the simple pad or club foot was often elaborated into the ball-and-claw. The flat surfaces were most often walnut veneered, but some were japanned and there was occasional use of marquetry.

The seat lost its square look, becoming rounded or serpentine, and was overstuffed or fitted with the familiar drop-in frame which necessitated strengthening the front corners, and may have prompted the change to arm verticals set back a little from the chair front—a line that suited ladies' dresses—curving forward to meet the rounded scrolls of the dished arms. In the early Georgian chair this shepherd's crook arm was largely replaced by a projecting end with a small, tight scroll or volute.

Many early 18th-century chairs had tall, wholly upholstered backs, such as the compass or spoon-back chair and that other dandy's chair, the reading chair. Walnut was in abundant use for chairs throughout the first half of the 18th century, but when mahogany took the lead from the 1720s onwards, early Georgians found a new pleasure in carved detail such as the lion masks of the 1720s and 30s. Until the 1740s, however, the general outlines changed comparatively little. Some attractive upholstered chairs date roughly from the 1730s, with low, squarish backs, wide seats (sometimes with richly carved seat rails), and back-curving supports to upholstered arms. In some of the most spectacular—restricted to a few wealthy individuals and too lavish to become a commercial vogue—the ponderously carved mahogany was enriched with gilding.

Already by the 1730s, however—and far more by the 1740s —splat-back mahogany chairs were beginning to show square-

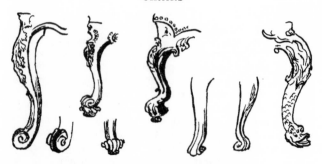

22. Chair legs of c. 1750s. Five views of the period's modified scroll feet; two views of the knurl foot; seaweed leg with dolphin foot.

shouldered outlines, which was the next major phase and produced what many collectors regard as the finest chairs ever made (Fig. 21). Here the cresting rode over the tops of the slightly outward-curving side verticals, typically ending in 'paper scrolls' or similar neat detail, while the splat gained much in ornamental value by intricate piercing: the heavy baroque style was giving way to French rococo. The metallic brilliance of the carving in hard Spanish mahogany has only improved with age, in contrast to the painted ornament of the last years of the century.

Matthias Darly, in 1752, offered designs for 'Chinese, Gothic and Modern Chairs', but Chippendale's *Director* of 1754 was the first widely influential collection of chair patterns. He had little use for the heavy ball-and-claw foot, although he allowed the dolphin motif, preferring the lighter French style of cabriole with appropriately undulating seat rail on a scroll or knurl foot. Even in upholstered chairs he approved a back which, while framed in carving, was 'open below' (i.e. with a space between the back panel and the serpentine-

23. Chair legs of c. 1750s. 'Chinese' with card-cut leg and fret-cut bracket and stretchers; fret-cut 'Gothic' with square foot; 'Gothic' cluster column; two 'Gothic' columns, forerunners of the tapering neo-classic legs of the 1760s; gutta foot, often with church window 'Gothic' leg; square moulded 'Gothic' leg (below).

fronted seat). He used straight legs on Gothic and Chinese chairs—some with stretchers—and in the third edition of his *Director* included tapering pillar legs.

A typical fashionable chair of the period from 1745 to 1760, however, was a restrained version of his 'modern' chair. It was of mahogany, crisply carved on back rails and splat, and possibly also on arms, seat rail and legs, or showing merely a little rococo work on the cupid's bow crest rail and C-scrolls or strapwork on the splat above plain cabriole legs. The splat piercings were chisel-trimmed at the back for lightness, but retained an impression of strength by being based on a mahogany shoe-piece rising from the centre of the back seat rail. The *London Tradesman*, 1747, noted that specialists shaped and carved the splat—known as a pedestal —and its associated cresting rail and shoe piece, often working at home and never without a job.

It is a mistake to look for many chairs of the period exactly

24. Chairs of c. 1750s. the 'Chippendale *Director* period'. TOP:
Chippendale design with pierced splat; Chippendale ribband back;
two details of arms; typical armchair. SECOND ROW: three *Director* designs which were offered as 'Chinese', 'Gothic' and 'French',
giving alternative details. BOTTOM: Ince & Mayhew 'parlour chair'
(two leg patterns); Ince & Mayhew burjair (bergère); everyday
chair of 1760s onwards, with wave moulded legs.

reproducing Chippendale designs, or those of such contemporaries as Robert Manwaring and Ince and Mayhew. Indeed, such popular designs of the period as the revived ladder-back (Fig. 27) found no place in the pattern books.

The neo-classical style appeared in Adam chair designs of the 1760s and 70s in the French manner. These were of painted or gilded soft wood with oval or rounded tapestry-mounted backs, padded arm horizontals and tapering, fluted legs. Dress fashions contributed to the shape: with stiffened coats and hooped skirts becoming outmoded during the 1760s, seats could be smaller and the arms brought forward over the front legs once more.

Even when the back was square, retaining something of the mid-century cupid's bow cresting, the effect was restrained and slender, with the splat sometimes shaped as a lyre. But the characteristic back outlines were the oval or rounded ellipse, the nearly square escutcheon and the vase (now usually called a shield). The back support of slats, bars (banister-back), or other decorative detail such as carved swags, was wholly contained within the framing. In each case the backward- and outward-curving back legs were extended a little above the seat to support the back framing, while the arm horizontals extended directly from the framing, but quickly curved downward in a concave sweep to the front legs. Seat rails became deeper from about 1780, and often entirely hidden beneath horsehair, mohair cloth, silk or printed linen, fixed with close-nailing. Ornament consisted of the acceptable classic motifs, carved in low relief, inlaid or painted.

Hepplewhite illustrated the current liking for these simple and increasingly light styles appropriate to prevailing dress fashions, and referred to the renewed interest in painted and japanned chairs. Some were gilded, and caning was in fashion again. He recommended a width in front of 20 inches, depth of seat 17 inches, height of seat frame 17 inches and total

25. Post-1760 armchairs. TOP, with escutcheon backs: transitional; with 'French' leg; 'Gothic' (V. and A. Museum). SECOND ROW: chairs in squarer neo-classical lines, with arms tending to begin higher on the back vertical rails and end over the front legs, and with the legs straight and tapering. BOTTOM: chairs with vase-shaped (now called shield-shaped) backs, one showing serpentine seat rail, one wave-moulded legs; also two chair legs.

26. Post-1760 armchairs. TOP: chairs with oval backs, the centre one with serpentine seat and French legs. SECOND ROW: chairs of the 1790s, based on Sheraton *Drawing Book* designs (1791–4). BOTTOM: upholstered chair; porter's chair, in leather; Hepplewhite winged design.

chair height about 3 feet 1 inch. It is interesting to note that his *Guide*, published by his widow in 1788, was re-issued in 1789 and was used by chair makers to the extent that an exact Hepplewhite design appeared on the trade card of William Perry (1790–95). The revised edition, 1794, included patterns for square-backed chairs which had been on the market for at least eight years before Sheraton's *Drawing Book* gave impetus to such designs in 1791.

Late in the 18th century the liking for ever lighter chairs was associated with this return to more rectangular outlines. The crest rail, very thin towards the sides, often formed or rode over a narrow central panel curved to fit the sitter's back, and offering opportunities for flat ornament. Below there was sometimes a vase-shaped splat or a group of narrow lattice bars rising from a cross rail only a few inches above the seat, and sometimes incorporating carved swags.

Turned work was of increasing importance, and Sheraton even incorporated a turned crest rail. His love of rectangular lines was expressed in chair backs (where the dominant line was a square enclosed by the uprights), a low but important cross rail, and a crest rail that was seldom entirely a straight line in the Adam manner. Within the square the range of fillings rarely included the vertical splat form of earlier design. Arms tended to be high-shouldered, with horizontal emphasis. Sheraton recommended satinwood quite as much as mahogany; he enjoyed touches of gilding and surface ornament such as inlay, marquetry or paint. Some of his designs were specifically 'suitable for japanning'; others for 'finishing in white and gold'. By 1803 even Sheraton was recommending that dining chairs should be 'respectable and substantial looking'. He approved of painted chairs for breakfast and tea rooms and touches of gilding on mahogany for the drawing room.

Early 19th-century design, however, reflected the archaeologist's wish to reproduce the actual furniture of the ancient Romans, Greeks and Egyptians. Thomas Hope, in 1807, rejoiced that the French Revolution had 'restored the pure

27. Later 18th-century chairs. TOP, backs: ladder, from the 1760s, breaking away from vertical splat; three from Hepplewhite's *Guide*, the Prince of Wales feathers taken from the third edition, 1794. SECOND ROW: typical single chairs of c. 1775, still showing traces of vertical splat. BOTTOM: four Sheraton designs, 1791–4.

taste of the antique reproduction of ancient Greek forms for chairs, etc.'. Sheraton, in his *Cabinet Dictionary*, showed something of the change in taste with the return to curves in scroll back and scimitar legs, in curricle and X-framed chairs, with such ornamental motifs as chimera, lion's mask and paw, eagle and dolphin. Regency chairs included severe examples of church-window Gothic, some gaily japanned chinoiserie and, in the same mood, some light beechwood turned and painted to suggest bamboo. All these receive individual mention. But the typical chairs of the period are immediately recognisable with their shoulder-high square backs, dipped seats and curving scimitar legs.

There was also a repetition of late 16th- and late 17th-century changes in chair design. The crest rail several inches deep was widened to ride over the uprights instead of being housed between them. Arms rested on extensions of the front legs, sometimes lion or leopard monopodia. Splats such as the revived lyre were less common than simple horizontal cross rails or diagonal lattice, and ornament was concentrated on the cresting. Often one notes a structural weakness in the deep, backward curve of the lower back immediately above the seat rail. This necessitated the curving back leg which continued through Victorian days and, at its most attractive, was matched by an equally simple curve at the front, usually in tapering square section and often reeded. The alternatives consisted of the straight front leg, sometimes a cluster column or a spavin type with appropriate paw foot, but most often a variety of the Greek leg, often eight-sided, small at the top, very broad at knee height and tapering quickly. Turned variants were sometimes reeded, often spirally. An attractive variant tapered from a circle of tassel-like gadrooning at knee height.

The classic Greek chair, adopted by Rome, was a Regency favourite that continued in post-Regency years, with a con-

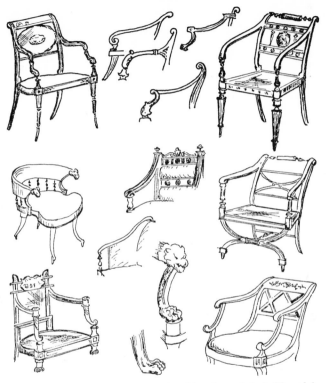

28. Early Regency chairs. TOP: painted beechwood chair (V. and A. Museum); four arm outlines from Sheraton's *Cabinet Dictionary*; painted beechwood chair, early 1800s. SECOND ROW: Sheraton curricle or curricule chair (from what he describes as a two-horse chaise); two Sheraton backs; chair in 'Greek' style. BOTTOM: light chair of cane and painted beechwood; leg and arm-terminal with lion motifs; chair with diagonal back bars and brass inlay.

83

29. Chairs of about 1815 and later. TOP: chair with more elaborate cresting, big arms, c. 1815; chair steps, a Morgan & Sanders design; desk chair. SECOND ROW: tub, developed from Sheraton's curricle; three leg designs; Regency version of scoop or spoon back. BOTTOM: characteristics include arm set back, diagonal stretchers, thick, well-turned leg; cane easy chair of bergère type.

tinuous curve flowing from the side verticals to the backward flaring back legs balanced by the forward sweep of the front legs and somewhat dished seat. The shoulder-high cresting board was supported on the forward curve of the side verticals. In some late Regency specimens the splat was in the shape of a lyre and the tapering front legs ended in heavy paw feet.

Another style associated with the Regency was the leg design composed of double reversed curves crossed in the centre (Fig. 28): the curves either dominated the front (with straight legs at the back), or were introduced to each side of the chair. The reading chair, the compass-seat or spoon-back, the curricle or arc-back and the bergère were also important Regency introductions or revivals. By 1820 R. Brown had to declare that 'it now baffles the most skilful artists to produce any new forms'.

In 1833 Loudon declared that the prevailing styles were still the Grecian or modern—'by far the most prevalent'—Gothic and Elizabethan. The post-Regency and early Victorian tendency, however, was away from the classical traditions of grace and proportion, although the extremely wide, deep crest rail, often brass-inlaid, was known as Grecian and was used on swelling 'Greek' front legs.

In the dining chair the wide overriding crest rail was either linked to the cross rail by an elaboration of carving, or was itself carved. Painted motifs on such splats included musical trophies, fruit, even pictorial scenes within formal patterns. As an alternative there was also brass inlay matching the table claws. The scimitar splay to the back legs continued, but in the front legs it was replaced disastrously in some specimens by the heavy Greek leg. Even some Gothic dining chairs had such front legs, and the church-window piercings were restricted to the back with appropriate card-cutting on the seat rail. In the more slender drawing room chair the legs were less obtrusive and often linked by thin double stretchers. But by early Victorian days even drawing room specimens tended to be aggressively heavy-legged, with stuffed and buttoned backs.

Meanwhile, from the 1820s onwards, the general tendency in chairs, as in other furnishings, was towards arched crestings. One important result was the balloon-back in various forms. This might be regarded as a return to the so-called Hepplewhite back, but in the post-Regency outline the shape was an oval rather than an ellipse. Such publications as the *London Cabinet Maker's Assistant*, 1832, indicate that in the single chair even upholstery was usually restricted to the oval or its heart-shaped variant.

In the drawing room, where the single chair was essential for wide skirts, the seat was often slightly nipped at the sides and serpentine in front. In the 1840s and 50s this lent itself to a version of the French or cabriole leg with a small knee and scroll foot, but by earlier rules it was too long in the back and too short in the leg.

For boudoir and bedroom, early Victorian taste was for chairs in the full exuberance of French rococo style, whether in walnut, gilded or painted soft woods boldly fashioned or papier mâché (Fig. 131) in seemingly endless scrolls. There is much of Louis Quinze in the chairs of the 1850s, but the close reproductions of Hepplewhite and Sheraton design may be dated 1870s onwards.

Particularly acceptable today are some of the bedroom chairs with cane or rush seats, the open backs suggesting whimsical variants of the open balloon or figure of eight, and with notably elaborate turning on the slender front legs, ending in outward turning tapers. Regency and early Victorian chair makers applied the term 'fancy' to chairs of painted or japanned beech.

In the upholstered armchair the round-topped back slightly narrowed at the waist and swelled again into low arms. Characteristically the whole shape was outlined in lightly

30. Chairs outside usual Regency range. TOP: two painted chairs in 'Chinese' style flanking detail of cross rail, c. 1820, carved around a shield of brass inlay. SECOND ROW, two work chairs: strut-back Windsor and a popular kitchen chair from c. 1820s which might have flat laths or turned sticks flanked by 'roman spindles'. (see also Fig. 40). BOTTOM: characteristics of George IV and William IV.

carved walnut or mahogany, the back border or frame flowing into the arms which were supported by scroll extensions from the front legs and had small, padded arm rests.

During the second half of the century chairs in self-conscious 'art' styles emerged. Both the familiar Morris chairs became popular in the 1860s (Figs 31, 32), and by the 1870s the features of the cult had become recognisable. Many fairly simple, lightweight chairs were produced, showing enthusiastic use of ebonised woods, with green-stained oak as an alternative. There might be touches of gilding, perhaps, and the splat or cresting was painted rather than carved, but often it was severely plain, with a tendency to include quantities of thin, turned members in severe rectangular shapes.

The more substantial dining chairs of the period tended to show shallow, many-ringed turning on only slightly tapering legs. For relief from such severity the tendency was towards circular forms—low in the back, high in the arm—typified by the Eaton Hall tub. With the change in dress fashion, arms became important on chairs again from the 1870s.

It is a mistake to underrate the importance of simplicity to furnishing designs of the 1870s and 80s. Country styles of rush-seated spindle-backs and ladder-backs and modified Windsors then took their place with equally simple cane as alternatives to the massive, fully upholstered, deeply sprung lounging chair. By then great numbers of chairs were being made, not as interpretations of earlier fashions, but as direct replicas of late 18th-century work. This is now an endless source of confusion to collectors, but at the time must have been welcome as an escape from the current 'quaint' chairs in

31. Early to mid-Victorian chairs. TOP: reclining chair: 'neo-Greek' chair, 1840s; chair by Jackson & Graham, 1851; early, buttoned 'Louis XV' chair. SECOND ROW: prie-dieu style; 'Louis XV' drawing-room chair; early version of fringed, straight-sided tub; buttoned and fringed chair. THIRD ROW: two people's conversation seat; upholstery buttons and tassel; Morris adjustable chair made from 1860s. BOTTOM: wicker chair, covered with home needlework, popular in 1870s; later waisted tub shown with fringe removed; leather library chair; bergère in late 18th-century tradition.

shiny rosewood with broad crest rails flatly ornamented with paint or metal inlay, spindly legs, low, awkward stretchers and curiously unwelcoming arms.

Abbotsford chair (Fig. 12): Created in the 1830s and 40s and still widely in use in this century, the chair was influenced by the style of Scott's house, and intended by Victorian romantics to be Elizabethan in design with renaissance carving. In fact, while remaining unmistakably Victorian, the features of the chair were more late 17th-century. The tall back had a central panel of upholstery or caning, flanked by twist-turned side rails and supporting a heavily carved crest rail. Below the seat the disproportionately short legs, and stretchers too, were often twist-turned or carved in S-scrolls. Usually the chair was of oak, sometimes walnut, with tapestry upholstery, and it was placed in the hall, library or dining room.

Adelaide chair: Name now sometimes given to the William IV chair (introduced earlier), with a balloon back, composed of facing C-scrolls.

Astley Cooper chair: Designed by Sir Astley Cooper F.R.S. (1768–1841) to preserve the child's straight back. The chair back was extra tall and straight with a broad crest rail and two much lower, broad, cross rails. The legs flared strongly outward for rigidity, linked by two sets of stretchers, including a flat foot rest.

Balloon-back chair (Figs 30, 32): From the 1820s onwards, popular especially as sets of dining chairs with heavily upholstered seats. The back lost all trace of the overriding cresting, and instead was a skilfully shaped curve to fit the sitter's back. To the front view it presented either an open oval or an obvious variant of the nipped-waist line such as the cameo, with carved

32. Chairs for the dining-room, bedroom, etc., early to mid-Victorian. TOP: clumsier version of Regency type; chair with cane in back and seat; two balloon backs with detail of balloon curving. SECOND ROW: two with shouldered balloon backs, the bedroom chair with stretchers in papier mâché; 'Elizabethan' or 'Abbotsford' back with 'Greek' leg; 'Louis XVI'. BOTTOM, chairs with more vertical lines: bentwood chairs (second from right) were popular from 1862. Morris chair (right) was adapted from a Sussex type from c. 1865.

detail on the inner frame of the O, and a back composed of two facing Cs. Ornament was restricted to crest and cross rails and the changing styles of front legs. Invariably the out-curving back legs were plain, being unimportant to the Victorian intent on 'show'. Most familiar are the dining and library chairs with Greek front legs which became somewhat more shapely and slender by the 1850s. Flimsier fancy versions in stained woods have tapering, out-curving legs, but by the 1850s showed more use of the French or modified cabriole.

Back stool: *See* STOOLS.

Bamboo chair: Imitation bamboo chairs were much used around 1800. Sheraton in his *Dictionary* described this cane-coloured furniture in turned beechwood, and in 1797 it was listed among the stock of the 'fancy chair maker', William Challen, at a period when even the potter enjoyed imitating the shapes and colours of cane. Chairs actually made of bamboo are associated mainly with the Oriental mood of the late 19th century, and they had become conspicuously flimsy by the 1890s.

Bended-back chair (Fig. 20): Mainly a dining room chair, sold by the set—of single chairs with a pair of armchairs. Introduced from Holland around 1710 when furniture fashion was taking a new delight in curves. Made of walnut, this chair was dominated by curved lines—in the cresting, curving roundly into side verticals shaped as elongated Ss, and in the seat curving roundly out from a narrowed back with the shoulders of the cabriole legs following the rounded line. But the most conspicuous detail was the splat which for the first time rippled vertically to fit the sitter's back. The phase soon passed, although bended backs in black walnut were still being made in the second half of the century, long after fashion had turned to mahogany, and a cheaper market was long served by bended-backs in japanned beechwood. In high fashion the squarer lines of the 1730s and 40s required more angular

33. Less usual 19th-century chairs. TOP: folding or steamer chair; rustic (sometimes ante-dated); rustic in terra-cotta with 'Gothic' crannies for ferns, c. 1890. SECOND ROW: step-ladder chair hinged at the seat, shown open and closed, including 'Gothic' variant. BOTTOM: bentwood and cane.

cresting and a square-fronted seat. Even the shepherd's crook arm was outmoded. As for the splat, it lost its ripple, becoming wider and tending to curve in the horizontal plane before losing its smooth beauty in a complexity of piercings.

Bentwood chair (Fig. 33): Familiar, slender, rounded frame and out-curving legs made of light birch wood, usually stained

black or mahogany colour with seat and back panels most
often of cane. The method of steam heating to bend the wood
was long familiar to the Windsor chair maker, but was
developed by the Thonet brothers of Vienna, and became
popular in England from the 1860s. The chairs ranged from
reclining rockers to round-seated chairs for children.

Bergère chair (Figs. 29, 31): French term for a winged armchair from about 1725. Ince and Mayhew applied the term

34. Children's chairs. TOP: cane-seated chair with movable foot
rest, 1690s onwards; rush-seated country specimen, early Georgian;
details of ball turning adapted to hold footboard and bar across
seat; mid-Georgian chair, with Cupid's-bow cresting. BOTTOM, late
18th and early 19th-century Windsor types: comb back and hoop
back; early 19th-century version of popular chair-and-table, found
also in Victorian balloon-back style, the two parts making a high
chair linked by a central iron rod; spindle chair with splayed legs.

to an excessively deep, low, reclining chair with padded, horizontal arms. In the late 18th century the name was sometimes given to a nursing chair with a low back and down-curving arms filled as a single entity with upholstery or caning. A detail revived in the later 19th century was the turned arm support only an inch or two in front of the framing. The bergère was frequently of bold design in the Regency with massive armrests carved as winged chimeras, for example, but the simple caned version was revived in the 1860s and 70s when the back was higher and the seat lower than before, and the wood often white or gilded.

Caqueteuse or gossip's chair: Sixteenth- and 17th-century design, probably from France, with narrow raked back and high seat, the arms and the back edge of the seat following a wide arc, to accommodate full skirts. An alternative in the 17th century was the farthingale chair (q.v.).

Ceramic chair (Fig. 33): Ceramic chairs and stools were made in the 19th century to introduce bright colours into the conservatory. A tub stool in the Spode-Copeland Museum is marked SPODE. This has a lifting hole in the seat and pierced ornament among the pictorial detail of the famous Italian pattern in transfer-printed blue. The Mason firm introduced vivid japan patterns on seat furniture in ironstone ware, which was also used for fireplaces. A typical Victorian notion was the rustic seat in terracotta with niches for growing ferns and mosses.

Child's chair (Fig. 34): Solid small-scale versions of panelled oak chairs remain from the 17th century. High chairs are known in 17th-century turnery, with wide, splayed legs; in substantial versions of the Charles II walnut chair; in Georgian mahogany with splat back and extended versions of cabriole legs linked by stretchers; in various Windsor forms and in splayed bentwood. In all these chairs the distinguishing features are the heavy leg and stretcher construction, including holes in the front legs for an adjustable foot rest and in the arm verticals for a safety bar.

An interesting design popular in the 19th century was the small armchair—typically with balloon back, upholstered seat and short, sturdy legs. This was mounted on a small, steady table, an iron rod from the centre of the chair seat passing down through the centre of the table to fasten underneath the top. When not required as a single high-chair unit, the rod could be released and the chair and table placed beside each other. *See* ASTLEY COOPER CHAIR.

Chinese chairs (Figs 24, 30): As explained in Part XVII, japanning was endlessly popular as a means of giving an attractive finish to chairs made of cheap woods. From the late 17th century onwards the ornamental motifs were frequently inspired by the lacquer imports of the East India Company. The so-called 'Chinese' furniture went a little further, including a few supposedly Chinese motifs in what was otherwise wholly Western construction. But it was still a fashion mainly restricted to minor rooms.

The most conspicuous phase, around the mid-18th century, produced many chairs, illustrated, for example, by Chippendale and Ince and Mayhew (who called them dressing chairs). These were, of course, Western chairs with 'Chinese' detail such as 'Chinese railing' for the back in place of a splat, and pagoda-shaped cresting. The angular trellis that filled the back and arms was sometimes built up piece by piece or fret-cut from the solid. Card-cut or fret-cut work often ornamented the seat rail and fret-cut brackets linked the rail to straight legs, either solid and card-cut, or L-shaped in section with both faces fret-cut. Such chairs were frequently strengthened with fret-cut stretchers, but in 1762 Chippendale noted that such backs were unsuited to the hard wear of the dining room.

Chinese chairs were popular again as a minor phase of Regency fashion. Many attractive little beechwood chairs

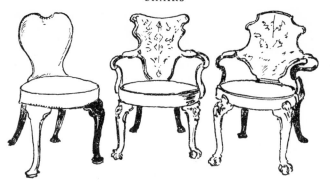

35. Early Georgian compass-seated chairs, also known as spoon- or scoop-back chairs.

were made, turned to suggest bamboo and appropriately painted. Others were white with touches of gilding, and others again were japanned and ornamented on deep cresting with chinoiserie subjects. Pierced frets were introduced as angle brackets to seat and back rails, but the general shape of these attractive chairs was unmistakably Regency.

Chippendale chairs: *see* CHINESE CHAIRS, GOTHIC CHAIRS, RIBBAND-BACK CHAIRS.

Cockfighting chair: *See* READING CHAIR.

Compass-seated chair (Figs 21, 29, 35): Also known now as a spoon-back chair. Derived from the round-seated stool and intended to serve the dress-conscious gentleman of the early 18th century when, as noted in *Read's Weekly*, 1736, 'The plaits of the coat stick out very much in imitation of the ladies' hoops'. The early compass-seat chair had a tall, rectangular, upholstered back, sometimes with a straight top rail but more often rounded. The deliberately narrow junction of tapering back and round seat gave the chair the characteristic spoon-back outline. A detail of the chair cresting of the 1720s was the cupped recess for the sitter's neck at a period when the wig was worn with a queue. The upholstered back was succeeded by a solid concave of walnut or rosewood veneer, or solid mahogany contrasting with vigorous carving on the cabriole knee and ball-and-claw foot. A design for the library was made from about 1720 onwards with a low back, nearly semicircular top rail or yoke, and swivel candlestand and tray in its flat terminals.

Arm or elbow chairs with compass seats were made to accommodate the huge dresses worn in the 1740s and 50s with the scroll-over arms in a continuous curve. In late compass-seat chairs the arm projected horizontally from the back, scrolling over and beyond the inward-curving uprights. The Regency liked the style with its opportunities for brass inlay or painted ornament on the smoothly rounded back support. This curved down to scroll-ended arms resting on the side seat rails or on backward-curving verticals above scimitar legs. The shape was emphasised by the placing of the back legs much closer together than the front legs. Compass seats, slightly dished, are noted on some late Georgian hall chairs, the wide seat and narrow back being particularly suitable for heavily coated callers. The shape proved welcome yet again for crinolined ladies in the early Victorian drawing room, when lightweight versions were known as pincushion chairs.

Conversation chair (Fig. 31): Early Victorian notion, with two seats sharing a central arm rest but facing in opposite directions (*see* Part VIII). Reading chairs (q.v.) were sometimes known as conversation chairs.

Corner chair, writing chair (Fig. 36): Early Georgian chair in walnut or mahogany, typically with four cabriole legs equidistantly spaced, but with one at the centre front. Sometimes only this front leg was in the elaborate cabriole shape, but later all four were frequently square with ovolo moulding on

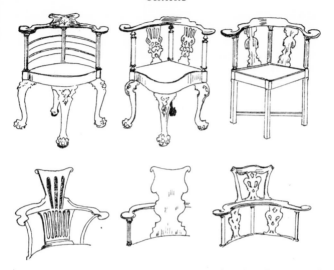

36. Early Georgian corner chairs. TOP: variations in splat, seat and leg arrangements. BOTTOM: modifications into so-called barber chairs, the one on left pierced in the lower, wide section but left solid (with dark markings) for strength above.

the outer sides. Some specimens from the 1760s and 70s had stretchers. The drop-in upholstered seat was a somewhat rounded diamond shape to correspond. Three short verticals rose above the legs, interspersed with two splats, all supporting a low, rounded crest rail extended as short arm horizontals. Eventually the stock size established for this chair was: height, 33 inches; seat height $17\frac{1}{2}$ inches; seat width 25 inches.

Such a chair looked attractive from the back, so that it was suitable for a writing table, and most especially for the current passion for card playing. Reference to corner chairs was made as early as 1734. Variants include a design of the 1770s on-wards, most often in beech with a back composed of horizontal rails, the main construction being turned. An inelegant variant with a high support like an added chair back in the centre is known as a barber's chair; this, too, had a variant made by the turner. Other corner chairs have been noted with bookrest and candlestand attachments, and some showing the Windsor chair construction with legs tenoned into a solid saddle seat. At the end of the 18th century various low-backed chairs were evolved with rounded arm shaping, but these lacked the leg arrangement of the corner chair.

Curricle (Fig. 28): Term used by Sheraton in his *Dictionary* (1803), presumably taken from the 18th-century carriage. In the same way Hepplewhite used the term cabriole for an upholstered chair rather than for a leg shape, presumably associating it with the cabriolet. Sheraton recommended the curricle as a conveniently low chair for the dining table. The style was familiar in a number of early 19th-century tub chairs of the smoker's bow variety (Fig. 10 etc.) *See* EATON HALL CHAIR with the body-hugging back continued along the sides of the chair as arms of the same height.

Derbyshire, Yorkshire chair (Fig. 37): Generally 17th-century, especially around 1660, probably copying Italian work. Details vary widely, but basically this was a sturdy oak chair with an open back, more elaborate than the familiar spindle-back, and dominated by an arched or arcaded top rail. Sometimes there was a wide, matching cross rail, and both were orna-mented with small pendant knobs or decorative spindles to fill the upper back. Back verticals had decorative finials and often split turnings attached to the front faces.

Eaton Hall chair (Fig. 10): Comparable with the plain smoker's bow and in library use by the mid-19th century. It acquired its name when supplied to the first Duke of West-minster at Eaton Hall, 1867. The nearly circular seatline was followed by the low back and horizontal arms hugging the sitter. A thick layer of upholstery matching the seat covered the arm horizontals and upper back, being supported on about ten decoratively turned spindles. The short front legs were turned, the back legs swept well back for rigidity.

Farthingale chair (Fig. 18): Late 16th- and 17th-century chair. Sometimes called a turkeywork chair from the knotted pile frequently used to upholster the seat and upper back. This was a single (armless) chair with a low panel of upholstery to support the sitter's back and a wide fabric-covered seat fitted with a deep cushion. The name does not date from the period but has been subsequently applied by those who attribute its success to its convenience in displaying women's dress with the hooped effect on the hips that became an exaggerated fashion at the court of James I. The general proportions of the chair suggest women's use in association with the footstool then required by the fastidious.

Folding or steamer chair (Fig. 33): A six-legged construction dating from the 1850s, with a wooden frame containing inner panels of cane for seat and back, all waved for comfort. The side seat rails were extended, curving down as raking back legs and forming folding crossings with the extended back verticals. The third leg of each side, projecting in a forward arch, also crossed the seat rail in a folding X, and was continued above the seat to support the arm, thus giving the chair great stability.

Gilded chair (Fig. 25): This was mainly massive architects' work until the 1760s, when Adam popularised elegant designs, and by the early 1790s London had more than 150 master furniture carvers-and-gilders. Adam style in gilded upholstered chairs reflected the Louis Seize fashion until the 1780s, whereas other drawing room chairs were lightly constructed of beechwood in the familiar 'Hepplewhite' and 'Sheraton' styles, but even gilding could not render this wood durable.

The demand continued through the Regency. Robert Jones, for example, is noted in the royal accounts as supplying nine light chairs, carved and gilt, at £75 each. Sixty bought in 1815 for the Gothic dining room at Carlton House cost £8 each. In the 18th century two qualities of gilding were in use: the

beautifully lustrous water gilding—a difficult, highly skilled craft—and the more durable, cheaper oil gilding. The methods are described in Part XVII. Sometimes the flat surfaces of a chair were oil gilded, and the carved detail water gilded and burnished. Sheraton noted in 1803 that water gilding required more care to keep it from injury.

Glastonbury chair (Fig. 37): A folding X chair of early form, associated from about the end of the 16th century with church use and comparable with Italian work of its time. The X was formed at each side of the chair by the crossing of front and back legs. Legs and seat members were flat rails, their junctions fastened by wooden pins.

Gothic chair (Figs 24, 41): A minor fashion of the mid-18th century welcomed by Chippendale and his contemporaries, who light-heartedly mingled Gothic features such as ogee arches and window tracery with familiar rococo detail. Cluster-column legs (Figs 14, 23) were popular on plinth or guttae feet (Fig. 23); some legs were five-sided. The style lent itself to severe dining and hall chairs, and some superb Gothic Windsors were made around 1760. The mood was revived in the early 19th century when the media included iron, which was approved for conservatory and garden seats. George Smith suggested Gothic chairs even for the drawing room, with backs almost or quite vertical, and high, square-cut arms, all with church-window tracery. Gothic detail may be noted occasionally in chairs throughout the Victorian era.

37. Regional chairs. TOP: folding chair originating in 16th-century, now known as Glastonbury; detail of joint; so-called Derbyshire, from mid-17th-century; detail of attached split-spindle ornament; so-called Yorkshire. SECOND ROW: now called Lancashire ladderbacks, popular from 18th-century, often rush seated, showing clumsy adaptation of earlier cabriole leg and pad foot and including typical 19th-century form. BOTTOM: North Country and Yorkshire spindle backs of 18th-century onwards showing cross rail swellings for spindles; 'drunkard's' chair.

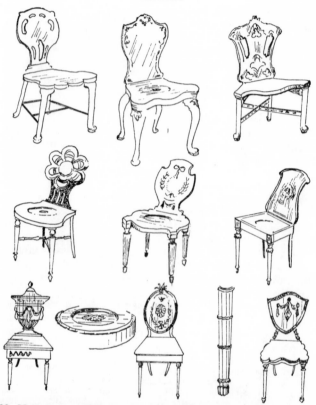

38. Hall chairs, 1750s–90s. The central specimen made for David Garrick, c. 1775 (V. and A. Museum). BOTTOM: three Hepplewhite designs and details of a dished seat with marquetry motif and typical column leg. The chairs were intentionally plain for use of messengers and people waiting in outdoor clothes.

Hall chair (Fig. 38): Developed as a distinct type in the first half of the 18th century. Chippendale suggested six designs in the 1762 edition of his *Director*. From the 1760s sets of 12, 18 and even 36 were made. The requirement was a strong, plain construction lacking upholstery or small intricate ornament, for the chairs had to accommodate messengers, sedan chairmen and others in rough outdoor clothing, and at the same time impress more important callers—hence the crest or cypher often painted on the solid wooden back as noted by Sheraton in his *Dictionary*. The seat might be slightly dipped or shallowly dished—just enough to keep the sitter from sliding off its polished surface.

In the late years of the 18th century an oval, round or vase-shaped back was joined to the seat by a narrow back rail, solid or perforated, and sometimes contained a painted medallion. In others the back was pierced to form a pattern of scrolling loops. The wood was most often dense mahogany, and through the Regency and later periods many were enriched with gilding on crestings, seat rails and scimitar legs.

Chairs of similar shape were sometimes considered suitable for garden use in summer house or gazebo, but these were more often of painted soft wood, easily transportable. Before the end of the 18th century even the villa entrance hall had its chair, which might be of oak. By Victorian days, however, demand had diminished, and none was included among the thousand or more chairs in John Ayres's catalogue of 1838.

Iron chair: For garden or hall, with slatted seat to throw off the rain and, for lawn use, flat feet to the narrow tubular legs. The finish was black, bronze or 'oak'. Some charming examples remain from the Regency—the low, square lines enlivened with Gothic detail—but they soon became involved in intricacies of foliate scrolls as they experienced the furniture designers' enthusiasms for Gothic, Elizabethan and rococo styles, from the naturalistic plant forms of the 1840s to the Japanesque of the 1880s. Some delicate examples made of bent wire, often gilded, have survived, and include rounded lattice effects comparable with Regency cupboard door grills.

Ladder-back chair (Fig. 37): Usually a rush-seated country chair, probably originating in the Low Countries and known as a Dutch chair in the late 17th century. The horizontal slats filling the back were bent slightly to fit the sitter, their number increasing to as many as five or seven, often in decreasing widths, with cupid's bow or double ogee outline, and sometimes elaborate ribbon shaping. For a long time the legs retained the swellings that were the rural craftsman's approximations to the cabriole, linked by a swelling cross-stretcher. A handsome adaptation of the ladder-back may be found in later 18th-century mahogany, with pierced, carved cross rails, and all the other members tending to be wave-moulded (Fig. 72). Proportions and general style usually distinguish these from innumerable subsequent versions.

Mendlesham or Suffolk chair (Fig. 41): Comfortable, low-backed 19th-century variant of the Windsor style with saddle seat and splayed, dowelled-in legs. The back was composed of square-cut rather than turned members, the side rails enclosing a double crest rail and double cross rail often separated by a row of small balls. Between cresting and cross rails there was sometimes a row of flat, pierced splats. The arms were flat, outward-curving and extending beyond sloping supports.

Morris chair (Fig. 32, 31): William Morris was not basically a furniture designer, but two chair designs are especially associated with the firm he and his friends established in 1861. One may be regarded as an adaptation of a rush-seated Sussex type of spindle-back chair. This had all its members plainly turned and so slender that the back and arm cross rails and leg stretchers were in duplicate. The arm verticals, slanting inwards and backwards, extended several inches below the chair seat. R. W. Edis (1881) praised a piece made to this design in stained wood and then costing 9s 9d.

The other design was an adjustable, upholstered chair with arms and back legs projecting beyond the chair's tall, square-cut back. The legs allowed for considerable rake to the back; arms were extended and notched at intervals so that a bar could be fitted across where required as a support for the inclined back. Sturdy spindles linked the arms and the seat rail which, as in the steamer chair, formed the back legs.

Papier mâché chair (Fig. 131): This was sometimes wholly of papier mâché but more often only the upper part was of this material, on extremely slender, tapering legs of turned, out-curving, black-japanned wood. The open back was either oval, with a double-C outline, or more elaborately shaped with arching crest and cross rails, the faces of back and seat frame inset with wisps of pearl shell and the seat usually caned. The acid method of shaping the shell introduced in 1840 increased the possibilities of this work (*see* Part XVII).

The other most familiar style had a solid back, rounded and outward-curving to include vestigial arms—all that could be permitted when wide skirts were in fashion in the boudoir. The front legs, when also shaped of papier mâché, were sometimes wide-kneed, excessively curved cabrioles, so that the whole front of the chair could be richly ornamented. Designs were registered to avoid copying, and impressed with a small diamond registration mark. Some were marked with the maker's name—usually that of Jennens and Bettridge. After its early Victorian heyday the work continued to some extent into the 1870s, when the background was often a mellow green and the ornament occasionally 'Persian'.

Periwig chair (Fig. 19): Late 17th-century version of the cane-panelled walnut armchair with an extra tall, raked back emphasised by an arching crest rail and narrow canework. Often the scroll motif was repeated in an arching front stretcher and in the outcurving arm supports and front legs.

Porter's or Watchman's chair (Fig. 26): Designed for halls and passages in draughty 18th- and 19th-century mansions. The general design was an overstuffed armchair with back and wings forming an arched top. Sometimes the shelter extended

beyond the front of the seat like a watchman's hut to protect the sitter's legs, and the usual covering was close-nailed, enduring leather. The draught-preventing shape was mentioned as early as 1649 by Randle Holme in a twiggen or osier chair for the infirm.

Prie-dieu chair (Fig. 31): Almost entirely early Victorian, a single chair with a very long, straight back, flat topped, and a low seat, intended for kneeling in prayer. Usually it was upholstered with the kind of severe pattern worked in cross-stitch that was considered appropriate for Sunday embroidery. For prayer use the top was padded and the upholstery was T-shaped. But even by the 1840s more chairs of this type were welcomed as drawing room furnishings perfectly displaying ambitious pictorial Berlin wool embroideries which were tasselled and fringed accordingly.

Reading chair, conversation chair, now often called a cock-fighting chair (Fig. 39). Others have referred to it as the horseman's chair, since the user sat astride a leather-covered padded seat that narrowed towards the back, and rested his arms upon the suitably flattened crest rail. Thus the general design was composed of a somewhat T-shaped back, an exceptionally long seat from narrow back to broad front, and massive backward-projecting legs, often linked by substantial stretchers. In this way the Georgian could preserve his coat uncreased when the occasion demanded more formal dress than his 'night gown'. In 1757 William Cauty of St Mary-le-Strand, London, advertised in the *London Gazette* 'mahogany

39. Reading or horsemen's chairs. TOP: late 17th-century chair; chair of about 1720, with padded leather and folding candle stands (V. and A. Museum); conversation type with massive stretchers. CENTRE: two views of early Georgian specimen with dished arms for candlesticks (Brufords). BOTTOM: Sheraton conversation design detail of padded rest enclosing book-rest; bookrest detail from Sheraton's *Dictionary* (1803); compromise of 1820s–30s.

and walnut-tree reading chairs, corner chairs, compass-seated chairs, shaving chairs and dressing chairs'.

Sheraton in 1794 called them conversation chairs, but in 1803 noted their convenience for reading and making notes, the crest rail serving as a miniature desk, fitted with bookrest and candlestand. Some were wholly upholstered for use in clubs, for example, and sometimes the seat contained a locking drawer. They became less substantial towards the end of the 18th century and on into Victorian days, when the back was ornamentally pierced and carved, often pictorially.

Reclining chair (Fig. 31): From the late Regency onwards throughout Victorian days. Viewed from the side, the back and seat formed a continuous, flowing S-curve. The arms ended in deep scrolls and in an early specimen the legs formed an arc, so that seat and legs from the side view showed the Regency's favourite, rounded S outline. Alternatively, tapering Greek legs at the front contrasted harshly with the scimitar curves at the rear. By the second half of the century the chair often depended for its effect wholly upon the upholstery, which was usually vertically striped and often buttoned, with a tassel each side to finish the scroll-over back. A similar line of back and seat was later used for a rocking chair with elaborate bentwood supports (Fig. 40).

Ribband-back chair (Fig. 24): Chippendale introduced this style in his 1754 *Director* but did not originate it. It superbly exploited the dense Spanish mahogany by brilliant carving in twisting ribbon effects. The silhouette of the design was cut and pierced from a solid plank and inserted with the grain vertical. Over this, small sections of mahogany were glued, arranged so that their grain suited their subsequent carving in the ribbon pattern, and minimised later cracking. The daring, pierced curves swept up into the lines of the crest rail to resemble a single piece of wood, and occasionally also linked the splat with the side uprights. Robert Manwaring in his *Cabinet and Chairmakers' Real Friend and Companion*, 1765, illustrated about 100 chairs he had actually constructed, including ribbon-backs. In his work the splats were composed of entwined ribbons rising from shoe-piece to cresting between scroll uprights. Trade cards through the 1770s and 1780s indicate continuing demand for such chairs.

Rocking chair (Fig. 40): From about 1760. The first design was a ladder-back or spindle-back chair with a pair of rockers

40. Victorian casual chairs. TOP: tubular rocking chair by R. W. Winfield, Birmingham, exhibited 1851; 19th-century Windsor, associated with the North; smoker's bow, (*cf.* Windsor and Eaton Hall chairs). BOTTOM: child's rocking chair; kitchen chairs developed from spindle backs and ladder backs of 18th-century.

linking front and back legs, comparable with cradle rockers. The rocking chair with a flowing S-shape to back and seat over intricately curving rocker supports was evolved by early Victorians in brass or steel strip (shown at the 1851 exhibition) and in bentwood. A late 19th-century design had a fixed base and the rocking movement was controlled by massive springs. This was comparatively straight backed, like the American rocker, and considered suitable for old people.

Rout chair: For use at assemblies known as routs around the beginning of the 19th century. Sheraton in 1803 referred to 'small painted chairs with rush bottoms lent out by cabinet makers for hire as a supply of seats at general entertainments or feasts'. These were in everyday use finished in black or imitating rosewood or bamboo and, in Victorian days, bird's eye maple. By then some lightweight chairs with cane panels for seats and backs were known as rout or soirée chairs, often in light-toned wood and sometimes touched with gilding.

Smoker's bow chair (Fig. 40): Variant of the Windsor type, associated with the 19th-century farmhouse and kitchen. This had the Windsor's saddle seat and splayed, turned legs, but the arms and low back formed a continuous horizontal hoop above the back and sides of the seat, supported by about eight turned spindles. The arms were flat, ending in flat scrolls, the back sometimes only a little deeper, fitting snugly to the sitter and rounded off on the upper edge.

Spindle-back chair (Fig. 37): The country turner's chair, associated especially with Lancashire and the North. An armchair might have three cross rails below the cresting board, and three rows of decoratively turned spindles, but for a single chair two rows of spindles were more usual. A simple form of the chair with a single row of spindles and a plain wooden seat has been associated with Cumberland. The spindles, grouped together, gave much the same support as a splat, and were housed in plainly turned cross rails scarcely thicker than the spindle ends, but swelling slightly where drilled for the spindles to be inserted. Randle Holme illustrated one with more spindles between seat and stretcher.

Spoon-back or scoop-back chair: *See* COMPASS CHAIR.

Thrown chair: Composed mainly of units shaped by throwing or turning on the lathe. In wide use in varying forms throughout the period under review, but mainly used for everyday work, so that comparatively few remain. Thus in 1615, for example, turned, matted (rush-seated) chairs were selling at 7s, a dozen. The turner's methods, his lathe powered by bow or wheel boy, are described in Part XVII. The chair, made in ash, elm, yew or beech rather than tough oak, was constructed of interlaced struts and rails, often turned with ornamental knobs and rings. Four main vertical members formed the back rails and legs, and the front arm supports and legs, with tapered dowel joints for the linking cross rails, including the rows of vertical and horizontal spindles that sometimes reinforced the main structure above and below the seat. Some were triangular on plan. Decorative thrown chairs were also made in the Low Countries and Germany and were imported, augmenting English work which included the Windsor, white Wycombe and spindle-back.

White Wycombe (Figs 40, 41): Mass-produced, unstained Victorian chair derived from the Windsor and Mendlesham styles. Loudon in 1833 indicated current acceptance of the type as merely cheap kitchen furniture, little different from many made this century. The seat, only slightly saddle-shaped, rested on four dowelled and well-splayed legs, ring and baluster turned, with H-stretchers. Side verticals, square-cut and wide at the base, were dowelled into the seat and somewhat S-curved for comfort, with plain top rail and cross rail housed between them. Alternatively, from around the mid-19th century, a similar saddle seat might support a row of decoratively turned spindles forming the back or flanking a

41. Windsor chairs. TOP, comb backs: probably from 1720s; probably from 1730s or 1740s; probably from c. 1740s–50s on, the cabriole legs less usual after 1770s. SECOND ROW, hoop backs and a leg detail: chair with hooped stretcher; Gothic Windsor of the one type now found; low-back chair, the wheel splat dating c. 1790s on. BOTTOM: four details from J. C. Loudon's *Encyclopaedia*, 1833; Mendlesham or Suffolk chair.

114

central pierced splat, all capped by a wide, slightly rounded crest rail.

Windsor chair (Fig. 41): The name has been noted in the 1720s, but it appears that it was already in use in palace library and country garden. Such chairs became popular for coffee houses because the construction ensured that they bounced rather than disintegrated under hard use. In fact ordinary people bought them for inexpensive comfort. The chair was assembled from members shaped of available local woods on the primitive pole lathe wherever the bodger could operate in woodland clearings. Its main features combined to make it entirely different from any other chair of its day, with saddle seat, round taper-tenon joints, a complete disassociation of legs from back and arms and, from the 1740s, the use of hooped wood in back, arms and stretchers. Beech—or occasionally ash or chestnut—was used for the legs, elm for the seat, and yew for the bowed work. Some were japanned or stained black, others green, but many for indoor use were merely sand scoured.

The first style was the comb-back, its back composed of nine or ten plain spindles supporting a slightly curved crest rail, comb-shaped until the 1740s and still illustrated in trade cards of the 1780s. Early legs were plainly turned, their splay not checked by stretchers. For greater rigidity the back was sometimes braced with a pair of struts projecting diagonally from a narrow bob-tail extension behind the seat. A major strengthening feature, however, was the horizontal hoop forming a half circle across the back and out to the front as arm horizontals, with the back spindles passing through it.

From this it was but a step to introduce similar curved buffering as a hooped crest rail with the bar of rectangular section raking well back and forming the entire frame of the back. On the low-back variety its ends were bedded in the seat; on the high-back it rose from the horizontal arm hoop.

Within the hoop a central vertical splat, eventually pierced, was usually flanked by plain stick spindles; the wheel splat was introduced at the end of the century. Cabriole legs—ill-suited to the seat line and seldom free of stretchers—were introduced on Windsors when they were already going out of fashion. They were followed by baluster turning, the main swell being situated high on 19th-century specimens. In the later 18th century the curved cow's horn or spur stretcher was used.

Some particularly sturdy Windsors are associated with the North of England, with decoratively turned arm supports, legs and stretchers—the whole chair being often of yew. Handsome yew-wood Gothic Windsors were made in the second half of the 18th century, from the 1760s, with splats of church-window piercing and occasionally with the loop itself given a Gothic point. These specimens appealed to the well-to-do romantic for furnishing the fashionable Gothic cell, but served also as hall chairs, for example.

In the 19th century, Windsors were of little interest to fashionable people, while large-scale factory production served cottage and kitchen, but there was a revival of interest among handicraft enthusiasts late in the century, and even more than a hint of Windsor style in some flimsy specimens of *art nouveau*.

X chair: Apparently in the 16th century the prerogative of royalty, but associated with wealthy households in the 17th century. The legs, front and back, formed two rounded X shapes, and between them on intersecting webbing a deeply cushioned seat was slung. Continuations of the back X supported fabric for the back, and those of the front X the arm horizontals, which were sometimes all finished with small pummels of metal—later of wood. The entire wooden framework, awkward to shape neatly with early tools, was covered with rich fabric held by the cofferers' brass-headed nails.

PART IV

Tables

Seat and table furniture are complementary and must have evolved together, the early chest proving an unwieldy substitute for either. Medieval constructions of planks laid across pegged trestles are represented today mainly by Victorian ideas, and the early tables that remain are generally the heavy, joined tables of oak that served the more important members of a well-to-do household in Tudor and early Stuart days. As with all early furniture it is important to realise that cheaper woods, more cheaply assembled, must have been used for a far larger amount of homely furniture which, for that very reason, tended to take the brunt of wear in kitchen and cottage down the centuries until it disintegrated.

Two of the earliest tables were the straightforward long table and—from Elizabethan days—the extending version known as the draw table. Side tables for games and the like included the simple little three-legged type now often known as a cricket table. There were early versions of the gate-leg, too—at first as folding tables and soon after as falling tables also, the distinction lying in the position of the flap or flaps when closed. The chair table—now known for no good reason as monk's table—has a long history, too.

Only at the end of the first period under review was the range of tables widened to include more specialised occasional tables, in particular for writing and cards. In the second or Queen Anne period dining requirements produced many extremely fine, large gate-leg tables. This was the period when the range of delightful pillar-and-claw tables really became established, and a very few date from the 1690s. Other pillar-

and-claw pieces included candle- and kettle-stands, but possibly the most notable development was the new demand for tables as decoration, created by the spate of building and rebuilding on more spacious, orderly lines. These pieces come under the headings of pier, side and console tables.

Early Georgian furniture makers, exploring the possibilities of mahogany, transformed the gate-leg table into the gate table for dining, produced the pillar-and-claw in its most enduringly popular form and concentrated the extremes of current fashion on pier and console. The range of tables was increased around the mid-18th century, again in response to the short-lived fashion for ornament. Chippendale illustrated a breakfast table, for example, and a number of light, galleried tables have survived in rich, mid-century rococo, Chinese and Gothic taste. These are generally known as tea, china, silver or supper tables. The spider table of the third quarter of the century was a variant of the earlier gate-leg also intended for such uses.

The later 18th-century period, while giving Adam grace to the pier table, produced also the lightly constructed extending table known as the Pembroke. Fitted tables became immensely important, and are considered among desk and bureau furniture: these included the so-called architect's table, various versions of the harlequin table, the Carlton House table and many work or pouch tables. The small occasional tables of the period included the light form of pillar-and-claw known for a time as the teapoy—another word of changing meaning—and the urn table. Sheraton referred to the nest of tables produced at the time as quartetto tables.

Social or wine tables evolved late in the century, continuing into the Regency when two important table shapes were notably popular. One was the sofa table, often equipped so as to come also under the heading of games and/or work table. The other was the circular table here considered in detail among late pillar-and-claw designs, but altogether more massive than the earlier type. Various names appear with little obvious differentiation for these cumbrous, handsome

42. Victorian occasional tables. TOP: five pillar styles, those with adjustable tops in papier mâché. SECOND ROW: folding table with late Victorian poker ornament; two tables liable to be antedated. BOTTOM: late Victorian bamboo; side table usually heavily draped; tea-table on castors; 1897 design by C. R. Mackintosh.

tables—dining, wine, loo, library and drum are such names.

Curiously enough, what is often regarded as the one new table style evolved by the Victorians—the Sutherland—can only be regarded as a return to the gate-leg in its very early trestle outline. The most numerous tables of this era were possibly the occasional tables, which were often classed at the time merely as ornamental, sometimes as Moorish, although covering a huge range of styles and treatments. These were drawing room tables of low, coffee table proportions and it is interesting to note a plain, slender-legged, two-shelf coffee table design of the 1880s by E. W. Godwin who decried the ill-proportioned copies then widely sold.

Breakfast table (Fig. 45): By implication this was a bedroom or dressing room piece, and as such had to meet the requirements also of a sideboard cupboards or drawers, while taking up little space. Pieces so named appeared around the mid-18th century and were illustrated by Chippendale, Hepplewhite, Sheraton and Smith. The Chippendale design was nearly square, but with small side flaps resting on fly brackets. A drawer fitted the framing, and below it was a deep cupboard with two concave doors to allow the sitter knee space. Chippendale suggested Chinese frets with brass wire as an alternative on all sides of the cupboard to allow ventilation.

Charming specimens may be found occasionally matching the japanned dressing room, or in mahogany with equally informal Gothic cluster column legs (Fig. 23) and small castors to the guttae feet (Fig. 23). Castors of brass and of leather are mentioned in references to such two-flap breakfast tables in the 1760s. It must be assumed that circular pillar-and-claw tables were often used, too, despite their lack of cupboard space. Southey, in 1807, used an oval one in the current fashion.

The rounded rectangle, a compromise between rectangle and ellipse, was much used in the early 19th century, a line then approved for silver, glass and china vessels. Smith suggested a breakfast table on a shortened version of the vase pillar, ending on a plinth of concave triangular outline: this may be found on heavy castors rather than Smith's massive paw feet. The Smith design had top and plinth of scagliola, and he suggested painting to match the china. The breakfast table was also considered suitable for Chinese decoration. In pedestal form it continued far into Victorian days, but with the Gallic name of déjeuner table.

43. Candlestands. Late 17th-century; early 18th-century with the period's shouldered or Silesian stem; mid-18th-century rococo; Hepplewhite design, 1780s; Sheraton design, 1790s.

Candlestand (Fig. 43): This was most usually of pillar-and-claw construction. Randle Holme in 1649 described it as 'a little round table, set upon a pillar or post, which in the front branches itself out into three or four feet or toes, for fast and steady standing. They are also made square, sexagon and octagon in the table part'. Through the 17th century the stand might be three to five feet tall, following the familiar sequence of twist and baluster turning on a pillar made of walnut or other easily turned wood; the claws were sharply jutting scrolls. The finest were made in pairs—to flank and match side tables and dressing tables, for example. The most costly were covered with embossed silver, and others were richly carved and gilded or silvered. A few were enriched with gilded gesso, and others were brilliantly japanned.

Early in the 18th century a vase-shaped unit was introduced between the pillar and tray, which might be as much as a foot across for a massive candelabrum. Early Georgian specimens became heavier and less graceful, the tray with a moulded border, the pillar baluster turned. In the 1740s many a sharply carved, handsome stand was produced in mahogany with a round or eight-sided tray, a slender shaft carved with foliage or composed of branching scrolls, and the carved cabriole legs raised on claw-and-ball feet. A low fret gallery sometimes surrounded the candlestick base.

Chippendale illustrated lavish rococo and Gothic designs with elaborate piercing and opposing C-scrolls. On the whole he favoured a somewhat shouldered design, in keeping with the bombé-shaped commodes and the shouldered pilasters of contemporary desk furniture and, indeed, in keeping with the 'Silesian stem' of early Georgian silver, glass and other fashionable wares.

Thomas Johnson in his *Collection of Designs*, 1758, illustrated ten stands to be elaborately carved with elongated pinnacles, C-scrolls and other rococo motifs; three showed full-length female figures. Trays were square, round or lobed, with carved rims. During the 1750s, Matthias Lock noted the carving of two candlestands each requiring 188 days at a cost of £23 10s. It is interesting to note among the rococo stands of Ince and Mayhew a splendidly plain Doric pillar. But far more candlestands were comparatively plain turners' work—round top, baluster pillar, plain cabriole, legs on club feet.

From the 1760s, the neo-classical style prompted increasing use of a smooth concave curve from tray to base, composed either of three slender shafts throughout or based upon a solid pedestal. This drew the eye upward to the tray ornament of carved rams' heads. It is interesting to contrast the change of emphasis between 18th- and 19th-century classical line, and the gradual reversal of the tripod. All too soon the upward swell leading the eye to a magnificent candelabrum was altered to an upward taper from massive pedestal to tiny lamp tray.

Hepplewhite suggested slender tapering pillars on round pedestals—the Herculaneum lampstand design—and he introduced classical detail that was much in evidence in the Regency period. This included lotus carving at the pillar base (later it also became popular immediately below the vase-shaped tray) and a small collar low on the shaft, which was sometimes distorted into a marble-topped drip tray on the Victorian lamp standard.

Sheraton favoured the alternative style—an open tripod with three upsweeping concave shafts from a small-footed platform base—and gave his designs dainty, vertical peg toes. But the characteristic Regency foot that followed was the shouldered or elbowed paw. Such tripod feet and the tall, tapering pillar above them were still much in evidence in the familiar drawings of 'Modern Costume' by Henry Moses, 1823, supporting diminutive lamps. Like George Smith he chose such stands to flank a drawing room sofa. Smith (1808) suggested a number of shapely vase forms for the tops of stands that look disproportionately attenuated when contrasted with the graceful baluster and plinth design by Hope, but which may well have been in deliberate contrast to the massive designs of some rivals. To the Victorian the stand might suggest interesting complexities of wrought iron. Soon, however, with more elaborate paraffin lamps, functional necessity made a travesty of classical design.

Card table (Figs. 44, 48, 51): Folding and falling tables of the 17th century, as well as many small versions of the ordinary joined table, must have been used for cards and backgammon, but the Queen Anne period saw the development of delightful tables specifically for the card playing widely enjoyed through the 18th century by those who could afford/superb materials and craftsmanship to serve their pleasure. A specimen of around 1700 might be circular when open, supported on two hinged gate-legs, additional to the four of the fixed section,

which were linked by a deep, shapely apron and waved stretchers. A few others of this period show the side or writing table design with four fixed legs and two extra legs swinging out from the centre of the front.

Far more card tables, however, date to late in Queen Anne's reign, when the usual table was a rectangle which unfolded to make a square. The customary piece of cloth, edged with braid or gimp and glued within a border of veneer, could then be hidden when not in use. Or there might be two folding flaps, so that even when open the table could offer a finely veneered top. The vertical, slightly convex moulding that edges such a table may be contrasted with the nearly flat ovolos of the late 17th century. By then, with the use of unfettered cabriole legs, the simplest support for the folding flap was for one of the four legs to swing out, complete with part of the underframing, constituting a kind of gate table.

44. Tables for games and cards. TOP: late 17th-century gate-leg shown open; drop-flap tripod, late 17th- to early 18th-century; early 18th-century card table showing hollows for counters and dished circles for candlesticks, its open top resting on hinged framing that closes concertina-fashion (similar in action to the table immediately below and explained by the diagram below this). SECOND ROW: early Georgian table with two opening leaves for cards and board games, the flaps resting on a movable leg in the gate-table manner; triangular table opening to a square with an additional gate-leg and with pull-out candle slides; table with extending framework shown half open, its back legs of inferior quality, its corners shaped for square candlesticks. THIRD ROW: 'Gothic' style of 1760s with three alternative tops on an extra gate-leg but lacking counter and candlestick sinkings; pillar-and-claw table for tredille; diagram of the concertina frame opening on rule hinges. BOTTOM: late 18th-century serpentine card table on gate-table principle with none of the earlier elaborations; detail of a Pembroke games table shown half open, its reversible top pulled out to reveal space for tric-trac behind the sham drawer; table for chess, etc., with shallow drawer and candle slides, late 18th-century.

Soon, as a more shapely alternative, half the underframing could be drawn forward, with two of the four legs, the underframing being triple hinged on each side so that it folded in on itself when closed. Often the projecting corners of the square table top were rounded and slightly dished to hold candlesticks. The framing frieze, square on early work, soon followed the rounded outline. Then, around 1740, the projections were given square shaping to suit the fashion for square-based candlesticks—so contradicting the theory that these were drinking-glass holders. Alternatively, pull-out slides were fitted into splayed corners. Dished receptacles were provided for counters, inlaid or cloth lined, a detail largely abandoned in the later years of the century.

The same changes in leg outlines occurred as on other fashionable early Georgian tables, and mahogany was adopted as the finest wood, handsomely carved with the current lion motifs on knee and foot. By the mid-century years the design was frequently very simple, plainly square when open, but through the 1750s and 1760s a great deal of elegance was introduced with shapely French legs, cabochon-carved on apron and knee, and richly scrolled feet. The top was frequently in serpentine outline, with shapely little corner projections, the edge carved. Some were in square-legged fret-cut Chinese style, others by the 1770s extremely slender legged with fluting or marquetry rather than carving on the frieze.

The neo-classical style filtered into card-table design in the late 1760s with tapering legs and plainer shaping to the top—most usually round, elliptical or a round-cornered square. Some were of satinwood, and all folded to make handsome side or pier tables. Card tables became less important during the Regency, although many were made with the characteristic tapering, outcurving scimitar legs of the period, also with the slightly grotesque version of this: the spavin leg of antiquity. Some were in rosewood. By then the coming fashion was the pillar-and-claw loo table (q.v.) with brass and ebony inlay (*see* also GAMES TABLES).

Centre table (Fig. 51): Through the 16th, 17th and 18th centuries this may be regarded mainly as a variant of the contemporary side tables (q.v.). The main difference consisted in shaping and ornamenting the four sides to match. Obviously this offered greater scope for graceful outlines, such as the serpentine pieces of the 1760s. To the Regency home-maker the piece was usually a pillar-and-claw table, with four claws or a four-footed pedestal base. Sometimes the top was square with rounded corners, occasionally with wide, clipped corners so that each of the eight sides was slightly concave, a notion illustrated by Sheraton (possibly because he delighted in problems of perspective), but more in keeping with the elaborations of the 1860s. Tables in the Victorian-Elizabethan manner—with distortions of late Stuart or Jacobean style—included the popular eight-sided oak centre table on straight legs linked by diagonal stretchers with an ornamental boss at their central crossing. Frequently all members were swash turned.

Chair table (Fig. 46): Sometimes now known as a 'monk's table'. A dual-purpose piece occasionally found in 17th- or 18th-century oak. A chair or settle shape with a solid vertical back and solid horizontal arms became a table when the back was tilted forward to rest upon the arms.

China or silver table (Fig. 45): Galleried table for displaying a few choice ornaments such as figures that needed to be viewed from all sides, and possibly for such important social niceties as the ornamental comfit holder with its tiny, highly flavoured cashews. It could provide a note of informality when billowing skirts made it hazardous to depart from the stylised arrangement of furniture around the walls. It must be assumed, however, that it was mainly in demand as a tea table (q.v.).

In Victorian days there was a fashion for a small display table of this kind, permanently crowded with ornaments. This was usually called a silver table, as its prevailing note through the later part of the reign was the bright silver of photograph frames and other articles. The piece was accepted as a light-hearted frivolity, and the shape was typically either Louis Quinze or Louis Seize—that is with serpentine top, wavy frieze and French legs, carved or ormolu-mounted, or else with oval top, straight frieze and straight tapering legs often linked by a lower tray instead of stretchers. In either case the aim was still a light decorative piece with a low metal gallery.

Clap table (*see* CONSOLE TABLE): So-called, for example, by Celia Fiennes (who visited many country houses around 1700 when they were not common). Later in the 18th century they were known also as 'frames for marble slabs'.

Console table (Fig. 45): A variant of the side table from about 1700, intended to be attached permanently to a panelled wall in hall or reception room. This permitted the legs to be in bracket form, the outline tapering towards the base. It was thus a particularly elegant form of side table, intended to be viewed from the front and, like the side table, could be ornamented on and below the frieze, as no one would have to sit at it. The bracket effect was emphasised when it was made to appear to be supporting a mirror hung on the wall above and ornamented to harmonise. Such tables were frequently made in pairs.

Early specimens were of walnut, some japanned and many, when not of gilded gesso, were topped with expensive Italian marble. The manner recalls the early carved and gilded stands for Oriental cabinets. The whole style tended to be Italianate in the William Kent manner, with massive carving of sphinxes, putti, swags or acanthus. Some of the most striking are of the 1730s, when an eagle with wings outspread appeared to support the table, its claws gripping a rocky base on a rectangular plinth considerably smaller than the area of the table top. As with any bracket, the wall behind carried much of the table's weight, and the bird's wing feathers barely touched the carved frieze. Sometimes dolphins served as the table support.

45. Various 18th-century tables. TOP, console tables intended for fixing to wall at back: marble top supported by carved eagle, c. 1730s; mid-18th-century rococo with central cabochon motif; neo-classic style with turned legs suggesting late 18th-century. SECOND ROW, tea or silver tables with tray rims or carved frets: walnut, 1700s; mahogany with frieze, legs and stretchers as well as rim fret-cut in different patterns, 1750s–60s; mahogany in slender style of c. 1770 onwards. BOTTOM, breakfast tables: c. 1750s–60s; last quarter of 18th-century.

This table was always subject to much Continental influence, as seen for example in the designs by Batty and Thomas Langley which leaned heavily on Italian and French decorative designs. It lost favour somewhat in the 1740s, along with heavy room panelling, although Chippendale suggested ornate rococo examples, the essential curving line from the wide top to the narrow base being expressed in foliated scrolls, opposed C-scrolls or cornucopias. Only the appearance of two legs instead of four in the design distinguished his 'frames for marble slabs' from his pier glass and table. Ince and Mayhew offered somewhat attenuated versions as slab frames.

Occasionally console tables were made through the rest of the 18th century, the outline changing in harmony with neo-classical style. In these the front legs were the normal straight tapers without the bracket effect, although back brackets concealed under the table top still took the place of back legs. Southey referred to console tables as a new fashion again in 1807, but the bracket line was out of keeping with Regency design. By Victorian days any marble-topped table tended to be called a console, and purists complained that even the modest home would have one loaded with pot plants upon every staircase landing.

Cricket table: In the style of the cricket stool, the turner-made milking stool with stick legs dowelled into a solid top. Being three legged, this stood firmly on the uneven flagstones around the hearth. The name appears comparatively modern and associated with the hearth-loving insect rather than with the game of cricket. Tables of this style with splayed, stretcher-free legs taper-tenoned into the solid wooden top have been illustrated in English manuscripts from the 14th century onwards.

Dining table (Figs 46, 47, 51, 57): Early dining tables of the 15th, 16th and 17th centuries are discussed under the headings trestle table, joined table and draw table; the gate-leg table of the 17th and early 18th centuries and the gate table of early Georgian mahogany also have their own sections. The tops of these tables show an interesting sequence of shapes; very long rectangle; short-rectangle with extensions; round or oval with only occasional rectangle, and finally a short rectangle with an occasional oval, but with extensions to form once again a very long rectangular table.

From about the mid-18th century an alternative was the two-flap gate table, extended by putting a semicircular pier or side table at each end of it: a Chippendale bill of 1769 charged £5 for 'two mahogany round ends to join his dining tables, with two pairs of strap hinges, hooks and eyes, etc.'. Such sets of dining tables with bolt-and-fork fastenings were required so that 'the whole or any part . . . join together at pleasure'. The neo-classical design of the 1760s and onwards produced immensely attractive dining tables with plain vertical fluting and corner paterae on the frieze, which projected in splayed corners above fluted, tapering legs. Each of a pair in the Victoria and Albert Museum, London, has a fifth leg that swings out to support a deep flap. Placed with the flaps end to end, they make a table over seven feet long with four legs at the corners, four intermediate side legs and two under the centre. This specimen also shows figured veneer in place of the earlier solid mahogany, bordered in patterns of dark and light woods which would be revealed when the low hanging cloth was removed for dessert.

A novelty illustrated by Shearer, 1788, was the horseshoe dining table. This was illustrated, too, by Sheraton in his *Cabinet Dictionary*, with the title of Grecian dining table. He suggested settees for the diners and a dumb waiter within the arc, topped by a candelabrum. This had the approval of Roman precedent, but the diners sat rather than reclined on the outer side, while served from the inner side. Smaller versions are noted as social tables (q.v.). Shearer's seven-foot example was composed of a fixed table on five straight legs and two flaps that folded back over the top when not in use and were supported on gate legs so that, extended, the top was a half-circle. This he costed at £25, plus oiling and polishing for an extra 2s, and a lining of hand-made blue paper in the drawer, another three halfpence.

The main change in design came late in the 18th century with a return to round-topped tables as heavy versions of the

light claw table, which by then was often used for informal breakfasts and suppers. The construction is discussed under pillar-and-claw tables. Sometimes a cluster of columns on a plinth was used instead of the pillar. D-ended tables came into favour at the end of the century. Round tables with their implied informality and equality of status continued popular from the late 18th century until Queen Victoria's reign. In one extending design an outer circle could be added, composed of four leaves that were bolted on.

In 1800 Richard Gillow patented a new way of extending a rectangular table by fitting it with telescopic underframing—wood or metal sliders to run in grooves so that, when extended, flaps could be laid upon them. In 1805 Richard Brown modified this device by shaping the table underframing as a horizontal 'lazy tongs' and resting the flaps upon this. George Remington introduced a further patent in 1807. When a combined table and sideboard was commissioned by Nelson for Merton from the patent furniture specialists, Morgan and Sanders, the result was a table frame opening on the lazy tongs principle with a slender turned leg under each section.

46. Tables, 16th–17th centuries. TOP: dining, typical Tudor-early Stuart, the table ends often cross-framed for strength; three leg details: 16th-century with the stretchers in T section, early 17th-century with corner bracket tenoned to top of leg, and late 17th-century showing the bulb modified to baluster shaping and the T section stretcher in a wide H plan. SECOND ROW: draw-table of Elizabethan period and later, shown (left) closed with only the tips of the raking bearers showing under table top and (right) with one end extended showing a bearer (black) also extended, its inner end pressing up against the table's central rigid plank and its slope ensuring that the extension is level with the table top—details that would be hidden by the table's deep frieze. THIRD ROW: three side tables of 17th-century, and thumb mould and baluster leg details. BOTTOM, early folding tables: so-called monk's table; early gate leg with three rigid legs; half-circle opening to circle as side or centre table.

Closed, the framing fitted into the open centre of the sideboard with the leaves in the sideboard drawers. This was marketed in 1806 as the Trafalgar table.

Nevertheless many Regency dining tables continued to be bolted together, the difference being the use of a pillar-and-claw support for each unit. Sheraton noted in 1803 that such tables were easily made to any size 'by having a sufficient quantity of pillars and claw parts, for between each of them is a loose flap fixed by means of iron straps and buttons so that they are easily taken off and put aside'. A compromise was the pillar-and-claw table flanked by two tables on straight legs, the outer legs hinged so that leaves could be inserted. George Smith in 1808 suggested a pillar on a round plinth for a dining table 'to do away with the necessity of claw feet [which he called a great inconvenience] and will answer as well for sets of dining as for single tables'. By the 1820s these plinths on paw feet were generally preferred to the claw legs for dining.

At the same time it must be noted that the table with four corner legs and telescopic framing continued also throughout the 19th century, the legs becoming more massive by the 1830s, often reeded and with a great deal of unimaginative turning. Eventually the worm screw simplified opening and closing.

Draw table (Fig. 46): Extending table which was introduced from the Low Countries in the early 16th century and has been in production on and off ever since. This was a development of the joined table inventoried at the time as a drawing joined table with a frame. Here the main area of the top completely covered the two half-size flap extensions that were mounted on slanting bearers. When one or both flaps were pulled out the top rose slightly, then sank again so that the whole extended top was exactly level. This design was largely forgotten in the late 17th century when the demand was for a

47. Tables with Regency characteristics. TOP: gate-table for family meals augmented by D sections. SECOND ROW: occasional tables. THIRD ROW: sofa table; Regency modification of the pillar-and-claw base; sofa table showing details of beaded drawer, turned handle and (below) the ball-and-reel turning and brass-mounted foot. This table was made in 1809 (Blairman). BOTTOM: end view of sofa table support; typical foot for centre table, c. 1815–20s.

135

48. Games tables. TOP: sofa table, the sham drawer containing tric-trac recess; drum or loo table, central square reversible; card table that opens and swivels. SECOND ROW: table with reversible slide for chess; table with fly-bracket ends and reversible board over tric-trac recess; multi-purpose table with top that folds and swivels. BOTTOM: table with well, side recesses, etc. (also detail of brass gallery); brass inlaid table and (below) typical tric-trac recess.

number of small round and oval tables, met by the gate-leg construction. But the draw table reappeared, its working fully described by the extremely practical designer, Thomas Sheraton, as the universal table (q.v.). It was widely made early this century.

Drum table (Fig. 47): Heavy, four-footed pillar-and-claw table. The circular top had a deep frieze fitted with drawers or bookshelves, often including shams.

Games table (Figs. 44, 48, 51): This implies a table specifically made for such games as chess, draughts and backgammon. An occasional early 18th-century specimen resembled the folding-top card table, but had an extra flap inlaid in the checkers and long triangles of these games. Often a drawer in the framing held the playing pieces. This style sometimes had two leaves so that it opened for both cards and games.

A complicated variant of backgammon, known as tric-trac, came into more general favour around the mid-century, however, and for this a shallow two-part well was required, prompting a change in design, mainly from the 1760s onwards. To cover the well a panel was introduced, at first removed by releasing trigger catches disguised as drawer knobs. One side of the panel was inlaid for draughts, with a small ivory rectangle on either side for cribbage scores. The recess for tric-trac was inlaid, painted or of tooled leather (the last recommended by Smith for quiet play). It was presented on the table frieze as a sham drawer with a real drawer below, and pull-out candleslides were fitted below two sides. From the 1770s the panel was extended to run from side to side of the table so that it could slide out. Such a table, carefully veneered, could easily pass as a Pembroke table through the later 18th century and, in appropriate shape, as a sofa table when this was the fashion.

For two-player games small trestle or 'horse' tables were popular, with fly bracket flaps and sometimes small end galleries. In the 1780s and 1790s a small square table of urn table style might be used. The top consisted wholly of a reversible panel over a tric-trac recess with a drawer below, and might be flanked by fly brackets or merely by candle-slides. Tapering legs were linked by cross stretchers. In the 19th century the table had a pillar-and-claw support.

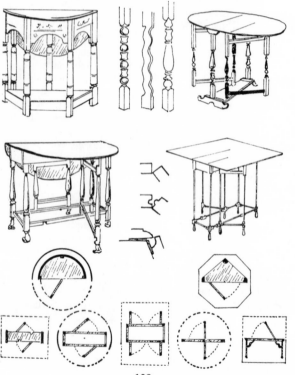

From about 1800 the sofa table with end standards was introduced, the D-shaped ends being sometimes lidded for storing games materials. By then cabinet makers were combining numerous games and desk requirements. Sheraton delighted in such pieces, and in 1811 Ackermann's *Repository* illustrated a table 'comprehending seven different accommodations', made by Morgan and Sanders. Such multi-purpose furniture was continued, and some charming games tables are noted in early Victorian Tunbridge ware. The tendency by then was to include such pieces also among pillar-and-claw designs. In 1851 a chess table was included among the furniture by the Coalbrookdale Company, made in cast iron.

Gate-leg table (Figs 44, 46, 49): Introduced in the 16th century. A table extended by one or two hinged flaps resting on extra legs hinged to the under-framing. The earliest were folding tables—that is, the flap folded back over the fixed section of the table top when not in use. This was augmented by the falling top table, the flap hanging down vertically to the side of the fixed section. In each there might be one or two flaps. In some early folding designs half of one back leg, divided lengthways, was hinged, opening to support a semicircular flap, making a circular table. Variants were six or eight sided when open, particularly in early 17th-century examples serving as shapely little side tables when closed. The top hinged on rule hinges which could be secured with nails, and the

49. Gate-leg tables with *falling* flaps and hinged *additional* support legs. TOP, 17th-century tables: table with one flap and, at left, the extra leg hinged to support it; three legs: reel-and-ball, joiner's flat copy of turner's twist turning, and baluster; early interpretation of the conventional gate-leg table. SECOND ROW: typical late 17th-century gate-leg table with one flap closed; alternatives for junction of fixed top and flaps: plain, groove-and-tongue, and rule joint; spider table, 1760s. BOTTOM: diagrams of usual gate-leg arrangements, the upper two 17th-century and (lower right) one that folds flat with whole top vertical and one for a single-gate-leg spider table.

gate-leg on a wood hinge into the table framing and the back stretcher.

The centre table with a gate leg on each side and falling flaps was developed in the 17th century. Early screws permitted the hinges to be fixed to the underside of the top even when the wood was thin, a sign of high quality timber that would not warp or split. When the top was thick the maker 'softened' or rounded the edge on the underside to appear thin. Dowel pins fixed the top to the under-framing until the more widespread use of screws in the 18th century.

There was a succession of outlines for the meeting of the fixed top with the falling flap, but these cannot be closely dated, and the early square cut to both edges may be noted on ordinary 20th-century pieces with no deliberate intention to deceive. An early alternative was the bead- or tongue-and-groove, but the most satisfactory and enduring favourite was the rule joint which concealed the hinges, leaving no gap between top and flap. Here convex shaping to the edge of the fixed top fitted a concave curve to the corresponding edge of the flap. Often the table was then rimmed on all edges with a similar plain thumb mould.

The early 17th-century gate-leg table might have four fixed legs supporting the framing; alternatively two end standards on projecting feet were linked by a base board. Sometimes the standards were turner-made pillars with baluster or, late in the century, swash turning. It is interesting to note joiner-cut planks for the end pieces in variously shaped and waved outlines intended to suggest such turners' work.

Most of the gate-leg tables found today, however, are in the straightforward form that has continued with little alteration to the present century. The four legs under the fixed framing are linked by stretchers which, like the framing, are halved to receive folded gate legs. In this style of table each gate leg is an additional leg, a construction of two verticals,

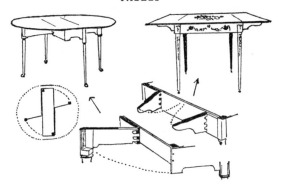

50. The two commonest alternative folding tables. LEFT: the oval gate table used especially in second quarter of 18th-century in strong mahogany, two of the four legs being hinged (wood hinges) to the under-framing as shown. RIGHT: Pembroke table with flaps resting on fly brackets, also working on wooden hinges. The gate table was popular in mahogany for dining and cards, the Pembroke in painted satinwood, etc., for lighter duties.

turned to match the fixed legs and linked top and bottom by stretchers. The inner upright pivots between the framing and stretchers, while the outer one swings out to support the flap. A large flap may have two supports, and some of these tables are square when open, but more are round or oval. Often a drawer is put in the central framing, which, because of the gate legs, has to run on a single central bearer.

A variant of the gate-leg table with folding top was the design with both gate legs on the same side. These offered a firm top and leg space for writing at what, when closed, was a decorative little side table. Many acquired interior fittings, and these are discussed as desk furniture. Late 18th-century gate-leg tables were different enough to be known as spider tables (q.v.). A Victorian variant was the Sutherland (q.v.), but the immediate successor to the gate-leg table for dining was the gate table (q.v.).

Gate table (Fig. 50): Associated mainly with the use of mahogany in early Georgian days. Gate-leg tables with their awkward multiplicity of legs were superseded by the table with two massive falling flaps, each a single piece of dense mahogany, adequately supported by swinging out two of the table's four legs, together with parts of the under-framing. Wooden hinges made this a sturdy construction, while the then universal rule joints concealed the iron hinges of the flaps. This design was made practicable by the freedom from stretchers permissible with mahogany. Such a table was often extended by fixing semicircular side tables to the ends of the flaps.

Joined or long table (Fig. 46): Now often called a refectory table, but without early precedent. It began as an early example of joined furniture as a supplement or alternative to the trestle tables of the dining hall. Early inventories distinguish between the table with a pair of trestles, the table with dormants and the table with a frame. This distinctive framed-up construction was permanently fixed under the table top and supported at the corners by hefty column legs given extra rigidity by similar mortise-and-tenon jointed stretchers. It was in use in the 15th century, and by the second half of the 16th such a piece was inventoried as a joined table.

The framing frieze under the table top was tenoned into the square blocks of the leg tops and carved with Elizabethan gadroons or early Stuart lunettes and some were inlaid with checker patterns. But by the later 17th century it was losing ground as a parlour dining table to the gate-legs. Some had glued-on ornament, but far more were plain. The legs went through the phases associated with 16th- and 17th-century furniture, cut square at first and chamfered on the inner

51. Tables. TOP: early Victorian massive central table used as a dining or loo table; butler's tray and its folding web-topped stand; Regency style chess table in Tunbridge ware made for the Prince Consort in 1845 (Tunbridge Wells Museum). BOTTOM: folding chess table in Clay's paper ware; exceptional design by Owen Jones, 1872; detail of the heavy-handed 'simple' notions of such reformers as Philip Webb, c. 1870 (V. and A. Museum).

corners, shaped hexagonally or in faceted baluster form. The Elizabethan bulbous cup-and-cover outline was sometimes used, and also pillars with crude Ionic capitals, but such detail is more often noted in Victorian specimens in black-stained oak. Plain, turned pillars and balusters soon returned, always left in square section for the joints and often with carved corner brackets.

Stretchers or foot rails were only a little above floor level, running directly from leg to leg or across the ends and down

143

the centre. Below the blocks left for the stretcher joints the original carved feet have often worn and been cut away, slightly spoiling the proportions. The stretchers raised the sitters' feet from the cold floor and permitted stools to be up-ended under the table between meals. Original stretchers might be moulded or in the 16th-century's T-section, but most

that remain are replacements. Plain tables of comparable massive style continued to be made for farmhouse and kitchen through the 18th and 19th centuries, but only on reproductions was there any attempt at carved ornament.

Kettle stand (Fig. 56): *see* URN STAND.

Loo table (Fig. 51): A card game resembling whist was often played in the 19th century on a circular centre table. Such tables followed the changing styles of pillar-and-claw or pedestal. Some tops were scalloped in the second half of the century, and some six or eight sided. Sheraton illustrated a design in 1804 with eight slightly concave sides. In 1822 Brown described as a loo table a specimen in the classic Hope style with a solid pyramid support on triangular plinth with heavy scroll feet.

Monk's table: *see* CHAIR TABLE

Moorish table: Late Victorian name for any exotic looking design, usually of low, coffee table proportions. The general style was most usually a six-, eight- or twelve-sided table with a straight leg at each corner and a deep apron between in arcaded outline. The main feature was its ornament of shell, bone, ivory, or other inlay. A comparable piece, but with an Indian flavour to its all-over relief ornament, was the so-called 'Benares' table: this had a dished tray of brass elaborately bordered with patterns in relief resting on a broad wooden rim, usually in lobed outline. Variants of these tables

52. Side tables. TOP, late 17th-century to 1700s: table with thumb mould to thin top, twist legs, flat waved stretchers; S-scroll legs, X stretcher; carved gilded gesso, shouldered legs, rounded H stretcher. SECOND ROW, first half 18th-century: gesso, shell in apron; shaped marble top, C-scroll frieze, double scroll legs; marble top, aggressively carved mahogany comparable with designs by Matthias Lock, 1746. THIRD ROW: 'Gothic' pierced frieze, cluster column legs, etc., 1750s–60s; neo-classic, c. 1765 on; table c. 1770s. BOTTOM: serpentine outlines, kingwood veneers and ormolu, c. 1780s; squarer table with turned legs, 1790s; table towards 1800.

TABLES

reflected the craze for Japanese work. An example at the Victoria and Albert Museum in ebonised wood has stencilled gilt ornament on its fret cut aprons which are in minaret outline, above turned, outcurving legs in the bamboo shaping of the period.

Ornamental table (Figs 12, 42, 57, 131): A term associated with circular pedestal tables of the 19th century, their interest depending on surface treatments that rendered them too decorative for much use. It may be claimed that the earliest were early 18th-century gesso side and console tables followed by the superb marquetry of around the 1770s, but the notion was greatly extended during the popularity of pedestal tables in the 19th century. Different treatments included: Regency penwork; Regency geometrical Tunbridge ware and subsequent Victorian Tunbridge mosaic; Derbyshire blue-john and local marbles in scrap work and ornate floral inlay; papier mâché, either shell encrusted or oil painted; boulle; painted slate; Berlin wool embroidery. The processes involved are described in Part XVII.

It must be noted that much marble inlay work was imported from Italy and only mounted in England. Already in the 1830s 'Louis Quinze trivialities' were ousting the heavier Louis Quatorze Baroque in drawing room and boudoir. Ceramics painted with designs after Raphael and Watteau were in fashion, and circular plateaux for table tops were made by the Copeland firm—despite the difficulty in preventing warping. Sometimes a plaque was inset in the table top, as in a specimen by Chamberlain of Worcester shown at the 1851 exhibition. By the 1850s porcelain flowers were sometimes inserted in the wood like other marquetry.

Pembroke table (Fig. 50): A variety of light table with small falling flaps supported on fly brackets instead of resting on movable legs. This is differentiated from the sofa table by the general shape of the top when open—a round cornered squarish rectangle, often about three feet across, or occasionally elliptical. The Pembroke dates from about the 1750s and was popular as a breakfast table. At that time it might have cross stretchers and was the kind of minor furnishing to lend itself to Chinese and Gothic detail such as cluster-column legs.

From the 1770s, for the same reason, such tables were often of satinwood with delightful ornament in marquetry, inlay or paint, and it is this type that has most often been preserved. Often a drawer in the ornamental apron is matched by a sham drawer on the other side, and the legs end in small castors—tapering, stretcher-free legs which were thermed at first and often husk carved or fluted, but turned at the end of the century. By then the alternatives were horse legs or the pillar-and-claw support. Sheraton recommended a height of no more than 2 feet 4 inches, including castors. He liked the oval table top to be a little fuller than an ellipse so that 'the flaps, when turned down, may better hide the joint rail'.

Piecrust table (Fig. 53): Popular design of pillar-and-claw table with the top turned in a repetitive cyma outline of contrasting straight and curved sections. The low rim about an inch wide following this outline suggested the crimping of pastry edging a pie. Popular around 1760 and much in demand for reproductions.

Pier table (Fig. 52): A variety of side table (q.v.), a pier being an architectural term for the wall between windows, which in an important 18th-century room would be of constant proportions so that a pair of matching pier tables could stand between three windows. They were frequently more or less semicircular and included some of the finest furniture ornament ever produced, since their purpose was mainly decorative, and they were restricted to lavishly furnished rooms.

Pillar-and-claw table (Figs 42, 44, 48, 53): This elegant Georgian table for tea, dessert etc. was the remote descendant of tables and candlestands for primitive homes requiring three-footed stands for stability. A few remain from the late 17th century, the design consisting of a small top resting on a slender pillar based on outward-jutting horizontal feet in square-cut massive little scrolls. This early claw had an angular point to the meeting of concave and convex curves, but became more graceful in Queen Anne's reign. The late 'black' walnut was occasionally used for such a table, the top made from a single piece of wood. As late as 1755 Thomas Hollinshed offered 'Turnery Good in Mahogany, Walnut-tree, etc.'. He gave a full list of claw furniture more easily shaped in the softer wood, including dumb waiters, claw tables, firescreens, tea kettle stands and candlestands.

With the development of mahogany furniture, pillar-and-claw tables became widely popular occasional tables in important rooms. As early as 1733 Sir William Stanhope owned 'a mahogany scollop'd Tea-Table on a claw'. The huge girth of the wood made it possible for the turner to shape a top of considerable size, most usually slightly dished so that it had a low, sloping rim, sometimes scalloped, sometimes in the familiar piecrust outline. Sometimes the rim was elaborated with carved foliage or beading on the table top, while the underside was rounded or softened so that the wood still appeared thin and light. By the 1750s an alternative was a low vertical gallery of delicate fret cutting, and on such a cabinet maker's piece the top was sometimes octagonal. On the simpler top, made by the turner, in round or waved outline, the gallery occasionally consisted of tiny, turned spindles.

Occasionally a table is found with low rims or dished circles to accommodate eight vessels around the scalloped edge. This is usually called a 'supper table' for informal meals. But its more obvious purpose was to hold light confections offered as the dessert or banquet at popular, informal social gatherings through most of the 18th century.

Below, the pillar, too, indicates the qualifications of its maker: cabinet men introduced shaping and carving of conjoined scrolls, but the more usual pillar is a turned baluster. This is sometimes carved with foliage on the well-proportioned

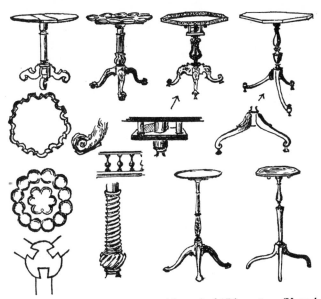

53. Pillar-and-claw tables. TOP: table, end of 17th-century (V. and A. Museum); early Georgian, its top sunk for dessert glasses; table with hollow carved pillar, fret-cut rim and 'birdcage'; Sheraton design with typical late 18th-century feet. SECOND ROW: detail of piecrust rim; foot showing 'shoe'; 'birdcage', removed with table top when horizontal peg is withdrawn; alternative leg arrangement by Sheraton. THIRD ROW: table top dished for dessert glasses; detail of spindle rim. BOTTOM: dovetailing of claw legs into pillar base; alternative to usual pillar; two 18th-century teapoys.

swell, or ornament may be limited to the turner's more simple spiral fluting. A mid-century alternative was a cluster of engaged columns dowelled into the solid block that held the claws or legs. This was an important constructional feature, the leg being dovetailed vertically into the block with a flaring tenon before the pillar was inserted.

Like the proportions of the pillar, the curve of the three legs or claws suggests the date of a table. The S-outline of the legs derived from the cabriole leg, and in the same way may show carving to enrich the difficult curve of the knee and to shape the foot so that it grips the floor. Late 18th-century design (and many reproductions) tend to skimp the wood with a weaker line and to sprawl rather than grip.

The shape of the foot follows that of other cabriole furniture, but it is a mistake to attempt too exact a dating. The most usual is the simple club or pad foot, sometimes called a snake's head. This, the wood turner's choice, is to be noted throughout the period of the table's popularity. But the hairy paw foot and the claw gripping a ball were variants in fashion in the 1740s and probably continuing into the 1760s. A more aggressive lion's-paw form was used on many massive pillar tables of the early 19th century, but otherwise these interesting designs are more common on reproductions. A dolphin head was an occasional variant from the 1760s, but more frequently then the leg ended in a scroll toe, and the foot was shaped with a heel that ensured a firm stance. Scrolls and knurls gave poise to some particularly charming, richly carved specimens.

An interesting feature of this type of table was the way the top fitted into the pillar. At first an applied turned collar was screwed on to the pillar. By the 1740s the top could often be tilted upright to stand in a corner; subsequently it was sometimes made to revolve—important when loaded with a pyramid of dessert glasses filled with sweetmeats—and from about 1755 the whole top could be lifted off when not in use. This construction was known as a bird-cage. The tilting top was equipped underneath with two small cross bearers bored for a pivot that acted as a hinge on a small square platform, fitting neatly between them and mounted on the pillar top. A brass spring-catch fitted into a socket on the platform edge when the top was horizontal.

In the more elaborate bird-cage version, the platform was made into an open-sided box formed with a second platform and small spindles at the corners. The lower platform was bored for the pillar top, which was secured within the bird-cage by a horizontal wedge passing through it. When the wedge was withdrawn the top could be lifted off.

Ince and Mayhew illustrated several ornately carved claw tables around 1760, including one with a triangular top with candleslides and wells for counters, but late in the century the tables lost their vigour, and by the 1780s the cabriole claws tended to sag in dipping curves. *The Book of Prices* showed a number of designs with neat scrolls and tiny turned feet for firescreens, dressing glasses, etc., as well as heavier legs on club feet for dining, and loo tables. Sheraton, in his *Drawing Book*, showed extremely slender pillars and claws in both arched and dipping line, ending neatly in his typical, turned vertical feet. In contrast to much 19th-century design, he made his claws flow smoothly from the pillar base with graceful vase turning above.

The *Book of Prices* (1793 edition) reference to dining and loo tables is a reminder that circular tables for many purposes became popular before the end of the 18th century, with ovals and rounded-corner squares as occasional alternatives. These are noted in a range of sizes and purposes, but three main styles emerge, derived from the 18th-century's popular pillar-and-claw. Much of the following description may be applied indiscriminately to what the period knew as dining, wine, library, drum, supper and loo tables.

The top was usually plain through the first half of the 19th century, and after that the rim was often carved and the top more elaborately shaped, becoming many sided or scalloped. For the support, three main forms were produced, with many minor variations. The most obvious immediate change, even among small tables, was the greater solidity and simplicity. The pillar tended to become straight, plainly turned, and sometimes divided into three slender, thermed, slightly dipping legs with no more than minimal ring turning at the join. From Regency days such legs were often reeded. Typically, however, the complement to such a casual line was the controlled merging of these legs with equal grace into a plain triangular plinth, concave sided, often mounted on castors or more elaborate feet. Sometimes the pillar was almost lost, and the division into three legs began almost immediately below the top—a pleasing line that became somewhat too loose in early Victorian work.

The obvious alternative of the 1800s was the turned or turned-and-carved pillar mounted directly on a floor-level pedestal or plinth. Smith in 1808, for example, showed this style with a square top and a four-footed plinth and it is noted again and again through the Regency and later. For a library table Smith introduced four flat, projecting legs, and illustrated a suitable scroll bracket to steady the table at the pillar top. By the 1810s there was a tendency towards a more massive pillar, and careful classical detail on a thick, solid plinth. The pillar was either gadrooned above the plinth or, with more extensive reeding, suggested an inversion of the Greek leg among miscellaneous knops by the 1820s and 30s. The circular plinth of the late 18th century was largely replaced by the classic polygonal outline, each side slightly concave to give additional emphasis to the corner feet.

The third alternative table support showed the disappearance of the three legs in a solid pyramidal pedestal of

54. Tables. TOP, quartetto tables: Sheraton design, 1803, with bowed stretcher; table with brass wires linking top and feet; design with turned stretcher and late-Regency feet; table with 'Gothic' supports and no stretcher, in Smith style. Each of these is taken from a nesting set. BOTTOM: stand for ornament; side table; late 18th-century teapoy; chess table illustrated by John Doyle.

similarly concave outline. This was the style popularised by Thomas Hope, in his design of 1807, which showed handsome inlay on the face of the pedestal, worked out in ebony and silver. Such supports were three or four sided with paw feet protruding below the similarly cornered plinth. The line was somewhat spoilt when the corners of the plinth flowed directly into huge scroll feet.

Yet another alternative consisted of ending a solid pedestal considerably above floor level and supporting its plinth base on three or four claw legs. Even before Victorian days four vertical, turned pillars sometimes replaced the pedestal, giving a wider area of support under the table top. In this platform style, too, the convex or concave line of the Regency claw table was used—but under a substantial table usually the latter—and the supporting legs or claws followed a sequence of styles. Thus the point of junction—the straight-turned base of the pillar—was extended downward, and the tops of the claws deepened to match, so that larger tenons could extend from the claws into the pillar. When the centre consisted of a platform, the same leg or claw deepening at the shoulder meant that it arched above the platform, and this was sufficiently approved for the same arching shoulder line to be introduced in the pillar design, making the tops of the claws deeper still by the 1820s. Subsequently the line of the claw shoulders was reversed into a horn, so that the general line of each claw was a C rather than an elongated S.

Quartetto table (Fig. 54): Defined by Sheraton in his *Dictionary*, 1803, as 'a kind of small work table made to draw out of each other, and may be used separately and again inclosed within each other when not wanted'. These were typical of many little tables for casual use towards the end of the 18th century. Made in graduated sizes, they were usually in trestle shape, but with a single long-ways stretcher to the back instead of across the middle to allow of close nesting. The slender legs often had simple, turned ornament, and the rectangular tops were sometimes decoratively veneered. George Smith, in 1808, showed rectangular end standards with Gothic piercing. He noted their use: they 'prevent the company rising from their seats, when taking refreshments'. He thus associated them with the small tables known as teapoys. Some of the tables were ornamented with brass inlay and had wire instead of wooden stretchers. Quartetto and trio tables have continued in demand ever since this period.

Refectory table: Recent name for the long, joined table used for meals, as distinct from the trestle type and the draw table (q.v.).

Side table (Figs 46, 52): Intended to stand against a wall so that the back is usually plain, these tables date from the 15th century onwards and include sideboard tables, writing tables and pier tables. Some 17th-century joined tables—probably forerunners of sideboards—resemble dining tables but lack carving on one side of the frieze. However, more small side tables date from the late 17th century onwards, as occasional furniture, intended to furnish a room rather than for any specific use. Here again it is only the plain back frieze and often a drawer in the front that distinguish the piece: sometimes the back stretcher lacks the waved line of front and sides. Many of these may have been intended as dressing tables. The top is a rectangle, usually about three feet by two feet, and the legs go through the changing designs of the 1690s and 1700s with S-scrolls, straight or set across the corners, or with the elegant turnings of their day. They are linked by flat or moulded stretchers, waved or looped, often meeting in a central turned finial. Feet are ball or bun shapes.

Some surviving examples from around 1700 are in the ornate style of Oriental cabinet stands, deeply carved and gilded, the legs with gadrooned capitals, the frieze in full relief foliated strapwork. Some of the finest have tops of gilded gesso; others of marble or scagliola. As with console tables, they were often massive in the William Kent manner with full relief gilded carving of female masks, putti and sphinxes among their huge scrolling legs and swirling acanthus leaves.

Often a greater resemblance to the console table was achieved with the legs based upon a solid plinth in shaped outline. By the 1730s the tendency was to mount a marble top on a deep frieze carved with C-scrolls, fluting, egg-and-dart or some other repetitive pattern above huge leaf-carved scrolling legs linked by a deep apron similarly carved around a central motif of shells, female mask, fruit, etc. Sometimes eagles' heads were introduced as leg terminals. By the 1740s, although still massive and often marble topped, side table design was more restrained, with richly carved cabriole legs, classic carving on the frieze and a large central apron motif. The handsome paw feet of the 1740s were followed by knurls and scrolls on the reversed scroll legs and in corner brackets of rococo charm.

These side tables continued to be made far into the 1760s with superbly carved legs in emphatic cabriole outline to declare the extravagant use of material and man-hours. But the fashion for straight legged, pierced and card-cut Chinese and Gothic tables in the 1750s was soon followed by Adam-esque designs from the 1760s, again offering chances for ornament on frieze and legs that could not be displayed so well on any other furnishing. Adam design included intricate relief carving in pendant swags, for example, below the frieze and rams' head terminals to the legs. An important motif still dominated the centre of the frieze such as a female or satyr mask or a pair of sphinxes. Many a side table of the 1760s and 70s had a pair of legs to each side of the front, either thermed or turned and fluted.

Chippendale and Ince and Mayhew illustrated designs for sideboard tables, but these may best be considered among dining room furnishings, as direct forerunners of the side-board. The ornamental side table delighted Hepplewhite and Sheraton who specified them as pier tables, Sheraton showing three in use between the windows of a drawing room. Charac-teristically these narrowed roundly towards the front so as not to impede passers-by. But Sheraton shows a marked change of mood. Hepplewhite delighted in richly ornamented table tops: Sheraton led the eye down to decorative stretchers supporting a central ornament a little above floor level. The outcome of this mood, observable by late Regency days, was the table with a low platform base backed with silvered glass 'to produce,' as Smith suggested in 1826, 'a reflecting effect from china objects which are usually placed in such situations'. Some of the most interesting that remain from the late 18th century are painted upon satinwood or a substitute such as birch.

Hope, in 1807, suggested a pier table with ornate end verticals or standards to a trestle or horse construction and this method of supporting a side table continued through Victorian days. Heavy Regency examples included much use of elbowed lion paw feet as cross supports to the standards. But other side tables, some marble topped, are found with a variety of supports. These include four fluted, tapering legs topped by lion or Egyptian masks and based on appropriately carved feet; legs in double reversed curves to make a rounded X outline at each end, linked by a single stretcher; front legs in the ungainly spavin or conventionalised scimitar line topped, perhaps, by leopard masks. Some tables were wholly painted and gilded, some of rosewood, mahogany or amboyna with gilded enrichment, some inlaid with brass. Marble was popular, including Derbyshire marbles and the red-spotted, dark green serpentine from Cornwall, but proved hazardous in the dining room, and in 1834 *The Architectural Magazine* reported that 'Nobody will buy such pieces of furniture now'.

Other side tables, leather topped, served as occasional writing tables. These were regarded as suitable for the Victorian-Elizabethan style in blackened oak with end supports in cup-and-cover swellings, the apron carved with strapwork, its corners dripping pendant knobs and the outward-jutting feet carved as pairs of dolphins.

Social or wine table: A horseshoe shape on castors to be drawn up to the fire. It dates from the last years of the 18th century, and remaining specimens generally suggest late Regency origin. The important feature was that a pair of coasters could be moved within reach of the drinkers sitting on the outer side of the curve by sliding from side to side of the table's inner curved edge. Brass fittings were attached to japanned coasters.

A variant illustrated in the *Cabinet Book of Prices*, 1792 edition, was a kidney-shaped table 'for use with a pillar-and-claw in the hollow part [that is the inner curve of the table], the top turned to receive the bottom of a tin or copper cylinder, two feet over and made to turn round, a mahogany top of ditto fitted into the cylinder and cut to receive five tin bottle cases'. This was costed at £1 8s. Circular wine tables were made also, with receptacles for coasters, etc., within the framing, accessible by lifting off part of the table top.

Sofa table (Figs 47, 48): An English design popular from the late 1790s as an elongated version of the Pembroke. This had similar flybracket supports to small flaps, which in this design were introduced at the table ends. The top was supported in the trestle or 'horse' manner of the day, and much of its elegance depended upon the design of the standards and the castor-mounted outjutting feet. Such a table could be drawn close to the armed sofa or settee and offer space for two people to work or play side by side.

Sheraton in his *Dictionary*, 1803, suggested that it should be 5 to 6 feet long, 22 to 24 inches wide and about 28 inches high. The many cheaper examples, factory made from about 1810, tended to be a little smaller. The top and its D-shaped or rounded-rectangular flaps might be of satinwood with contrasting border banding, but in the early 19th century many were veneered in exotic woods such as zebra or amboyna. Both sides of the table were identical which meant that, on each, one of the two drawer fronts was a sham. Sometimes they were flanked by small, square-fronted drawers to pull out and swing sideways, fitted for inks and pens.

On an example of fine quality all would show lines and cross bandings of contrasting woods and the drawers would be oak lined whereas cost-cutting drawers in cheaper work would have sides of soft wood concealed by linings of blue paper. Similar delicate detail of boxwood lines was popular on the simple standards and smoothly flowing legs on socket castors characteristic of the early sofa table, but reeding was a cheaper substitute. Here the quality of the construction permitted legs to appear free of the usual cross stretcher which, however, might be introduced almost out of sight below the framing. The stretcher rail itself was of varying quality, often rectangular in section and slightly arched. The heavy late Regency design sometimes included a massive turning with lotus or tassel capping each side of a central ball motif, touched with gilding. Coarse turning on a low-placed stretcher was common in factory specimens.

In the opulent style of the early 19th century the table standards, too, were elaborated. Many were lyre shaped, with brass rods to suggest strings, which were popular on factory-made tables from about 1815. Smith suggested a design with lion monopodia supports, two at each end, but many late Regency designs showed square-cut standards supported by the truss-shaped brackets of the 1820s above massive paw feet which were double gilded and highly burnished.

Like other Regency furniture, the sofa table from about 1810 was often supported by a single central pedestal based on a rectangular platform with four corner feet in dipping curves. This style with its changing foot outlines is described among other pillar-and-claw tables. Brass inlay on the pedestal became coarser from about 1815. One variant had four turned spindles instead of the pedestal, and there was a brief period of success for a turned, central pillar with a gadrooned base. A successor to the lyre-end standard in the 1820s was the open vase outline, but with concave shaping

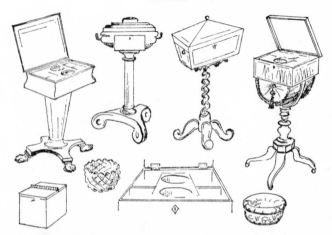

55. Teapoys, in the early 19th-century meaning of the word, when the piece consisted of a tea-chest mounted on stem and foot. TOP: on right, a specimen of c. 1820s (V. and A. Museum). BOTTOM: details of a typical compartmented interior with lidded teabox and cut-glass bowls for sugar and for blending the teas.

to the sides. In the mid-1820s the table lost its distinguishing end flaps and became no more than an occasional table—the name used by Smith in 1826. A rare variant was the draw-top sofa table. In this the ends pulled out by a mechanical device patented by William Bullock in 1801: pulling one end automatically extended the other.

Spider-leg table (Fig. 49): Form of gate-leg fashionable in the third quarter of the 18th century long after other gate-legs had been outmoded. This may, in fact, have eight legs like a spider, all very slender turnings—two at each end of the fixed framing and two for each gate: the stretchers are so slender, too, that the inner leg of each gate was extended to the floor.

The spindles were left square for each joint. Such a table may have one gate leg and flap: in this case the fixed portion has a modified front stretcher arrangement allowing more space for the user's feet.

Supper table: *see* CHINA TABLE.

Sutherland table: Victorian, named after Harriet, Duchess of Sutherland, Mistress of the Robes (d. 1868). A gate-leg table, the central portion very narrow in contrast to the deep flaps and supported on the trestle type of leg construction with out-ward-jutting feet, each standard often composed of a pair of turned spindles.

Teapoy (Figs 53, 54, 55, 131): A word often confusing to beginner collectors. In the 18th century, when tea was fashionably served in the gazebo or rustic summerhouse, each guest had a small individual table of slender pillar-and-claw construction—a teapoy. There are many references to such 'little tables from which we each drank our tea' by Mrs Delàny and others. Typically such a piece would be some 30 inches high and 15 inches across the top, light enough to be lifted easily with one hand. The joint of pillar and legs was sometimes strengthened by a metal bracket attachment screwed to the underside. Teapoys thus took their place among the dainty pillar-and-claw stands in use through the 18th century for candlesticks and tea kettles, with similar attention to delicate claw feet. Style followed that of the more substantial pillar-and-claw table in its light 18th-century form, the rimless octagonal top becoming straight edged from about the mid-century instead of moulded.

The change in the teapoy's purpose came in the 1780s when tea prices were reduced drastically and teapots—and therefore also tea canisters—much enlarged. The big new tea canisters were mainly of wood, a pair enclosed in a rectangular cabinet-made tea chest of tapering sarcophagus shape, complete with cut glass bowl for blending the teas. Sheraton in 1803 noted that the tea chest was now implied by the word caddy. Such a massive furnishing could no longer stand on the tea table or beside the hostess on the floor. Instead it was placed on a teapoy matching the tea table. Thomas Hope and George Smith illustrated such teapoys. But for safety, after about 1810, the caddy was fixed directly to the pedestal, so that by 1850 Simmonds' *Dictionary of Trade* could define the piece as 'an ornamental pedestal table with lifting top for holding tea'. Pillar-and-claw were soon modified to pillar-and-pedestal.

After about 1820 the caddy became larger again, with four compartments and two bowls and sometimes provision for caddy spoon and sugar tongs. Some Victorian examples have a mirror in the lid to reflect light upon the contents. Such a caddy might be mounted on a heavy octagonal pillar on a cross-shaped plinth or four massive castored feet, caddy and plinth often inlaid to match. Lighter teapoys were made in papier mâché throughout the long vogue for this gleaming material, richly japanned. As late as 1886 they were on display in the London japan shops, and black grounds became general in the 1830s. The word teapoy should not be applied to the porcelain or pottery vessel for dry tea: this was a tea jar.

Tea table (Figs 42, 45): Through the 18th century a succession of small tables served the hostess when after-dinner guests took tea and bread and butter, and often cordials, too, in slender glasses 'flowered' to harmonise with the tea equipage. For such an exotic drink as tea the japanned style was considered especially appropriate, but most of these in japanned soft wood with rimmed oblong tops have disappeared. However, there were many alternatives. The collector finds details of some of these among folding card tables, for example, where an additional leaf might be provided so that the table could be opened to reveal a worthy surface of elegant veneer

56. Stands. TOP, tea-kettle stands: two styles by Chippendale, one protecting the spirit flame; design with alternative legs by Ince & Mayhew; typical specimen of 1760s with small fret-bordered top and wide legs. BOTTOM, urn stands: 1760s; 1770s–80s; detail of usual pull-out slide for teapot and detail of such a slide in a Hepplewhite diagram; 1780s–90s.

and among the handsome pillar-and-claw tables (q.v.) fashionable throughout the long supremacy of mahogany. Many of these were rimmed or galleried to protect the fragile wares, and with the bird-cage device the whole top could be lifted off and carried away by the servant.

Early silver trays were sometimes referred to as tea tables: the development of tea trays in wood with ornamental galleries, in silver and almost indistinguishable Sheffield plate through the later 18th century, meant that more stable four-footed Pembroke tables and later sofa tables could be used

163

freely. Ince and Mayhew suggested four designs for trays with elaborately fretted rims; Hepplewhite some twenty-five years later suggested four with rich patterns for inlay or paint. At the same time more elegant alternatives to the hazardous pillar-and-claw were suggested, for example, by Chippendale as china tables. His designs had waved outlines to top and fretted gallery, one with carved, scroll-footed French legs linked by scrolling rococo cross stretchers, the other an early return to pairs of straight tapering legs, plainly thermed but with Gothic piercing in the slight swell of the foot.

Through the later 18th century, when the tea equipage had its own elegant tray, any side, Pembroke or other occasional table would offer a substantial alternative to the pillar-and-claw. The light simple form of claw table, known in the 18th century as a teapoy (q.v.), was often supplied for individual use, or quartetto tables (q.v.) were set out among the guests. In the early 19th century, occasional tables of the long sofa type, with or without end flaps, were widespread. Designers listed specific uses for their horse, claw, and pillar-and-pedestal tables as for reading, breakfast, loo, work and the like. Tea had lost its mystique.

Trafalgar table: *see* DINING TABLE.

Trestle table: The early dining table for the retainers in a great house, although the family might dine separately at a joined or framed table. The usual inventory reference is to a table with a pair of trestles. Planks of oak, walnut or elm held together by cross bearers cross-framed at the ends for hard ware were mounted loosely upon two or more heavy trestles or 'horses'. Rough finish to the early wood was masked by deep table cloths. The trestle might be a thick, flat board shaped like an I, or a pillar on substantial cross feet: board or pillar might be cut or turned to an ornamental profile. An early variant had a heavy central stretcher linking the trestles by being tusk-tenoned through the trestle uprights and the protruding ends secured by wooden pegs. Some collectors consider this design to be implied by the early term 'table dormant'. But this term, implying a table not to be moved or dismantled, might refer to a joined table. Reference to trestle tables continued into the early 18th century, but many more remain from subsequent revivals, especially from the 19th century as a result of the early Victorian delight in medieval furnishings (Fig. 9).

Tripod table: *see* PILLAR-AND-CLAW TABLE.

Universal table: A folding table illustrated in detail by Sheraton in his *Drawing Book*. This was, in fact, the draw table of the Tudors with the flaps pulling out of the central framing to rest on raking sliders. In the Sheraton design its square frame was mounted on thermed tapering legs with socket castors. He noted that with both leaves in the closed position it would serve as a breakfast table.

Urn table (Fig. 56): Boiling water was supplied to the 18th-century hostess so that she or her tea blender could make the tea in view of her guests, the tea kettle on its spirit lamp placed on a small pillar-and-claw stand. This was wide footed like a candlestand for safety, but otherwise followed the changes of other pillar-and-claw furniture at its most ornamental. The top resembled a silver salver of its day, at first with a moulded rim, but in the second half of the 18th century with a gallery. From the 1760s, however, fashion preferred a charcoal-heated urn to a kettle, with a short-lived vessel known as a tea fountain as a transitional piece, kettle-shaped but emptied with a tap.

The urn soon became a massive piece with an interior box iron heating unit and the pillar stand was no longer adequate. Chippendale and Ince and Mayhew in the early 1760s illustrated sturdier four-legged stands shaped as metal-lined boxes, such a box still being called a tea kettle stand. With a slit at the back—facing the hostess—such a stand would serve the fountain or early urn, perhaps with a pull-out slide for a basin to catch the inevitable tap drips. But fashion soon changed to an open table top that would display the graceful neo-classical urn. This urn table was square with four outspread

legs usually linked by stretchers and with a dished slide or pull-out tray as an expected detail for the drip bowl under the tap and for resting the teapot for filling. The slide became wider as the century progressed and by the end was often the full width of the table apron.

Early specimens were sturdy, with fretted galleries. Some tops were serpentine, and from the 1770s many were in light woods with inlay or marquetry. Hepplewhite's *Guide* illustrated delightful urn stands, with square, round and octagonal tops and free-standing tapering legs: he recommended a height of about twenty-six inches. Japanned urn tables, according to Sheraton, were for inferior drawing rooms. Even urn stands in the 1800s might be pillar-and-claw pieces. Sometimes one is noted with carving more recently added in an attempt to make it acceptable as an earlier kettle stand. By the end of the Regency, however, the urn table was largely forgotten, the urn dominating the tea tray.

Wine table: *see* SOCIAL TABLE.

Work table: This will be found among other desk and bureau furniture.

Writing table (Fig. 44): The fitted writing table is described among desk furniture. Others followed the same changes of fashion as simple side tables and are distinguishable only when the top is covered with leather, often associated with drawers, sham or real, in the frieze. Tables for cards or board games were often fitted for writing too.

---

57. Nineteenth-century table details. TOP, legs: development from Regency 'Greek' leg; popular design for cottage styles; heavy bobbin turning; two varieties of twist. SECOND ROW: turned motif for meeting point of stretchers; spindle turning: legs ringed to suggest bamboo; thermed leg, the central area serpentine waved; ultimate in purposeless turning on sturdy dining table. BOTTOM: three details of mid-century expanding circular table; detail of work-table frieze.

PART V

Chest Furniture

Occasionally, as at Anne of Cleves House, Lewes, Sussex, one finds an early chest shaped from a hollowed log. From such dugouts developed a diversity of chest furniture composed of boxed-in sides and lifting lid. These range from the massive medieval chests still found in some churches, triple locked and even bolted to the floor, to minor 19th-century knife boxes and salt boxes of sand-scrubbed oak with simple leather hinges. Dug-outs were superseded gradually by heavy boarded chests, including some inventoried as pegged chests, and the richly ornamented Flanders chests.

In the 14th century design was sometimes modified to a still clumsy joiner-made construction, but the main advance was introduced into England towards the end of the 15th century with the panelled chest. This skilled joinery, consisting of a framework linked by mortise-and-tenon joints and enclosing loose panels, is described in the survey of craft techniques Part XVII. The lid, composed of flat boards, was secured by cross battens fitted on the underside, outside the chest. The lid was thinner from about 1600 and this too was often panelled after about 1625.

Panelled chests are found under a number of names and uses. Blanket chests are associated especially with the first and second periods under review, but continued through the 18th century; counters, linenfold chests, Nonsuch chests belong to the first period. From the 16th century onwards metal and metal-bound chests must be included, such as the Armada chest and the plate chest known as a standard. For travelling there were trunks or portmanteaux and coffers.

As people acquired more numerous and diverse possessions, the chest storage space was augmented by one or two drawers —the 17th-century mule chest. From this evolved the chest wholly subdivided into a number of layers, becoming the chest of drawers of the later 17th century. In the following period this was further developed into the tallboy and the ornate drawing room commode, followed by the chiffonier. Small chests include the so-called Bible box and Derbyshire desk and a range of boxes now called lace or glove boxes; also small caskets which at their most elaborate qualify as fitted desk furniture, together with workboxes and compendiums of the later 18th century onwards (Figs 6, 8, 9, 131).

It must be recognised that small chests have proved exceptionally popular reproduction furniture. Also the collector must realise the popularity of amateur chip carving around the end of the 19th century and assess correctly the many 'medieval' caskets, chests and boxes of the period.

Ark: North of England term for a sloping-fronted chest. An arkwright had a smaller range of skill than a carpenter.

Armada chest: Dating from the late 17th and 18th centuries and not connected with the Spanish Armada. An iron strong box imported from Germany and copied in this country, mainly in simpler versions. Typically the whole lid is an elaborate lock with a dozen or more bolts to catch under the turned-in edges of the chest's sides. The keyhole is hidden in the lid, revealed when a knife is pushed under one of the metal straps. There may also be looped hasps for padlocks. A false keyhole is often added on the front and the chest's considerable ornament includes a decorative lock plate and sometimes much wrought iron scrolling, also paint. Wooden chests heavily banded with iron were listed as standards.

Bible box: Seldom found today predating the 17th century and mostly, like the Bibles themselves, far later. Such small, flattish boxes were in general use for storing and conveying books and papers. They are frequently of oak, with a little ornament carved in low relief, sometimes including initials or date. Careful examination of such details as hinges, lock plate and lid rim may guide in dating.

Blanket chest (Fig. 60): Among the earliest furnishings, usually standing at the foot of the bed for storing all the 'costly apparel, tents and canopies, fine linen, Turkey cushions' and

the rest that Gremio stowed in cypress chests in *The Taming of the Shrew*. Moth-defying chests of cypress wood were introduced in the 16th century and long remained popular, covered with incised or burnt low relief ornament. Sixteenth-century blanket chests had panelled fronts and sometimes also the ends ornamented with rich carving, boldly projecting pilasters on the stiles and muntins flanking panels with arcaded ornament. In the 17th century carving was comparatively shallow but often prolific, with lunettes, guilloche and similar repetitive patterns surrounding panels carved with lozenges or inlaid with flower groups. Some still show traces of paint. Feet were still merely extensions of the corner stiles, but a detail sometimes noted in early 17th-century work is the addition of a horizontal moulding along the chest base matching the projecting lid framing. This sort of oak chest continued to be made through the 18th century.

The heavy style of projecting panels, applied mouldings and split turnings is associated with the middle and later years of the 17th century, and is sometimes noted with further enrichment of bone inlay. In the last years of the first period and into Queen Anne's reign, extremely handsome blanket chests were made in walnut, some inlaid in the solid, some

58. Early chests. TOP: pegged chest, for storing flat, with canted lid revolving on horizontal pivot, the flange of the lid working in a slot in the back stiles, a type of 13th–16th centuries; detail of pegging; 13th-century onwards, the heavy frame reinforced at end with cross-bars and with wide uprights (standards) originally brightened with paint and with roundel of chip carving (detail below). SECOND ROW plank chest nailed and iron-banded with strap hinges, frequent from 14th-century (often originally decorated with tempera and sometimes with the banding in scrolling patterns although this often is Victorian); detail of linenfold panel carving; linenfold chest. BOTTOM: plate chest, 4′ 5″ long of wrought iron with painted ornament and dated 1557 (V. and A. Museum); detail of lock plate; early 17th-century chest with low relief carving (detail above), painted ornament in arched panels and glued-on base mouldings.

veneered and ornamented with marquetry. Others from this period were of imported Oriental lacquer with characteristic corner strappings, or were japanned in imitation, being popular dressing room furniture. All these conform to the general style of their day, entirely smooth-surfaced with projecting lid and base rim, and raised on bun feet or a low stand.

Cedar chests for blankets were popular at this time, many imported from Holland. Blanket chests continued to be made through the rest of the 18th century in mahogany, often in mule chest style in attractively simple, rectangular outlines, entirely lacking ornament apart from the rich pattern of the veneer, the cock beading of the drawers, the moulded lid rim and the metal mounts of handles and key escutcheons. Some of the finest are lined with dry, sweetly scented cedar wood.

Chests may be noted occasionally, too, in the bombé outlines of the fashionable commode, with gadrooned lid rim and carved corner ornament. Ince and Mayhew illustrated two clothes chests in 1760.

Boarded chest (Fig. 58): The front and back were composed of heavy planks pegged to the ends so as to present a flush surface that could be bound with iron straps. The ends might be prolonged slightly to serve as feet. This style continued through the 17th century but has lasted badly, as the boards tended to shrink and split. Design was somewhat modified in what may be regarded as the earliest type of framed chest, with a front composed of two side vertical planks that also serve as feet, with an even wider horizontal plank between them. In such a chest the lid may revolve on a horizontal pivot. Strap hinges became more usual from the end of the 13th century.

Casket (Fig. 9): By definition a box or small chest for valuables that is itself of value. In the 16th and early 17th centuries the finest were often of oak elaborately carved and sometimes inlaid, box-shaped or given a canted lid. But from the later

59. Seventeenth-century chests. TOP: Nonsuch chest, around 1600, with (below) two details of the inlay, different from Tunbridge ware (see Fig. 129); mid-century chest on bun feet with glued-on ornament (details below). BOTTOM: typical chest with moulding on stiles (detail in silhouette below) and low-relief lunettes below lid (detail); mule chest, mid-century, with drawers below.

17th century onwards a ascinating range of materials might be applied, reflecting passing fashions among the rich for surface ornament of incised leather or floral marquetry, tortoiseshell or lacquer. Much of this elaborate ornament persisted through the 18th century—paper filigree, shells and straw

173

work. But the collector finds also a range of more sophisticated treatments, including japanning, carved mahogany, marquetry in the handsome manner of the 1770s and 80s, painted satinwood and, by Regency days, exotic woods contrasted with bandings of brass. So many of these pieces were treated as multi-purpose compendiums, fitted with great elaboration and charm through the 19th century, that they are considered more fully among desk furniture.

Coffer (Fig. 60): Chest with handles but without feet, made for travelling. Also known as trussing coffer and sumpter chest. Randle Holme, in the 17th century, stated that they differed from chests merely in being round topped. This was in order to throw off the rain, and for the same reason it was customary to cover them with oxhide leather—sometimes cloth—and the term cofferer was applied to the specialist leather worker. The leather—*cuir bouilli*—might be patterned with incisions and painted or gilded, many coffers being imported from Holland and Spain. The close-studding of brass-headed nails securing the leather was usually ornament enough, however, sometimes including initials in the pattern: a royal monogram indicates no more than association with some government ministry. Round-topped coffers might be used for storing valuables, the outer covering being of velvet studded with silver gilt, or of Russia leather scented with oil of birch bark. Around the beginning of the 18th century the domed lid was introduced on many a coffer of lacquer or the japanned imitation, but here the obvious intention was to ensure that the delicate lid ornament was not damaged by use as a table.

Coffer bach or little chest: The Welsh variety of Bible box, sometimes with a couple of small drawers below the box section. Those found today date mainly from the second half of the 18th century, and include 20th-century copies. Oak and elm are most usual, and there may be holly inlay.

Counter: Chest of table size, its flat top marked or scored for reckoning.

Dansk, also Spruce, Overseas: Term for imported chests from the 15th century, commonly found in Elizabethan and early Stuart inventories for chests of coniferous wood imported from the Baltic regions, many probably made in Danzig. An Act of Tonnage and Poundage, 1689, indicates that they were imported in threes, fitting inside each other; iron chests were taxed singly and small leather-covered coffers by the dozen. Cypress chests were heavily taxed.

Derbyshire desk: Simple writing box of the so-called Bible box type, the most attractive being of oak with carving on the sides, but the occasional initials and dates must be regarded with caution. There may be a drawer below the lidded well. Many were made in walnut around 1700 when drawers were coming into general use.

Dowry chest: A comparatively recent name for the chest of linen expected of a woman when she married. This may be initialled and dated in the style especially favoured in the early 17th century.

Flanders: Name often found in inventories and now associated specially with chests of the framed flat-faced type which are richly decorated with low relief carving in church-window arcadings and tracery, although some of this may be English 15th- or early 16th-century work. Some of the ornament may be applied instead of carved in the solid wood, and the association of the term with glued-on ornament continued. Some collectors use it to indicate 17th-century chests ornamented with applied mitred mouldings, split turnings and bosses.

Forser, fosser (and in smaller versions the forset or fosset): Bailey in 1730 defined it as a small chest or cabinet, but the word had long implied an early form of strong box such as the Pewterers' Company's 'great joined forser painted with the

60. Early 18th-century chests. TOP: fine specimen covered with leather close-nailed and with pierced mounts in style associated with lacquer, etc., the top bearing the crowned monogram of William and Mary, c. 1690 (V. and A. Museum); detail of metal strap and handle escutcheon; trunk or coffer on stand with paw feet, c. 1720s. BOTTOM: japanned, early 18th-century chest; early mahogany chest and drawers in one piece in mule-chest tradition instead of chest on stand.

arms of the Company and locked with two keys' noted in 1488–9.

Jewel chest: Often a small trunk of coffer shape with a massive lock plate and metal corners. Those dating to the late 17th century and later may be mounted with silver or brass instead of iron. *See* CASKETS.

Lace box: Name now applied to the type of decorative, flat-tish box conspicuous in the late 17th and early 18th centuries.

Lace was then immensely important and the typical marquetry ornament harmonises with that on many an early chest of drawers, but at a period when the bed chamber served for guests, business callers and staff instruction, it would be foolish to attempt to limit the box's possible uses. There is reason to think that many were comparable with the ornate purses of the period, made to grace the presentation of gifts to those in high places.

Linenfold chest (Fig. 58): Probably originally Flemish—a carved pattern on the chest panels suggesting the folds of vertically pleated linen. The parchemin or parchment panel has similar association with rolls of parchment. There is little reason to adduce that the carving indicated the purpose of the chest, but the slight corrugations might check any tendency to warp.

Military chest: Regulation furniture for army officers until the 1870s. A compact chest of drawers in two sections, usually of cheap mahogany with sunk brass handles at the sides and on the drawers, brass to protect all corners and no protrusions of any kind. These are found in a range of sizes. Sometimes a sham drawer front between two drawers at the top reveals a small central fall-fronted bureau. This may be fitted for writing and/or toilet needs. The lower section is usually composed of three plain drawers.

Mule chest (Figs 59, 60): Associated especially with the middle years of the 17th century but continuing through the 18th. The name suggests a link between box chest and chest of drawers. The early chest frequently contains a small till or framed-off corner for coins and the like, but in the mule chest the usual undifferentiated storage space is supplemented by one or two full-size drawers below. Many are in oak in the cumbersome style of the 17th century with glued-on mouldings, including a sub-cornice between the chest and the lower section of one or two drawers.

Nonsuch chest (Fig. 59): Late 16th-century name of famous palace built by Henry VIII at Cheam, engraved prints of which were published in 1582 and 1598, showing buildings somewhat like the inlaid ornament on some chests now known by this name. Alternatively a resemblance has been noted to the Nonsuch House on London Bridge, a timber building brought from Holland in sections early in Elizabeth I's reign. The style of these chests suggests that they were the work of German or Flemish craftsmen.

Pegged chest (Fig. 58): Made to take apart for storage by removing wooden pegs like an early trestle table. These were popular among romantic early Victorians.

Plate chest (Fig. 58): For keeping table silver etc. Extremely strong, often of wrought iron.

Sumpter chest: Another name for trussing coffer: a pair would be slung across the back of a pack or sumpter horse.

Standard (Fig. 58): A great chest bound with iron (as defined in 1549). Its use was for moving valuables from place to place and typically it was fastened by two or three locks. To counteract the jolts of travel by wagon, the chest usually had heavy iron bands bolted to the thick wood, corner plates and massive lock plates, the early metal being shaped cold by sawing like wood. Modern replacement locks are often poor and the hinge pins too vulnerable for any measure of security. For weather protection the standard might be covered with leather or stout cloth, and as further protection from dust the interior was lined with closely woven linen or soft, quickly worn but decoratively printed paper—yet another minor specialist job. Valuables might be safeguarded by linings of quilting, widely sold by the yard in the early 18th century.

Trunk (Fig. 60): Common name for a travelling box suggesting man's earlier attempts to make something stronger than baskets of skin-covered osier. Like portmanteau, a word introduced in the mid-16th century, this became an accepted term for the larger version of the round-topped, leather-covered coffer. It is mentioned in references to the cofferer's trunk nails, trunk and portmanteau saddles, etc. Moxon, in 1677, differentiated between trunk locks, chest locks and padlocks. Nineteenth-century coach travellers were served by innumerable trunks studded with brass rosettes over their coverings of tough hair-cloth.

Workbox, compendium (Fig. 9): From the 17th century onwards women were supplied with wooden boxes to ensure privacy at home and convenience when travelling, while meeting their needs throughout the day. These are sometimes so elaborately compartmented that they may be considered as cabinets or desk furniture, but it is easiest to survey all kinds together.

In a typical 17th-century box, for example, covered with velvet and edged with silver galon, the opening lid might release a falling front or cupboard doors and show silver toilet bottles, a tray of sewing needs and corner vessels at the front for ink and pounce. From this developed the familiar 'miniature cabinet' design of drawers and pigeon holes around a central recess where there might be some attempt to include a really secret hiding place.

Among the most familiar of 17th-century specimens are the cabinet style of compendium with a square or domed lid over a fitted tray and a cupboard front enclosing small drawers. Such a piece made in whitewood depends for its great value today upon ornament contributed by well-to-do children, scarcely into their teens, who provided panels of exquisitely stitched pictorial embroidery. This raised embroidery, mounted on white satin, was known to Victorians as stump work. It is worth detailed mention because in some examples an outer case of wood has preserved the embroidery in remarkably fine condition. Similar ornament, such as figure

179

groups from Old Testament stories, is found in contemporary bead work, similarly mounted.

Such a box was intended not only for a few pieces of jewellery but to house writing materials, cosmetics and combs. Often there is a precious looking glass in the lid—a detail expected of the 19th-century compendium where it is angled to reflect the owner's bejewelled hands. Sometimes a central well in the 17th-century box is lined with small pieces of mirror glass reflecting a hand-coloured print pasted upon the bottom.

Many of these early workboxes and their 18th- and 19th-century successors were wholly professional, however, covered with leather or shagreen or veneers of parquetry with corners of gilded brass. Some of the most attractive are covered in semi-translucent tortoiseshell over a red or yellow ground and edged or inlaid with ivory. A padded lining of silk taffeta confirms that even the most personal belongings of those who ever travelled were subject to rough handling, a consideration that ensured a sturdy wooden basis for the workbox throughout the period under review.

Those intended for travel may show holes that allowed for screwing to the coach floor where they would, of course, be supplemented by other well-padded boxes for the traveller's drinking vessels and silver-mounted bottles. The 18th century saw the development of the traveller's tea equipage; the 19th century was particularly rich in travellers' games compendiums, the most elaborate catering for as many as thirty games.

Sheraton in his *Drawing Book* describes a travelling box to meet the woman's needs for writing, dressing and working. This includes a dressing glass, a desk and writing drawer and a roller for her lace—the shuttle netting or tatting of the day—together with boxes and compartments for scissors, cosmetics, jewellery. Such a box, mounted on a stand, served as an alternative to the increasingly popular work table.

In the 18th century, case making was a specialist trade. John Folgham, for example, supplied such compendiums in shagreen and green- or blue-stained dogfish skin and issued trade cards showing them compartmented for bottles and fitted with recessed trays for scissors etc. Marquetry in neo-classical style vied with etched ivory and ivory-mounted ebony. Light-toned satinwood might bear a coloured stipple engraving and there was a revival of paper filigree. In 1791 Princess Elizabeth received a 'box made for filigree work with ebony moulding, lock and key, lined inside and outside'. An alternative associated especially with the 1800s was a parquetry covering in glistening split straws, but the most enduring of these surface elaborations was the wooden marquetry known as Tunbridge ware.

Lock and handle fitments are important. Early keyplates and escutcheons are hand sawn from the brass plate; later in the 18th century they were cast, and from the 1770s might be stamped. Japanned specimens received especially elaborate metalwork in Oriental style. Many Regency boxes are brass enriched in name plate, key escutcheon, lion-and-ring handles and claw feet. Heavier mounts, too massively florid for 18th-century rococo, must be dated to about the 1830s.

Collectors have to be on their guard not to pre-date specimens associated with the 19th-century revivals. Often the workbox's shape is revealing, however, with the top and base shaping elaborated out of all proportion to the useful body of the piece. Many Victorian mounts are easily recognised, of course—even the popular pseudo-Gothic frets in antique bronze. Later came some beautifully veneered boxes with an absolute minimum of visible metal work. Victorian surface treatment includes oil painting under clear varnish, shell-glinting papier mâché, rosewood inlaid with brass or pearl shell and the ultra feminine effects of mother of pearl set into tortoiseshell. Inside, the lid may be perfectly lined with silk or gold-stamped leather or perhaps satin printed with an engraving.

Equipment may include silver-mounted ink bottles, pen holders of amber, perhaps, needle and silk holders of finely carved ivory. An early treasure may include blades and points of hand-wrought steel set in handles of silver; green-stained ivory handles are associated with the mid-18th century, rivalled later by mother of pearl, tortoiseshell, ebony, bronze, the Victorian's adored cornelian and even Derbyshire marbles.

Chest Stands (Fig. 60): In use from the late 17th century. The stand has a rebated frame to receive the chest and its apron and legs are in the style of the side tables of the period. Those of the early 18th century may have stumpy cabriole legs and drawers in the deeply curving apron. Chests and coffers in rich Oriental lacquer or imitation japanning are found occasionally on stands enriched with highly decorative gilded carving such as that used to support Oriental cabinets.

PART VI

Chests of Drawers

Chests with drawing boxes gradually evolved into the chest of drawers during the 17th century. Around the mid-century a liking for privacy or security required doors over the main drawer section, however, and a tall chest-like structure might have a full-width drawer above a pair of cupboard doors enclosing smaller drawers. Sometimes the hinged, lifting top was retained over a well above the drawers. The drawers themselves continued the early arrangement with grooves in their sides to fit bearers attached inside the carcase. Such pieces continued the weighty Stuart ornament with corbelled frieze, bevelled mouldings and occasional inlay of bone or mother of pearl (Fig. 61).

By the 1680s, however, the chest of drawers was acquiring its common form. Some, like chests, were mounted on stands, followed in Queen Anne's reign by double chests of drawers or tallboys. By this time it was fully established as a simple, straight-fronted chest some forty inches tall with five drawers and often a flat slide above—for additional table space since it lacked a kneehole—pulled out by two tiny handles. Only the back showed the panel construction, while front and sides presented a plainly outlined, smooth-surfaced field for balanced veneers in walnut, burr elm and so on, or patterns in marquetry or japanning.

Additional details are ovolo moulding to the top edge, matched by inverted moulding on the plinth above bracket feet, which often enclose square blocks to carry the weight in place of the earlier bun or ball outlines. Some, like chests, were raised on stands. The oak drawers were now running on

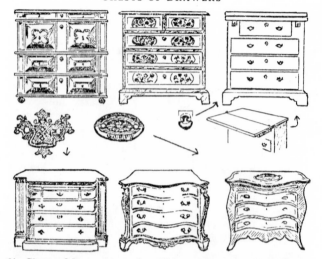

61. Chests of drawers. TOP: late 17th-century chest with projecting panels and applied mouldings; design c. 1700 with 'Dutch' flower marquetry; variant with folding top opening on rule hinges to rest on runners (detail below). BOTTOM: early Georgian with slide above drawers (pierced handle shown above); serpentine design, 1760s, with corner pilasters and ornate handles with inconspicuous key plates; late 18th-century chest with veneers of satinwood, kingwood and mahogany (stamped elliptical handle shown above centre).

bearers and fitted with brass pulls and escutcheons in place of earlier turned wood knobs. This brass work itself changed entirely between the 1670s and the 1700s, from pendant knobs to loops and thereafter loops and backplates reflected successive differences of mood and advances in techniques. (Figs 61, 64, 65 and *see* Figs 2 and 3).

Other drawer detail to note includes the lap dovetailing (Fig. 62) required for veneered work on the drawer fronts and the treatment of drawer surrounds, where exposed veneer edges were subject to wear. Until about 1705 or 1710 half-round mouldings might edge the drawer openings, but by as early as the last years of the 17th century an alternative was the double or reeded moulding. Most interesting, perhaps, was the development from about 1710 of a small lip moulding on the drawer itself, projecting around the drawer edge to hide signs of wear when the drawer was closed. This was a fore-runner of the cockbead introduced about 1730 and universal on mahogany drawers from about 1745. Changes in the veneer bandings on the drawers are discussed in Part II (Banding) and Part XVII (Veneer).

Chests of drawers of the early Georgian period (Fig. 61) continued to be mainly of walnut, but in early mahogany the cornice mouldings may show dentil or key ornament, and by the 1750s–60s canted corners might carry Chinese frets instead of fluting, harmonising with carving on top and plinth mould-ings. At this time the chest of drawers might be taller, with five or six long drawers below the top half drawers, for it was essentially a useful piece: for ornamental display the rich householder chose the lower, curving version now described as a drawing room commode, although the word was used somewhat indiscriminately around 1760. The chiffonier was the 19th-century successor to the commode.

By the 1760s the straight lines of the chest of drawers might be modified somewhat too, however, with serpentine front shaping, ogee bracket feet and occasionally a plinth base. The serpentine line brought the canted corners into greater prominence as pilasters—with architectural capitals, perhaps, or Gothic cluster-column forms. The drawers themselves, still of oak or oak lined, from perhaps 1770 show a con-struction change, the wood bottom no longer running from front to back but across in two half-width panels with a central bearer to prevent sagging. The fitted top drawer with a drop front dates from about 1765 onwards, making the chest a form of bureau (*see* Part X). One may find, too, a handsome mahogany chest of drawers with a top drawer compartmented for the toilet as a capacious dressing table for a multi-purpose room (*see* Part XV).

Changes in the later 18th century include greater use of lighter woods and many cheap, painted chests of drawers. One also finds cheap-quality mahogany veneered on pine and chests of plain oak that may be pre-dated. A frequent detail in keeping with the light tone and often effeminate ornament is the omission of a plinth so that the vertical corner pieces can be carried uninterruptedly to the floor in the outward curve of the French foot. To harmonise, the bottom framing has a

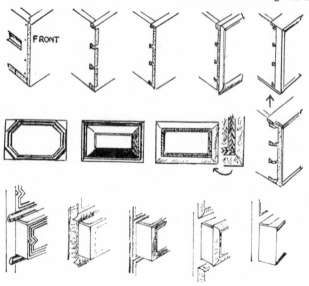

shaped apron or the bottom drawer is extended in shaped carving. Late 18th-century design returned to the straight front flanked by reeded quarter-column pilasters ending in tapering, turned feet, but included also the more formal bow front that ousted the flowing serpentine outline and has been admired and copied ever since.

Ornament around the turn of the century included the interplay of boldly figured exotic woods in cross bandings and diagonal parquetry and the provincial cabinet maker's favourite lines of stringing and conch shell marquetry motifs. Some chests of drawers of this period are exceptionally tall and the sense of height is emphasised by a deep cornice projecting only slightly—if at all—beyond the vertical line of the sides. Such a piece, slightly bowed, with bracket feet in the out-thrust French form, is an attractive bedroom piece.

Chests of drawers suited the simple weighty outlines of the Regency, with heavy corner pilasters reeded or rope-twisted, and often with deep base moulding above attractive, elaborately turned feet. Victorians continued the piece, but

62. Important drawer details. TOP, junction of front and side: Elizabethan, nailed, showing groove for side runner; 17th-century through dovetail; from c. 1700, lapped dovetail to avoid end-grain under veneer; frequent variant from c. 1710 with strip of walnut projecting round front edge of drawer with veneer over it; the cockbead, used in walnut from c. 1730 and in mahogany (the outline immediately below showing the same drawer detail with the side bead removed, disclosing the rebating required to give a flush finish). SECOND ROW, three drawer treatments: 17th-century applied mitred mouldings; 17th-century coffered panel; early 18th-century panel effect in veneers, including a band of herringbone (shown in detail, with the mitred corner expected in good work). BOTTOM, surrounds to drawers; applied moulding to mask join of stile and muntin; half-round moulding veneered with cross-banded walnut, typically around marquetry: two or more reedings, typically around drawer with herringbone banding; plain surround because drawer has outward-projecting lip; plain surround because drawer has forward-projecting cockbead—typical on drawers since 1750.

design no longer stemmed from purpose. An impressive-looking front with boldly projecting panels flanking the drawers, a deep frieze below a top square-cut to impress with its substantial weight of wood and a heavy plinth base all constitute wasted space so far as drawer capacity is concerned.

Collectors must be on their guard against judging a chest of drawers by its handles. Even among turned wood handles there is a world of difference between the patera-turned, flat-fronted knob and the rounded shape that fits the palm, but often knobs have been replaced by 'antique' brass bail handles.

Chiffonier (Fig. 63): Like the commode, a French word which acquired its own English meaning. In France it was a chest of drawers popular in the second half of the 18th century. In England it took the place of the 18th-century commode, a decorative piece with cupboarded front, low enough at first for pictures or mirror to hang above its flat top, which might be in serpentine outline. The O.E.D. defines it as a movable low cupboard with a sideboard top. George Smith in 1810 suggested its use for books in frequent demand but, like Nicholson in 1826, made no distinction between commode and chiffonier.

In a small home the chiffonier could serve in the dining room, its solid front better suited to small dimensions than the double pedestal of the early Victorian sideboard. The characteristic rounded, 'comfortable' outlines of the period are typified in the frequent addition of open, curved shelving flanking the central cupboard doors: sometimes the whole front is bowed. Regency doors might be of brass lattice backed with pleated silk, and this feature is sometimes noted as a modern replacement on a Victorian chiffonier which originally had cupboard doors of wood or glass. The design was variously elaborated, with drawers in the top, for example, and bookshelves in the centre above with supports of brass or the 19th century's characteristic shallow-turned spindles. As

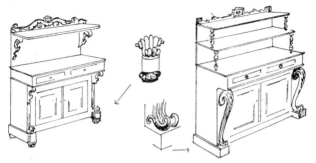

63. Chiffoniers, sometimes called cabinets for the morning room. LEFT: design showing Regency influence. RIGHT: proportions associated with mid-Victorian furniture.

with the sideboard the mid-Victorian chiffonier is often backed by a tall, arching mirror.

Commode (Fig. 64): The word was defined as early as 1718 in Sowbry's *Architecture*, but became important in England towards the mid-18th century when cabinet makers produced 'French commodes' in mahogany with gilded brass mounts, attempting to copy the most sophisticated drawing room creations of the French cabinet makers and metalwork artists. The piece was still basically a chest of drawers, but throughout the second half of the century those in the French taste most frequently show drawers covered with a pair of cupboard doors as a suitable basis for superb surface ornament. This is the sense of the word commode usually accepted by collectors today, although Chippendale and others at the time applied it more widely—for instance to the dressing commode that served as a drawer-fronted dressing table. Certainly many japanned specimens were intended for the dressing room to meet the rich vogue of around 1760–70 for minor rooms in Chinese taste.

Some splendid mahogany specimens date from the 1740s and 50s. These were in the massive architectural style with deep frieze and console-shaped pilasters at all corners on heavy feet. The top, shaped to project over the pilasters, may have a gadrooned edge and much carved detail picked out in gilding. Some delightful specimens of the 1760s show a fascinating interplay of planes with scrolling front combined with a serpentine plan. The front corners project sharply as ormolu-mounted ridges curving down to outsweeping French feet balanced by a shaped dipping apron below the doors.

Neo-classical influence in the 1770s prompted the creation of the commode with a straight front and six short tapering legs on spade or guttae feet. Sometimes the front is semi-

64. Post-1760 commodes. TOP: commode with bold carving of 1760s and rococo handles as in detail below; bombé shape with marquetry on top and doors and ormolu mounts, 1770s–80s; bow front, late 18th-century, with simpler marquetry on single door. BOTTOM: asymmetrical handle; more elaborate shape of 1790s (V. and A. Museum); details of flower ornament and oval stamped handle.

circular, divided by the front legs into three areas of equally important ornament. Hepplewhite noted that the commode might have one principal door or one at each end, enclosing shelves but declared that they were 'never intended for use but for ornament'.

Always on these superb pieces the surface ornament is the main feature. Being low, they could display the work on top as well as front, whether in the superb marquetry of the 1770s and 80s in neo-classical motifs around panels of classical figures, or partly or wholly painted. Painted commodes of the 1780s owed much to the style of such decorators as Kauffmann, Cipriani and Pergolesi, but the work tended to deteriorate towards the end of the century. Regency commodes returned to severe rectangular lines and Sheraton suggested brass inlay in the frieze and brass trellis to the doors (Fig. 13). George Smith, 1808, suggested satinwood, rosewood or gold on a white ground, or a japanned surface to resemble a finer wood, and with a top, too, that might be japanned, resembling marble, but already the piece had lost its significance.

Tallboy (Fig. 65): The double chest of drawers now so named tended to oust the chest mounted on a stand from about 1710. This reflected current interest in architectural furniture with a cornice strongly emphasised in cross-grain veneer, sometimes with a secret drawer in a swelling frieze which was then an alternative to the concave outline. The upper chest of drawers is slightly narrower than the lower, often made more graceful with canted, fluted corners. Frequently the upper chest has three long drawers topped by a row of two or three short ones; the lower chest may have three or more, which are deep unless space is allowed for stumpy cabriole legs.

Some fine tallboys were made in the second half of the 18th century, occasionally with swan neck pediment and fluted pillars flanking the upper drawers in the style of some long

65. Double chests of drawers. TOP: late 17th-century chest with drawer in stand (showing handle detail); chest, c. 1700, with doors over upper shelves (detail of key escutcheon); early 18th-century chest (detail of early, weak loop handle). BOTTOM: Queen Anne to early Georgian design with reeded splay corners (detail of marquetry sunburst and stronger loop handle); chest, c. 1750, with typical desk drawer (detail of handle); late 18th-century chest with urn ornament and corner pilasters (detail of handle and cabriole bracket foot).

case clocks. Others show low relief carving on frieze and canted corners. Feet are usually in the ogee bracket form and may be handsome details.

Late 18th-century design is associated with Hepplewhite's graceful lines. One notes moulded cornice and fluted frieze with paterae spaced between the flutings, harmonising with embossed circular or elliptical handle plates. By the Regency a range of wardrobe furniture supplied the bedroom.

PART VII

Stools

Chairs long retained something of their early value as status symbols, but 16th-century inventories show clearly that by then even the middling home of merchant or shopkeeper would probably contain a chair or two in each major room, while, for dining, built-in wall benches were made comfortable with an abundance of cushions. Nevertheless stools long remained the most readily available seating—in the kitchen regions the simple three-legged stick stool, and for diners the joint stool. Both have been in production ever since. The back stool, too, received occasional Elizabethan mention and the term continued in reference to a specific piece of furniture through much of the 18th century, although now widely misunderstood.

Inventories distinguished between the high stools suitable for men and the low stools, with only slightly shorter legs, for women. Thus a well-found Stuart room might contain chairs, back stools, high stools, low stools and foot stools. Upholstered buffet stools are recorded as early as about 1600, and from the early years of the 17th century the tabouret or drum-shaped version of this padded seat was acceptable as a fashion from the Continent.

The 18th century produced immensely decorative upholstered stools, including double stools, and a new outline in the window seat. But the stool's heyday was the Regency, when designers found abundant Graeco-Roman example which they could copy to supply attractive furnishings. Footstools, too, came into widespread use and continued through Victorian days when every drawing room and parlour had its music stools and fender stools, its beadwork footstools and Berlin work mounted on reproduction-Louis Quinze and its ottomans inarticulate with drapery and fringe.

Back stool (Fig. 66): Also known as a back chair and as a chair stool. Few collectors appear to have recognised that the term designated precisely the construction of a stool with a back, and not merely a single chair. Chairs and back stools were listed separately in many early inventories. In Medieval England, when the chair was a seat of authority and the women of the household were accommodated on low stools, their comfort might be given consideration by 'a low stool with a back thereto', as inventoried in the Howard House accounts in 1588. Such a back stool was often upholstered and the wood too might be covered with rich fabric. In 1614 the Earl of Northampton's dining room contained two chairs, (one high, one low), two high stools, one low stool and 'one little back chair of cloth of gold embroidered in gold twist'.

The piece may be regarded as a chair without arms, suited to the vast skirts of ladies' fashions, but it was distinguished also by the fact that it was basically a stool and went through the phases of other 17th- and 18th-century stool construction. Unlike a chair it was made with four identical legs, and for this reason was particularly suitable for use in a bedroom, as often noted in inventories, where it might be viewed from the rear. Randle Holme in his *Academie of Armory* (heraldry), 1649, shows a back stool with four identical legs and a short padded back between uprights springing directly from the back legs. Charles I's furniture sold that year included twenty-four wooden stools with backs painted and gilt.

Through the rest of the century references to back stools continue, carved and gilded, with brocade covers, or japanned with cane bottoms (seats), meeting the needs of fashionably dressed ladies. Georgian trade cards showed back stools and chairs side by side, the former more costly. Their low seats,

66. Back stools. TOP: late 17th-century example, with comparable stool; early 18th-century back-stool with four cabriole legs. BOTTOM mid-18th century back stool and similar stool with 'Chinese' legs and guttae feet; 'back stool chair' by Ince & Mayhew.

fourteen inches from the floor, indicated clearly their purpose· Ince and Mayhew suggested burnished gold and a blue damask cover for one of their back stools. Measurements showed that theirs were still low-seated with all four legs identical, but differed from other stools in having the front seat rail wider than that of the back.

195

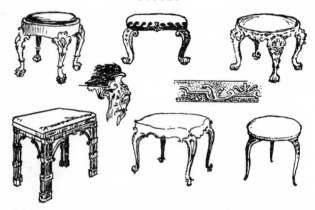

67. Stools. TOP, early Georgian: c. 1720 with drop-in seat, ball-and-claw foot; William Kent style with C-scroll ornament and heavy scroll legs; lion mask and paw, often in gilded gesso, a style popular in many media, such as silver salts. SECOND ROW: detail of hipped cabriole leg with typical carving; detail of gilded gesso, the ground matted. BOTTOM: stool with cluster-column legs of c. 1760; serpentine frame, hipped scrolling legs; slender Hepplewhite design.

Banquette: *see* DOUBLE STOOL.

Buffet stool: often, but not always, an upholstered stool (q.v.). In 1706 Lady Grisell Baillie commented on the cost of buffing or stuffing the stools she had bought, but by then the stool as a fashionable furnishing was almost invariably upholstered, so that the distinguishing adjective was no longer required.

Coffin stool: Not a specific type, but a name associated with joint stools used for supporting a coffin awaiting burial. Pepys in 1661 referred in his diary to his uncle's coffin 'standing upon joint-stools in the chimney in the hall'.

Double stool: Joint stools from Elizabethan days might be wide enough for two and the style persisted—for instance to stand at the end of a bed, upholstered to match chairs and footstools. Early inventory references to 'banketts' might mean such long stools rather than the simple benches provided for household servants. Their name may be associated with the banquet, a social gathering, informal and often crowded, when sweetmeats and fruits were served—a casual style of party continued through the 18th century as a dessert. As late as the Regency years the name banquette may be noted in Ackermann's *Repository*, referring to a long seat with high scrolling ends linked by low bands of caning—a compromise between long stool and settee.

Double stools are noted among caned stools of Charles II's day when, like day beds, they would be given squab cushions. An upholstered stool in walnut of the 1690s at Hampton Court is over seven feet long. This has eight legs, the waved stretchers suggesting three conjoined stools.

'Long stools' to stand between the windows and in window recesses were in some demand through the 18th century, some that remain being leather covered, with close nailing. These usually have six legs and the frieze and stretchers in duplicate. They are noted in the styles of their day with stuffed-over upholstery or drop-in seats of early Georgian mahogany and more especially in the neo-classical style of the 1770s onwards when they retained their place against the walls in formal reception rooms, while French stools were placed in the window recesses and became known as window stools (q.v.) Horace Walpole, describing Strawberry Hill in 1782, mentioned 'high stools of common Norwich damask mounted on black and gold frames', which were ranged 'all along the wall'. Smith, in 1808, called them tête à tête seats, suggesting heavy plain designs with neo-classical ornament.

Folding stool (Fig. 70): Noted in early references as a faldstool.

68. Stools and footstools. TOP: now termed a window seat; formal Hope design, 1807; 'Greek' version. SECOND ROW: two 'classic' specimens inspired by Hope designs; music stool simulating bamboo; adjustable music stool recorded by Henry Moses, 1823. THIRD ROW, footstools in the same mood: a Hope design; two Smith designs; a bolder specimen of the same period. BOTTOM: three designs from Ackermann's *Repository*; design recorded by Moses.

In the most usual design the legs were crossed, front and back, each pair being joined near floor level by a stretcher. These have a long history: an early 17th-century specimen at Knole, Kent, has beechwood legs and stretchers covered in velvet and an upholstered seat. This outline became widely popular again in the Regency. Royal furnishings at Whitehall in 1886 included 'three dozen of leather folding stools'.

Footstool (Figs 68, 69, 131): Common in Tudor days as luxury furnishings and often noted in pairs. Some listed at Nonsuch were 'covered with needlework green, red and white, in knotted wise [that is, in turkey work] fringed in red silk and gold', the feet painted and gilded. References to footstools are noted through the 17th century: for example, suites of furniture for each of three bedrooms at the House of Binns, Scotland, in 1685, included two arm chairs, two back chairs (back stools), four stools and a footstool, all upholstered with 'cloth of the curtain and fringe of the colour of the bed and lining'.

As chairs lost their symbolic importance they lost their accompanying footstools. These were of little significance through the 18th century but became important little details, if somewhat self-conscious, in the Regency's heavy-handed attempts to reconstruct the classical home. Hope might place a footstool under each handsome curule chair, but their more usual function then was to go with couch or settee, while every Grecian bed had its suitably ornate little bed-steps. Sheraton mentioned them in his *Dictionary* 'generally stuffed with hair and covered with some sort of needlework'.

A number remain in the neo-classical outline, with scrolled-over ends emphasised in scrolling shoulders to briefly tapering outcurving feet, somewhat comma-shaped. The front and back of the frame, like the feet, might be brass-inlaid with classical honeysuckle, for example. The most obvious alternative was the stool with ends scrolling inward over the flat cushion. This might have straight, tapering feet, the side silhouette suggesting a diminutive version of the settee. Smith in 1808 and Henry Moses as late as 1823, among others, illustrated both these dominant forms, although Smith suggested variants with Egyptian motifs.

It may be noted, too, that many a table in the current trestle style, with a low stretcher between the end standards, might have a footrest built on to the stretcher, a detail that was continued in Victorian days. Another detail introduced at this time was the pair of ears for lifting—in Hope's design composed of corded tassels.

By the 1820s and 30s footstools were tending to become larger, ungainly and shapeless, like the sofas they served. The most attractive design, perhaps, was the neat little sloping stool, the support a slanting S-scroll. Some were made in papier mâché, others heavily carved. Footstools especially were loaded with pictorial Berlin embroidery, but even at the time critics realised the unsuitability of mounting royalty groups and reproductions of famous paintings to be trodden underfoot.

Joint stool (Fig. 70): This was the joiner's version, constructed on the framed-up principle with mortise-and-tenon joints securing the rectangular seat frame to the block tops of the legs and linking the legs with stretchers. The seat might tilt slightly forward and the legs were somewhat splayed to ensure rigidity, but only forwards and backwards, since a sideways projection might cause trouble when the stools were ranged along the dining table.

Those that remain from the first period are in enduring oak, usually with edge-moulded top, often with an arcaded or shaped underframing and sometimes carved ornamentally. Occasionally the top hinged forward and the frieze was formed into storage space. Legs followed the changes noted on minor tables of their day, being left square for the mortise-and-tenon joints that secured the seat framing and low stretchers between them. Thus the 16th-century slender, fluted swellings gave way during the 17th century to heavier turnings often more ornately shaped, including balusters, spools and the like. Some stools, by the second half of the century, were rimmed for loose squab cushions filled with horsehair or tow. The seat might be as much as twenty-seven inches wide and perforated for easy lifting.

Post-1660 design included, too, the change of stretcher arrangement noted also on chairs, with an H formation augmented by a higher, ornate front stretcher matched, on the stool, by a similar one on the opposite side of a piece that could never have a back and front like a chair.

Through the 18th century various forms of upholstered stool were in demand and the plain wooden seat became largely a hard-working country piece. But its qualities of strength and cleanliness recommended it as a hall seat and specimens may be noted following the fashion of the 18th century, occasionally painted with a coat of arms or crest. As in hall chairs, the later 18th century eased the hard seat by giving it a slightly dipping outline and scrolled-over sides: this was counterbalanced by incurving supports resting upon arching, outward-jutting legs.

Sheraton called them corridor stools 'for persons waiting'—sedan chair men or servants with messages. His design had scrolled wooden ends like a window stool. The hall stool was simplified into the Regency's favourite curved-X outline with gilded paterae, perhaps, fronting the scrolled sides of the seat. Smith, however, suggested uncompromising rectangular bench seats of marble on scroll supports flanking massive honeysuckle ornament, all mounted upon marble plinth bases.

Tabouret (Fig. 69): The tabouret etiquette of the Continent was introduced to England in the reign of James I. This meant that certain ladies, whose husbands were of appropriately high rank, were allowed to be seated in the presence of the monarch. Charles II extended the practice to the homes of nobles and merchant princes, but after the end of the century it was continued only at court, where it was strictly observed until 1760. The word tabouret appears generally to have been applied to a woman's stool with a round top covered in fabric.

Such stools continued through the 18th century in the styles of the more usual rectangular specimens. For example,

Hepplewhite (1788) suggested an entirely simple design without even the elaboration of feet to its three slender tapering French legs. This, he suggested, 'is proper for a dressing stool', the framework of mahogany or japanned 'or to match the suit of chairs'.

Circular stools appear to have had no place in Regency classicism but were the delight of Victorians (Fig. 69). Most collectors will be familiar with the 'hour-glass' stool at the Victoria and Albert Museum, circular topped and based, the 'body' of pleated damask drawn into a tight waist by tasselled cords. But most familiar of all, perhaps, is the Victorian adjustable music stool with a screw pillar on heavy carved claw feet of rosewood, mahogany or walnut. The ugly screw was sometimes cased in by 1850. Many were covered with embroidery and beadwork and edged with fringe.

Three-legged stool: The turner's simple furnishing that would stand steadily on the most uneven floor. The top might be square or triangular but was more often circular, a substantial slab of elm or other available wood, drilled on the underside to receive the plainly turned legs, well splayed for steadiness. The legs might merely be dowelled into the seat or their ends might penetrate to the upper surface where they were secured with foxtail wedges.

The design is associated with plain stick legs, but these are mainly 19th-century workaday specimens. In their heyday many must have been more ornate, like turners' chairs, but of soft, easily turned wood that did not last. Randle Holme, 1649, described these turner stools as 'wrought with knops and rings'. Three-legged stools, including small versions for children, were in demand well into the present century.

Joint stools with three legs and triangular seats were made occasionally as late as the 17th century and again in the romantic mood of the 1840s. But a more interesting development was the stool comparable with early Windsor chairs.

In this design the three legs showed the characteristics of the cost-cutting countrified cabriole associated with 18th-century Windsor chairs and linked by swelling stretchers in T formation. The legs were dowelled into the solid block of the seat, which in such a piece could be fully saddle shaped.

Trestle stool: Occasional specimens remain of what must once have been common 15th- and 16th-century stools comparable with late Gothic benches and tables. The rectangular seat was supported on two wide end-boards or standards, splayed for greater steadiness. The ends of the seat underframing were slotted through these standards to make them rigid. Both standards and underframing were given decorative outlines and the underframing might be carved. Collectors must remember, however, that the trestle construction appealed especially to early Victorian romantics.

Upholstered stool (Figs 1, 66–69): Reference to 'quilted and lined' stools has been noted as early as 1596. While stools were more numerous than chairs they were often made in matching sets or upholstered to match and accompany chairs. Some were covered in the knotted pile known as turkey work, some in leather. Rich velvets and damasks soon became faded and worn, but gilded metal thread work proved bright and enduring. Some of the most hard wearing were in the fine home embroidery known as tent stitch.

Valuable upholstery was protected by linen cases, as noted, for instance, among the many owned by the Earl of Northampton in 1614. His upholstered stools are described in unusual detail. His dining room, for example, included two high stools and a low stool upholstered to match two chairs, all of cloth of gold, the ground maidenhair with fringe and tassels of gold, lined with damask watchet (pale blue) and maidenhair, and six high stools of russet velvet fringed. His winter dining chamber included high and low stools of tawny velvet and wrought (embroidered) purple velvet and a low

69. Stools. TOP, first half of 19th century: pleated fabric (V. and A. Museum); with modified Greek leg; modified 'Elizabethan'; 'Louis XV' with detail of foot. SECOND ROW: illustrated in *The Queen*, 1870s; mid-Victorian pouffe with typical fringe and tassels; heavy machine-carved walnut; bamboo. THIRD ROW: music stools, one (left) in papier mâché. BOTTOM, footstools: carved walnut; with lion paw feet; with plaited braids; painted black and gold.

stool of black velvet embroidered with a row of slips (flower sprigs) of silver.

Upholstery in the 16th and 17th century consisted of a deep cushion mounted on a plain framework masked by the period's deep straight fringe, above simple turned legs linked by plain stretchers. An occasional specimen remains from the 17th century showing the ornate Continental style with supports, front and back, composed of rounded X shapes in flat wood, entirely covered with fabric to mask construction difficulties and often fringed. Such a stool would be in harmony with the familiar X chair, the earliest form of comfortable upholstered seat. But as such fabric covering implied the use of soft wood, few have survived. Some were covered with leather.

Queen Mary II had eighteen stools in her withdrawing room at Windsor, covered with green damask. Apart from tabourets, upholstered stools were still mainly rectangular, their legs and stretchers delightfully ornate in the shouldered scrolls of the 1680s and the variously capped pillars, often square or octagonal, of the 1690s. These might have the intricately carved front and back stretchers associated with late 17th-century walnut chairs or the flat stretchers in waved-X outline typical of the small tables of the period. Many had shapely little turned-in knurl feet. Upholstery frequently covered the seat rail, close nailed or edged with fringe, the sumptous effect increased with gilded or silvered wood.

During the early 1700s, however, stools were transformed by the arrival of cabriole legs, some square cut, some in the 'broken' or spavin line, some narrowing at the knee which was edged with C scrolls. When the tops of the legs were carried into the seat rail—as in chairs, too, from about 1710—the stool no longer needed stretchers and strong cabriole legs were developed, often hipped around the corners of the seat frame and usually wide-shouldered. These were carved with escallop shells on the knee and the early pad foot gave place to the ball-and-claw popular from the 1720s to the 1750s.

Seat rails had to be made deeper to allow for tenoning into the blocks left at the tops of the legs. This gave a clumsy look to overstuffed upholstery. An alternative method was to halve the thickness of the upper part of the seat rails and fit a drop-in seat, strengthening the joints between seat rails and legs with screwed-in triangular blocks. Walnut continued popular for stools until the 1750s. Some were of japanned softwood, and others again enriched with gilded gesso. The dense mahogany of early Georgian days lent itself to vigorous carving and some magnificent stools were produced, frequently still with cabriole legs and hipped at the seat frame to give wear-resistant corners. Some legs bore lion masks, some were carved with hair, to end in shaggy paw feet. The drop-in seat permitted elaborate carving of the seat rail, sometimes including a central heavy motif of shell or mask.

By then the stool had lost its early importance, but a pair might match a set of chairs. These styles of the first half of the 18th century are probably the most often found among Victorian reproductions, sometimes square rather than rectangular. Stools are found in the Gothic and Chinese mood of the 1750s and 60s appropriate to minor rooms and their current status is emphasised by Ince and Mayhew who illustrated them as 'lady's dressing stools', giving them scrolling seats and curving crossed-over legs. Hepplewhite illustrated graceful little stools as simple as his chair seats and legs.

Upholstered double stools and window stools were popular through the later 18th century, but the stool as an important furnishing emerged again in the enthusiasm for archaeological classicism in the 1800s. The books on house furnishing by Hope (1807) and Smith (1808), for example, show the current delight in a seat form directly associated with antiquity. The most elaborate were in the Egyptian taste such as an example at the Lady Lever Art Gallery (Port Sunlight, Cheshire) in X form with saddle seat, ram's head arms and hoof feet. This would have tasselled draperies or a deep cushion laced to the arms. Ackermann's *Repository*, published throughout the Regency years, illustrated a wide range intended 'as ornamental and extra seats in elegant drawing rooms'. Many of this period were in mahogany, others in rosewood and many more in soft woods painted, gilded or stained black. Many from about 1818 were bronzed.

Victorians devised innumerable stool designs, covered them with embroidery and hung them with fringes and bobbles, but most characteristic, perhaps, were the ottoman entirely covered with fabric and upholstery, and the box ottoman which at least was functional within its fringed and tasselled covers (*see* Part VIII).

Window stool (Figs 68, 72): Popular from around the mid-18th century and noted, for instance, by Ince and Mayhew as French stools for recesses of windows. Short versions served as music stools. Such a stool, often japanned or gilded, had a long rectangular seat, its ends raised in scrolling curves upholstered like the seat in the manner of settee arms and similarly fronted with curving panels of wood carved in low relief and topped by paterae. Sometimes a central pair of legs was included, but more often the seat, between three and five feet long, was supported on four corner legs, free of stretchers, linked by a carved seat rail that was often slightly serpentine on plan. The waved outline or pendant scrolls of the seat rail thus emphasised the ornament on the legs. These might be the French modified cabriole with cabochon knee and scroll foot, or the Gothic cluster column with pierced corner bracket and gutta foot or the neo-classical taper, leaf-carved and fluted. Hepplewhite illustrated window stools, their ends to be stuffed or of openwork. Some of these stools were made with cane filling the seat and ends.

207

Late in the century the arms were straighter and Smith in 1808 suggested 'library seats' with vertical ends. But the curving X outline of the Regency resulted in some particularly graceful window stools with the arms and seat forming the upper curve of the X and the legs the reverse curve, linked, perhaps, by a central patera and lotus bud carving under the centre of the seat. Smith's low rectangular window seats had slightly raised corner pieces above stumpy feet or paws.

PART VIII

The Day Bed and its Successors

Both for comfortable lounging and for pretentious display the standing bed in all its textile glory served the Elizabethan man of wealth night and day. His own constrictive clothing, tightly padded, slashed and quilted, adequately proclaimed his aloofness from physical labour. If it necessitated more austere accommodation for daytime resting there was always the cushioned settle across the bed foot. Only late in the 17th century came more orderly home planning with greater differentiation between living and sleeping quarters and, therefore, opportunities for more specialised occasional furniture.

The first day bed was not very different from the ratchet-backed sleeping chair and, one suspects, was mainly regarded as a comfortable summer alternative to the settle. But, by the middle and later years of the 18th century, furnishings had been evolved in the taste and style of the most lavish reception room. There was then marked distinction between the design and the purposes of various long seats, although inevitably some confusion of terms.

In general one can distinguish between the settee which was a modified chair intended for two or three people sitting up and the couch, a modified bed, for one person in a reclining position. With the settee can be grouped the settle belonging as a fashion piece to the first period under review, the settee, including hall and bar-back varieties and the late 18th-century confidante, the small settee now sometimes called a love-seat and the ottoman and sociable and late 19th-century Chesterfield. The 17th-century Knole couch may be regarded as a dual piece. Also the sofa, important from the 1760s, in

70. Settees, settles and stools, 17th-century. TOP: Knole type of adjustable settee often reproduced, the ends on ratchets; two contemporaneous stools. SECOND ROW: two later 17th-century settles, one with wooden seat part-hinged for box space below, and one bored and grooved on seat rails for ropes to support long cushion; between them, a joint stool with legs splayed back and front for steadiness but not sideways as this would prevent close seating at table. BOTTOM: end-of-century elegance in two-seat settee or loveseat, caned stool, and upholstered stool with Spanish feet.

settee style but usually made wide and welcoming enough to be used on occasion for reclining. Specifically for resting, the day bed was succeeded by the couch, chaise longue, duchesse and meridienne which, by their very names, indicate their French origin.

Chaise longue (Fig. 72): French name for the day bed suggesting an extended chair, but more specifically an upholstered chair, with arms. Chippendale illustrated two in the 1762 edition of the *Director*, the long mattress or squab on either six or eight legs extending from an upholstered chair-head but in one example ending in a foot rail. He noted that 'they are sometimes made to take asunder in the middle; one part makes a large easy chair, and the other a stool, and the feet join in the middle, which looks badly,' and he recommended a 'pretty thick mattress'. A similar design was offered by Ince and Mayhew.

Sheraton noted its use 'to rest or loll upon after dinner' and illustrated two. One in the upholstered chair style was made in two parts, but the other in an asymmetrical couch style with a low support extending from the rounded head all down the back and curving attractively round the foot. Smith used the term for the asymmetrical furnishing surveyed here as a couch.

Chesterfield: From the 1880s, a late Victorian name for a large overstuffed sofa.

Confidante: A piece of French origin illustrated by Hepplewhite as a form of upholstered settee with a corner chair at each end, presumably to avoid the blank end usually offered by a settee set against the middle of a wall. He pointed out that the end pieces were removable, to use as bergère chairs and suggested a length of about nine feet (Fig. 73). Similar seats, with fixed ends, were in use in England from the 1770s.

Couch (Fig. 71): Defined in the 18th century as 'a sort of movable bed to lie down on'. It was thus an alternative term for the day-bed, a word associated mainly with Stuart days. The style with a modified chair-back as its head-board continued far into Georgian days and can be dated by similar chairs, but through the third quarter of the 18th century there was a tendency for wide, luxurious sofas for daytime rest.

Only towards the close of the century did those with an eye for comfort discover the charm of the couch in more or less classic outline. To add to the confusion this was often called a sofa too and was served by the sofa table (Figs 47, 48) characteristic of the Regency. But those with a liking for

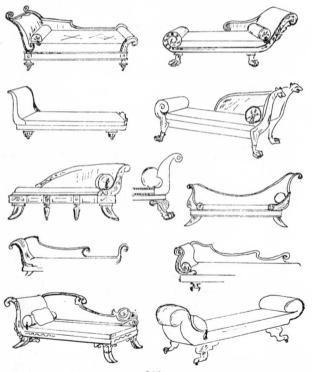

exactitude prefer to retain the name couch or use the clumsy term sofa in the form of a Grecian couch. At the time the Nicholsons' *Practical Cabinet Maker*, for example, used the phrase 'couch in the Grecian style'.

The term covers some of the most delightful furnishings that remain today, in mahogany, satinwood and japanned, painted and gilded softwood. In design, the backward scroll of the head end might be counterbalanced by a lower forward scroll at the foot, both curves often emphasised by outcurving scimitar legs. But there were several alternatives. The foot might be plain and often at one side a half-back curved down from the head. A carved and gilded specimen of 1805 made by the Gillow firm and now at the Victoria and Albert Museum, has leopard monopodia supporting the head and a forward scroll at the foot with similar carved legs with the leopard head carved into the scrolling. This has a round-ended back for about two-thirds of its length (it is 6 feet 8 inches long), and typically is free of stretchers. Often the feet were on castors.

By then the couch was to be found in almost any room in the house: *Ackermann's Repository* in 1809 called it 'an indispensable piece of furniture in a library'. The Nicholsons' design (1826) referred to above, was in mahogany with gilded detail (Fig. 71). It had the thick, reeded legs of the 1820s and decorative detail included the fan-shaped honeysuckle that dominated George IV ornament. The single-ended couch form

71. Regency couches. TOP: two Sheraton designs, early 1800s. SECOND ROW: simplest version of 1800s, sometimes with small arch at foot; made by Gillow, 1805 (V. and A. Museum). THIRD ROW: from Henry Moses drawing, 1823; scroll end from Hope, 1807; chaise-longue design by Smith, 1808. FOURTH ROW: progressive elaboration, 1810s and 1820s. BOTTOM: 'couch in the Grecian style' by P. & M. A. Nicholson, 1826, *Practical Cabinet-Maker, Upholsterer and Complete Decorator*; over-stuffed type with some Regency features, 1830s.

was approved by Loudon and retained its popularity during post-Regency revival of Louis Quinze fashion, the vogue being boosted in the 1830s under the name of the Adelaide couch. But the Victorian liking for massive, rounded symmetry was met more successfully by the sofa.

Day bed: An occasional reference has been noted in 16th-century records and in Shakespeare's plays, but it was largely a 17th-century development as a simple bedstock with panelled head and long cushion mattress augmented by graduated cushions harmonising with fabric bases hanging to the ground all round. After the Restoration of 1660 the fashion-conscious welcomed delightful day beds of carved walnut lightened with panels of resilient cane. The style suggested an elongated single chair, the 'back' or head being strongly raked and sometimes having the panel hinged at the bottom and adjustable at the top between the uprights.

Comparison with chair detail gives approximate dates for these day beds. But it may be noted that whereas the chair would have one broad carved stretcher at the front, the day bed with six legs frequently showed two at each side. These followed the changes of fashion in scrolling styles and the end-of-century X arrangement in flat, waved mouldings. The period's delight in upholstery was met then by the day bed with an upholstered scrolling head. The bed tended to be longer—often more than six feet—and required eight legs.

The elongated single chair style was continued through the early 18th century in splat-back, cabriole leg designs and ingenious early Georgians were already planning a wider form that could be folded to resemble a settee. Chippendale illustrated an extending day bed, calling it a single-headed couch, and this may be accepted as the term for what later developed a character distinct from chair furniture.

Duchesse (Fig. 72): A couch of French design made in England from the late 1770s. It consisted of a pair of tub-shaped easy chairs with a stool between them to form a couch. Hepplewhite suggested their use in a spacious ante-room. Each part had a loose squab or was stuffed over the

72. TOP: four settees of 1750s–60s in styles recorded by Chippendale and Ince & Mayhew, showing change to flowing curves. THIRD ROW: Hepplewhite duchesse; Sheraton chaise-longue. BOTTOM: long stools now known as window seats and, between them, details of wave-moulded leg chamfered on inner corner.

73. Settees and sofas. TOP: Chippendale sofa design, 1762; traces of mid-century in settee of 1760s based on Adam design. SECOND ROW: simple neo-classic example of 1760s; Hepplewhite design for confidante from the 1788 *Guide*. THIRD ROW, details of ends: 1790s; 1780s; 1790s. BOTTOM: Hepplewhite style of bar-back sofa.

frame. Sheraton in his *Drawing Book* constructed it of two rounded sofas separated by a stool, all on massive castors and linked by straps and buttons.

Hall settee (Fig. 74): This may be regarded as the successor in style to the settle which became a homely farmhouse piece in the 18th century. The hall settee was an early Georgian introduction that continued fashionable well into the 19th century. By 1750 sets of mahogany hall furniture were in fashion, a set consisting of a seven-foot settee and at least four chairs. The hall settee might be in oak, apple, elm or yew, but most fashionably in mahogany.

Comparison with hall chairs aids in dating. The back soon lost its traditional panels in favour of ornamental treatment, the arched cresting rail often decorated with a single expansive carved motif. Often the smooth wood of the back was painted in full colour with a coat of arms, but an alternative was an openwork pattern of carved scrolling. In the Regency specimen the detail might be picked out in gold. The seat might be dipped slightly to suggest a row of chairs like other settees, but more often was a smooth sheet of mahogany from end to end, being about eighteen to twenty-four inches deep. Sometimes the seat rails were deepened and the seat hinged to form a box.

Knole couch (Fig. 70): From the early 17th century and much reproduced. A simple form of upholstered settle or settee but to some extent adjustable for reclining. The flat-topped arms were low and above these, to the height of the back, were padded head or back rests which could be made to slope outwards by means of ratchets. The specimen at Knole, Kent, in velvet-covered beechwood, has been dated 1610–20. In such a style it would originally have matching chairs.

Loveseat (Figs 20, 70): Recent name for the double-chair or twin-back settee—called a half-settee in a reference of the 1740s. This probably began as a single seat, fully upholstered, made extra wide for the wide-skirted late Elizabethan or early Stuart lady. The intention was a small settee to go with a set of chairs and it acquired its usual double-chair back shaping, in walnut or beech, when chairs were displaying their Charles II characteristics of carving and cane. Some were fully upholstered with high arching double backs. Thereafter their development closely followed that of high quality chairs. Such seats are noted even in the Windsor style for garden or summerhouse. Their obvious successor in Victorian days was the sociable (Fig. 75).

Some collectors restrict the term loveseat to the particular style with back and seat suggesting wide, single units rather than a fusion of two chairs. Such a piece was usually upholstered but occasionally had an exceptionally broad single splat. Clearly here the purpose was to meet the needs of wide skirts and for one person's weight there was no need for a central leg. It is interesting to note that construction suggests a back stool (q.v.) rather than a chair. It is easy thus to trace the evolution of this piece from the complaints of women whose wide skirts had condemned them to stool seats and to note its disappearance with the dress changes of the 1760s.

Méridienne: Regency name for the couch in more or less classic style with one scrolled end higher than the other and usually paw feet on castors.

Ottoman (Fig. 75): Sheraton referred to a Turkey sofa as a low seat backed by cushions against a wall, and Smith in 1808 suggested that they were particularly useful in picture galleries as they kept the visitors from reaching and fingering the pictures. It became popular as a simple construction of a fully upholstered back serving seats on two or four sides. The circular version was sometimes known as a chaperon's seat. A variant was composed of separate, fully upholstered units that could be assembled round a group of statuary or as a curved sofa in a bow window. Not until the 1840s did it begin

74. Settees or sofas. TOP: Sheraton *Encyclopaedia* designs and detail of 'Egyptian' lotus foot. SECOND ROW: Hope design, 1807; Hope 'Egyptian' foot; 'Gothic' design, Smith, 1808. THIRD ROW: painted, with brass paw feet (V. and A. Museum), c. 1810; variant with lion heads and paw feet of brass; detail from hall settee. FOURTH ROW: William IV style. BOTTOM: two designs by P. & M. A. Nicholson, 1826–7 and leg detail shown by Doyle in 1833.

75. Victorian settees. TOP: buttoned chaise-longue; Victorian 'Elizabethan'. SECOND ROW: Victorian 'Louis XV' and 'neo-grec'. BOTTOM: ottoman for middle of large room, a piece that could be separated into a settee and four chairs; 'sociable sofa'.

to show its wooden framework, turned ends to the partitioning arms and short legs on castors. The backless box ottoman was also popular.

Settee (Figs 73–6): This was the piece usually made to accompany and match a suite of chairs. Basically its composition suggested a row of three chairs fused together. This

76. Settee and two chairs in the simple style of much Morris & Co. furniture, late 19th century.

was satisfactory in the earliest type based on the simple half-back Cromwellian chair, but it became somewhat top-heavy late in the 17th century when constructed in the style of the period's extremely high-backed, massively upholstered wing chairs. Even in the less unwieldy two-chair or loveseat style this was a somewhat weak construction. When cabriole legs became the fashion in the early 18th century the settee lost its imaginative back shaping in a generally smooth, flat-topped outline, the wings lacking the earlier earpieces and the arms flat, often outward scrolling.

It is interesting to note, on some early Georgian specimens, a closer association with accompanying chairs (two settees to a suite of chairs) expressed in plain wooden arms in the shepherd's crook or projecting volute. But the closest association with chairs was expressed in what Hepplewhite later called the bar-back settee.

The full development of the settee for three or four people dates from the 1730s but became more frequent from the 1750s. In walnut specimens of the 1740s and 50s the splats were usually vase shaped with the full complement of curving verticals to suggest a row of chairs: the rounded outlines made this inevitable, and often they had to be linked at the top rail with small shell carvings. With straighter backs, however, a single intermediate upright might separate each of the splats so that a triple chair design would have four uprights, three splats and a total of eight legs.

So many chair designs were repeated that the collector may note Chinese, Gothic, ribband and other familiar pierced splat patterns. Manwaring in his *Real Friend and Companion*, 1765, suggested lime or yellow deal for the backs of scrolling acanthus leaves. The upholstered seat might be of the drop-in type but, as often, stuffed over the wide seat rail and the richly carved legs might be linked by carved aprons, occasionally harmonising with carving on the arm ends of a fully upholstered settee.

The development of the Georgian upholstered settee is particularly interesting as it lost the plain chair style with open arms and by the middle years of the century had typically a unified, gently undulating back and high scrolled-over stuffed arms, the flat-faced front line of the arms curving forward to form a low, vertical end-piece above the front legs.

In upholstered settees the neo-classical taste found expression in a simplification of outline, the back often a single oval or rectangle of upholstery with open arms, the wood often beech, painted or gilded. The style of Hepplewhite's day might be as much as ten feet long, but less deep than formerly. In the open or bar-back version the back was composed of three, four or five open chair-backs following the elliptical or vase outline of the day, filled with decorated vertical bars or perforated splats. Late in the century the settee followed the chair into severe, square-shouldered outlines, but the Regency style was expressed in emphatic contrasts of curves and such leaders as Hope and Smith sought to decorate them with archaeological motifs and much Egyptian ornament. During the 19th century, however, the sofa again tended to overshadow the less luxurious settee as the square-ended 'Grecian' style was softened and rounded. The term continued in use where derivation from a chair style remained obvious, as in the simple Morris settee matching the rush-bottomed Morris chair of the 1860s.

Settle (Fig. 70): The most obvious development of the fixed bench built into the wall panelling. This had panelled back and ends and usually a chest seat with hinged lid and obviously long retained its usefulness when big open fires in many-purpose rooms associated comfort with all-round protection from draughts. Cushions ensured comfort, but the early foot rail was more often replaced by the Elizabethan's separate footstools. For lordly medieval splendour the settle might be surmounted by a canopy, more practically replaced later by the bacon cupboard projecting above the sitters' heads.

Collectors note the same changes in detail of rails and panel shapes, remembering that in farmhouse and inn the piece became traditional in the 18th century with no further impetus to change in response to fashion. Elizabethan and Stuart inventories indicate that it fitted conveniently at the foot of the bed, reducing the need to disarrange the bed's daytime splendours.

Comparatively few early specimens remain of what eventually became a cumbersome farmhouse piece. But there was a marked change from the fully panelled Elizabethan settle to the mid-17th-century specimen with bobbin-turned legs and arm supports and thence to the late 17th century's extremely high-backed piece. In the 18th century, as a provincial piece, its style changed slowly and collectors may find a low-backed early Georgian specimen with the period's fielded panels but with arms and leg features of the previous century. Details to note include the holes and channels in the seat rails for the cords that supported the long mattress and the contrast between ornamented legs at the front and plain at the back. The settle's fashion successor was the hall settee.

Sociable sofa (Fig. 75): Briefly popular around the 1840s in a wide range of designs as a successor to the 18th-century

77. LEFT: early 19th-century 'Gothic' settee for public use from illustration of the Chelsea Bun House. RIGHT: Iron seat, originally bronzed made by the Coalbrookdale Co., 1840s.

duchesse. It was composed basically of two conjoined padded armchairs half facing each other. These might be on shared seat rails and four legs or given two extra legs in the centre under a shared central arm, perhaps supporting a table. Among minor subsidiaries, collectors note also a circular three-seat variant and the conversation sofa with the sitters in two conjoined chairs facing in opposite directions (Fig. 31) —still advertised in the 1880s.

Sofa: Term used as early as the 1700s but only coming to the fore in the 1760s when it was made to sound glamorous by being called Chinese or Turkish. The design was basically that of the settee—symmetrical and with a back and arms to seat several people as contrasted with the headed couch— but at this period it became long and deep enough for reclining. The 1760s and 1780s produced many upholstered on the grand scale, finished with much lavish gilded carving.

The introduction of carved mahogany along the back was suggested in Chippendale's 1762 *Director* and popular again with the Victorians. By the 1760s the whole composition might be a delightful play of curves culminating in a magnificent scroll to the front of the arms, curving into the front legs to complete the serpentine shaping to the seat and the flowing line of the French legs. The play of contours in the upholstery of such a piece is comparable with the bombé shaping of a contemporary commode.

Towards the end of the 18th century and through the Regency the couch proved vastly popular and to Smith in 1808, as to Brown in his *Rudiments of Drawing Cabinet and Upholstery Furniture* (1822), the sofa was still a formidable, somewhat unwelcoming 'Grecian' piece. Smith's more gracious couch designs appeared as chaises longues. The Nicholsons mostly made their sofas low backed, on extremely massive feet, but suggested one design with deeply scrolling ends and dipped back, topped by the inevitable honeysuckle (Fig. 76). Carved arms are noted on some post-Regency sofas, continuing the Regency vogue for winged chimeras and the like; swans were especially approved and around the mid-19th century the vogue for ornate narrative carving associated with sideboards and fireplaces involved also the back of the sofa above the upholstery.

Thus the collector may trace the change from the low square-ended Regency classic through the early Victorian phase which gave back, arms and seat softened, rounded lines, expressed in buttoned upholstery and the restless scrolls from arm end to castor-mounted toe. From this, in the 1850s, emerged the arching back with a carved wooden framing, but it was only in the last years of the century that critics could observe much popular reaction against the shapeless, overstuffed sofa in favour of thinner, less shape-defying upholstery.

PART IX

Cupboards and Cabinets

Even after the term cupboard lost its medieval meaning of a side table to augment the dining trestles and gradually became accepted in its present day usage, the compilers of Tudor and Stuart inventories rarely used it explicitly. Instead, the vague 'little cupboard with a cloth' was a usual alternative to a variety of terms now difficult to apply with any certainty to the range of ancient cupboarding found today. Here confusion is increased by innumerable hotch-potch pieces put together from earlier remnants in the 19th century and later. Many that remain are of oak, but many more made of elm, fruit woods, deal or walnut have failed to survive.

The main specialised storage needs in the early home not met by the chest were for food—requiring shelves and ventilation—and for clothing—requiring length for hanging and shelves or drawers for folded garments. Here the terms hutch, credence, livery cupboard and perhaps aumbry, as well as bacon and game cupboards, are assumed to indicate food storage; armoire, press, wardrobe suggest the clothing store.

A well-run home would also need ordinary shelved cupboards for the trenchers, pewter and other dining equipment and a miscellaneous assortment of non-perishables, and many very old cupboards suggest such general storage duties. Some were further partitioned inside and listed as cupboard tills. These store cupboards may be noted bearing the same successive characteristics of skilled joiners' work as 15th-, 16th- and 17th-century chests. Some from the 16th and 17th centuries may retain their original metal work, showing ornate iron key escutcheons. Sometimes, as an alternative to the iron strap hinge with fleur-de-lys head, there may be H hinges or the attractive cock's-head hinges (Figs 2, 79).

Some of these cupboards are lightly carved in the 17th-century manner, but probably far more were still painted. During this century some were made with frieze drawers. Although many rested on brief extensions of the side stiles, an occasional example was raised on turned legs supporting

78. Corner cupboards through the 18th century: with rounded front and shelves above, early; with broken pediment, straight front, c. 1750s; ornate specimen of 1760s; glazed, with neo-classic ornament in marquetry, c. 1780s; bow front with pear-drop moulding, late.

a lower pot board on ball feet, and then frequently a drawer was added in the central framing. But the notable cupboard developments from the 16th to 17th centuries were among the varieties now classed as livery and hall or parlour cupboards—cupboarding at its most ornate climax before the joiner was outclassed by the cabinet maker. The Welsh *cwpwrdd deuddarn* and *tridarn* carried the traditions of the hall cupboard through the 18th century.

From the late years of the 17th century the most favoured cupboards were cabinets. Cupboards continued as invaluable furnishings in many parts of the big house, of course, and in farmhouse and merchant's villa. Cabinets of English make, as distinct from the rich curio collector's Continental show-pieces, date little earlier than the last decades of the 17th century: these include finely japanned imitations of costly Oriental lacquer. Cabinets on stands and on chests of drawers may show a range of small drawers and other superbly made fitments within their handsome doors, but lack the facilities for writing available in desk and bureau furniture.

With more books available, the fashion developed for mounting the plainly shelved bookcase over drawers or cupboards and restricting the name cabinet to the more decorative piece guarding or displaying collectors' treasures in drawing room, library or lady's closet. By such a definition the cabinet then merited an equally decorative stand or 'frame'. With the development of crown glass and the use of mahogany which could be cut into slender, shapely glazing bars, early Georgian fashion thereupon welcomed the glazed cabinet or 'china case'. Remaining specimens remind collectors that cupboards for general storage in rooms of fashion continued to be made throughout the 18th and 19th centuries, but lack distinctive features and are impossible to classify: they may be dated by material and style of treatment.

Through the Queen Anne period hanging corner cupboards might be considered in the category of cabinet. These, too, included glazed specimens around the mid-18th century. In its double, standing form, the corner cupboard was direct successor to the niche or buffet in the panelling. This was a space-saving notion used for the clothes press which, as a piece of furniture, was comparatively rare until the vogue of papered rooms. Late in the 18th century it was augmented by the vast, handsome wardrobe. But the corner cupboard, even in its more elaborate standing form, soon came to be regarded as a yeoman piece for villa parlour or farmhouse kitchen—as handsome, but frequently as unfashionable, as the dresser.

The other main furniture that might be classed among

18th-century cabinet and cupboard furniture, the commode (Fig. 64), has been considered among other chests of drawers. By Regency days homes big and small were accepting its successor, the all-purpose chiffonier (Fig. 63), with drawers, bookshelves and often a general store cupboard. Victorian cabinet makers, renowned for superb manufacturing detail, contributed little new or notable in cabinet design, but much to question among their near copies of earlier styles.

Armoire: Continental term for a clothes cupboard with ornament comparable to that on linenfold and arcaded chests. It is doubtful whether many of these were made in England.

Aumbry: Perhaps associated with the French armoire. The word occurs in many 15th- and 16th-century inventories, such as the familiar 'cupboard of aumbries' now assumed to indicate an enclosed piece of furniture; a number suggest a primary use for books. But a more likely association is with the wall receptacle for left-over foods to be distributed as alms.

Bacon cupboard: The most notable is the settle type with a tall shallow cupboard serving as a panelled back to a seat which is itself a box chest and sometimes with further cupboarding projecting above the sitters' heads. This massive piece went out of favour in the first half of the 18th century, but simple panelled oak and pine cupboards for hanging home-cured flitches continued far into the 19th century.

Corner cupboard (Fig. 78): When a shelved niche was fitted into a corner of a panelled room it offered opportunities for charming carved detail to set off a collection of porcelain, but this style of buffet was eventually supplemented by free-standing corner shelving at least partly enclosed by cupboard doors, suitable also for a room that was papered instead of panelled.

Queen Mary II is known to have had a buffet for her porcelain collection in the 1690s, but the free-standing double-tiered corner cupboard seldom dates before early Georgian days and is found more often in later styles. Meanwhile, however, an alternative for the corner, also probably Dutch inspired and certainly often imported, was the hanging corner cupboard. This, too, was mainly a product of the second half of the 18th century and later, but was found occasionally from around 1700. The third alternative, the low corner cupboard, was a comparative rarity in England.

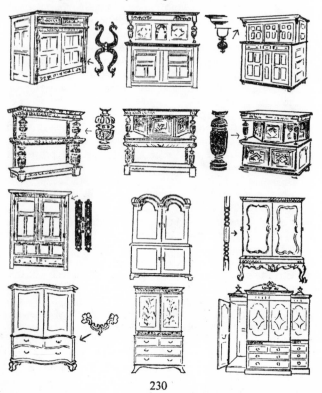

Hanging corner cupboard: Charles I had a 'little three-cornered cupboard', but very few remain that can be dated earlier than the 1690s when japanned specimens were a popular notion from Holland. These were particularly suitable for the precious china ware used by the fashionable hostess for evening tea. Dutch imports were advertised in Queen Anne's reign, and some that remain show the familiar double-ogee outlines and occasionally also the stiff, flowered wood marquetry produced in Holland. More in japanning suggest English work, and may show the bow-fronted design that permitted considerable storage space without undue width: this appears to have been too difficult for the early English veneer craftsman, but was less hazardous when the rounded surface could be japanned—in black or colour with chinoiserie scenes in colours and gilding. Sometimes receding shelves above offer space for a few china ornaments.

The arched effect popular in the Queen Anne period was achieved on a straight-fronted cupboard by shaping the cornice and following the same curve for the single or double door. In japanning then, instead of shelves, there might be carved and gilded cresting. In the walnut veneered specimen, always straight-fronted, the door might be flanked by fluting, and from about 1720 it became customary to chamfer these sides,

79. Cupboards. TOP, 17th-century parlour or hall cupboards: early, panelled and carved (detail of cock's-head hinge); design with small upper cupboards set back over bigger ones; plainer style that continued through the 18th century, the corner pillars reduced to pendant knobs. SECOND ROW: court cupboard (detail of cup-and-cover pillar, end of 16th century; an associated piece, perhaps a livery cupboard; late 17th-century enclosed parlour cupboard. THIRD ROW, for clothes: 17th-century cupboard with drawers below (detail of 'H' hinge); c. 1710; c. 1750, with rococo carved stand, applied moulding on doors (detail of door beading) (V. and A. Museum). BOTTOM: serpentine outline (detail of rococo handle); Hepplewhite; Sheraton breakfront wardrobe with applied mouldings.

again with the purpose of rendering the piece less obtrusive while giving considerable depth. Such an early cupboard might be some 4 feet tall and 2 to 2½ feet across. Inside it would reveal two cyma-fronted shelves comparable with the delicate fittings of the open buffet, since the hostess would be liable to open it in front of her visitors.

An occasional hanging corner cupboard may be dated to early Georgian days, fronted with mirror glass and topped by a broken pediment, as in cabinets of the day. Or the single door, still in the pleasant arched outline, may contain an arched, fielded panel, a style long retained in the occasional ornate oak cupboard. A few are comparable with early Georgian mirrors, the bold broken pediment and base moulding carved and partly gilded and the coffered door panel edged with a carved and gilded fillet. Glazed doors were sometimes used when manufacturing techniques made these easily available in decorative designs.

Some hanging corner cupboards reflect most of the changes of fashion seen in cabinets, but in a restrained manner, and retaining the distinctive, straight-fronted, chamfered-corner outline well suited to the swan-necked pediment, and with a plainly moulded base. A japanned cupboard might have two doors, the join masked by rounded moulding and the key escutcheon imitated by a sham on the second door, but the glazed cabinet of the 1760s would have a single door for a clear view of the contents.

Such pieces, however, are by no means representative of the hanging corner cupboard which in general was regarded as a minor parlour or living room furnishing, ignored by the leading furniture designers. As such it was mainly a simple mahogany piece made in quantity and almost datelessly from the 1760s until far into the 19th century, with cheaper versions in native woods, notably consistent in general design and size, although found in a considerable variety of finishes.

Typically the plain cornice rises about two inches above the cupboard top, suggesting that the piece was intended to hang above eye level. Shape in the plain mahogany specimen follows that of the glazed corner cabinet, with chamfered corners, fluted or decorated with applied or card-cut lattice. H hinges were long retained, but butt hinges may be noted on a late piece of good quality. The broken pediment continued as a feature of the more elaborate piece, frequently in scrolling swan-neck outline to set off a central pedestal-mounted finial and occasionally lightened by piercing.

Far more often the cornice was plain or dentil moulded; peardrop moulding was popular in the 1770s and onwards. Occasionally too the front might show richly figured veneer, the panel outline suggested by stringing, or there might be bandings of satinwood or tulipwood. In the country version there were mahogany bandings on oak. Simple marquetry motifs such as a conch shell or patera might be introduced on a plain door or frieze, but rarely anything elaborate.

The most popular probably were those plainly constructed or veneered in glowing mahogany in bow-fronted outline, a shape far commoner for corner cupboards at the end of the 18th century than it had been at the beginning. This involved making each of the two twelve-inch wide doors from three four-inch planks suitably curved and fitted together with tongue and groove. Such doors were rebated to close together, with no interruption to the curving line. Cornice and base mould, too, had to be constructed in short sections of wood to keep end-grain from coming to the front on the curve under the cross-grain or straight-run veneer.

Corner cupboards appear in two paintings by David Wilkie, painted 1805–10, *The Card Players* and *Rent Day*. One shows a convex-fronted cupboard with brass butterfly hinges; the other is open to reveal shelves and base holding toddy bowl, glasses and a silver tea service. The popularity of japanning may have prompted the oil painting found on some late corner cupboards of oak or deal, on the fronts and inside the doors. This may be in floral patterns against light-toned grounds, such as pale green or ivory and occasionally one finds groups of figures in the style of Watteau. Interiors of such cupboards were painted in opaque washes of red, green, yellow or the favourite sky blue.

Standing corner cupboard: This was a convenient alternative to the built-in buffet, substantially made with no pretensions to grandeur, so that many remain, including some early Georgian. These occasionally retain such buffet features as the half-domed top in fluted shell design. Here, again, dating is difficult. Some early Georgian detail continued far into the later 18th century and the versions that followed have a simple grace defying Victorian inventiveness.

In general design the cupboard resembled a hanging corner cupboard resting on a lower section of perhaps half the height, usually consisting of a plain, straight-shelved cupboard with one or two doors, the dividing line of moulding governed by the dado of the panelled room that had determined buffet proportions. In the same way, too, the cupboard acquired something of the buffet's architectural effects of heavy cornice supported by carved capitals and classic pilasters contrasting with the arch of the upper doors which corresponded to the lunette shape of the buffet's open recess.

Their use was largely prompted by the swing of fashion away from heavy architectural furniture towards rococo whims in gaily papered rooms, but nevertheless the piece retained the heavy, classic cornice with dentil moulding and frequent pleasure in broken arch and swan-neck pediment. This was supported on fluted pilasters ornamenting the broad, chamfered corners that carried the cupboard's attractive receding line right from the cornice to the broad, bracket feet.

Like the hanging version the upper section was often glazed

234

when crown glass and strong mahogany glazing bars made this popular. Many an extremely simple late specimen with a straight cornice and plain, narrower, chamfered corners has a single upper door delightfully glazed and a door below as a panel of fine mahogany veneer. Others are mahogany veneered throughout with applied mouldings to suggest panels and ornamental paterae to associate the design with current neo-classic ideas.

An occasional rarity shows use of satinwood or panels of marquetry, but a more likely find is a late 18th-century modification of the design such as a couple of drawers or a lower section entirely of drawers. There may be a writing flap of the fall-front secretaire type enclosing desk fittings. Sometimes a cupboard is found resting on a three-legged stand with an open pot shelf near the floor. Such pieces usually suggest country work and may be of oak with bandings in richer woods or minor inlays. Sometimes one notes small drawers inside the cupboard doors. Here dull green paint might set off china arranged on shelves that were often grooved, since by then the china on display would be more likely to be pictorial plates than Chinese vases.

Court cupboard (Fig. 79): A frequent term found in early inventories, and long assumed to refer to cupboarding in the modern sense. In particular the ornate hall or parlour cupboard was often so named by earlier collectors. This is no longer accepted and the court cupboard takes its place as a tiered variant of the dining room side table, forerunner of the sideboard. (*See* Part XII).

Credence cupboard: In early days not restricted to ecclesiastical use but serving as a small side table: a cupboarded table with canted sides narrowing to the front and often with a shelf below.

Cwpwrdd deuddarn and cwpwrdd tridarn: The deuddarn is the Welsh form of the hall or parlour cupboard described below, in widespread use from the late 17th century and throughout the 18th century, often showing handsome fielded panels and a high standard of joinery. Many examples bear the initials and wedding date of their original owners. Sometimes, however, a specimen is noted that has acquired much more recently a third, topmost stage consisting of canopied shelving: it thus follows the form of the more ornate cwpwrdd tridarn. The canopy made the tridarn an extremely impressive piece of furniture, the open shelf being high enough for massive platters or pewter vessels protected from dust by the canopy with its supporting side balusters or spindles—a vestige of the Elizabethan hall cupboard corner pillars.

Game cupboard: Type of food cupboard dating from the 16th century onwards with a sloping lid or door and ventilated front panels. The slant ensured that the opening was left unobstructed, whereas a chest tended to be used as a table or a seat. One design associated with the eastern counties has heavy front stiles topped with turned knobs.

Hall or parlour cupboard (Fig. 79): In Tudor days side tables were arranged so that foods could be set out and the handsome cups prepared for serving the diners. These tables included the dresser and the open-shelved court cupboard. For storing the dining accessories and for general cupboard use the need was for a piece comparably handsome but partly or wholly enclosed. Such was the hall cupboard, called with equal justification a parlour cupboard, as more and more well-to-do families sought privacy in a dining parlour. The essential difference between this and other cupboards of its day was that it followed the traditions of display furniture and can be regarded as an enclosed version of the medieval dresser and subsequent court cupboard (*See* Part XII). Thus the dominant features throughout the cupboard's existence as a fashion piece were the wide, ornamented cornice frieze and central shelf moulding and the pillars at the front corners.

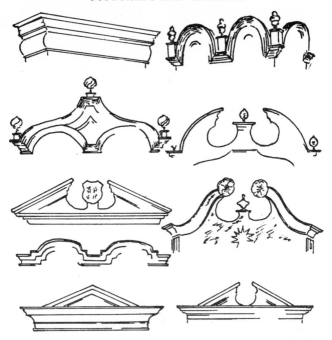

80. Cornices and pediments for cabinet furniture. TOP: late 17th century (often with drawer in swelling frieze); exaggerated arches with cavetto moulding of 1700s. SECOND ROW: 1700s and the rounded broken pediment of about 1730. THIRD ROW: three examples typical of the 1730s. BOTTOM: 1730s–40s.

This piece was important in Elizabethan and early Stuart days, but lost ground after the Restoration in 1660. As a substantial workaday furnishing it continued through the 18th century and in Wales, as noted above, the cwpwrdd deuddarn and cwpwrdd tridarn were in widespread use, showing little change throughout the century. Inevitably it prompted many Victorian imitations.

The cupboard averaged about 5 feet 6 inches high, 4 feet 6 inches wide (but occasionally wider than its height in a late specimen) and perhaps 1 foot 9 inches deep. The main portion consisted of a two-door cupboard, the corner stiles extended as feet. The top of this cupboard formed a shelf with deep ornamental moulding, and upon this rested shorter upper cupboarding. Most typically this superstructure consisted of a central panel flanked by small cupboards receding to the sides to leave considerable space towards the front corners of the shelf. Here two massive, stumpy pillars rose to support a deep cornice and frieze construction of the same dimensions as the cupboarding. By the 17th century the upper cupboard section might be straight-fronted but set back so that it still allowed space for the two pillars which harmonised with the style of the finest bedsteads, tables and other furniture of the day.

The Elizabethan cupboard might be spectacular, lavishly carved and often inlaid, or enriched with gilding and paint. Many were of oak, some of walnut, constructed on the joiner's sound panel technique. The pillars then reflected the Continental fashion for bulbous outlines, often in the familiar cup-and-cover form, carved, perhaps, with acanthus leaves and capped with gadrooning. Often the cost was reduced by using wood of a diameter to suit the turned sections of such a pillar, augmented by four additional facings to shape the bulbous swell. The upper cupboards or superstructure between and behind these pillars were frequently carved, too, on panels and framing. The central panel was flanked by pilasters, carved perhaps as caryatids and covering secret receptacles. Often, too, the central panel itself was opened by a hidden catch.

In the 17th century the tendency was towards flatter, less imaginative carving and the pillar swells became longer and less pronounced, eventually showing vase or double baluster outlines, and by the mid-century they were often replaced by short pendant bosses. At this time carved ornament occasionally gave place to glued-on mouldings, bosses and split spindles, but many specimens that remain from the second half of the century are plainly handsome pieces with well-proportioned panelled cupboards, the stiles and muntins decorated perhaps with incised patterns. A late specimen might have a row of three shallow drawers in the shelf apron. These were never intended for storing plate, which required iron-bound chests. Locks fitted to early examples tend to be late additions, usually with anachronistic brass keyhole escutcheons.

The oak of antique specimens has a hard, metallic surface and displays a rich lustre. Spurious examples abound. These, within a very few years, may show a lifeless surface with a yellowish brown tint; in some cases the tone is faintly green. Victorian-Elizabethan hall cupboards were popular in middle class homes during the 1830s and 1840s. Instead of being nut-brown they were stained black and they were fitted with up-to-date locks. Loudon's *Encyclopaedia*, 1833, gives a description of this trade.

Hutch: In the 13th and 14th centuries and later a primitive riven oak chest-form, turned with its end or side uppermost so that the lid came to the front as a door, usually a single slab of wood. There might be shelves resting on pegs or nails driven in horizontally from outside. Some collectors reserve the name hutch for the type raised on legs. Hinges might be of leather or primitive iron pivots, but iron straps proved more enduring and prevented the door from splitting or warping.

It is thought that such primitive construction continued long after the best hutches were panelled and raised from the floor by extending the corner stiles. An obvious alternative was to hang the cupboard on the wall with huge nails driven through the back boards. A solid plinth suggests that originally the piece had a matching stand. The ornament current on chests might be introduced, such as linenfold carving.

A feature of this type of cupboard was the ventilation piercing. A few examples from the 15th and 16th centuries show carved piercing and even occasional Gothic tracery, but many in this manner tend to be discredited as 19th-century primitives. More, it seems, were pierced with innumerable small holes originally backed by coarse hair cloth. A substantial food cupboard of the 17th century may show decoratively turned spindles in the current range of outlines—bulbous, bead-and-vase or baluster—to fill an open panel in the door. Wedge or butterfly hinges and the ornamental scrolling cock's-head may be noted, but more of the H outline, plain or engraved. In the mid-17th century small butt hinges might be required for full-width doors.

Livery cupboard (Fig. 79): In Tudor days dinner and supper were usually communal meals, but members of the household took other food to their rooms and this, along with necessary candles, was set out each day on a cup-board, the livery cupboard, where these victuals were delivered to their recipients. When enclosed cupboards became usual the liveries could be protected from flies and dust, and in a wealthy home each individual would have a livery cupboard in his room. A suitable cupboard sometimes given this name, although probably of wider usage, is a small version of the hall or parlour cupboard. This has cupboarding comparable with the upper stage of the hall cupboard, including the canted shaping, but an open shelf below. It is thus a half-way stage between the open-tiered court cupboard and the fully enclosed hall cupboard. Sixteenth-century references to the livery cupboard sometimes indicate a lower shelf. By the late 17th century the hanging corner cupboard was often used for candles, for example, in the richly furnished bedroom or dressing room.

Press (Fig. 79): The Tudor and Stuart cupboard fitted with yew wood pegs for hanging clothes. Subsequently a shelved cupboard for linen or folded clothing. References of the 16th and 17th centuries suggest that it was usually a plain wainscot piece; some were very large and fitted with locks. Charles I possessed a press cupboard covered with embossed leather and doubtless many were painted, while others again were but part of the room panelling. Some that remain from the 17th century are ornamented with carving on the frieze and below the doors in flattish repetitive motifs.

Presses from the reign of Queen Anne and early Georgian days tend to be pleasantly plain with square cornices, their decoration restricted to the ogee-headed fielded panels that are among the most attractive features of early 18th-century oak construction. A few are in walnut veneer with the double arch cornice and doors. The lower section may be of drawers, or doors may enclose open-fronted sliders, but like double corner cupboards they seldom suggest luxury work at this period when panelled rooms prompted much built-in cupboarding.

Magnificent presses were made in mahogany, however, at first with bold cornice, carved moulding and broken pediment in the early Georgian architectural manner. The broken line of the period persisted to suit the room dado, frequently with carved moulding between the long, upper press doors and the nearly square cupboard doors below that rested on a plinth or plain or ogee bracket feet.

By the 1750s the square cornice and straight sides of the piece might be relieved by panels in serpentine outline: a two-door specimen of about 1750 at the Victoria and Albert Museum rests on a stand with a scrolled, convex apron carved with rococo ornament on brief cabriole legs and paw feet. This handsome piece has a lining, shelves and drawers of cedar wood.

241

Chippendale and his contemporaries sometimes raised the almost square front of the press on a drawer unit composed of two half-drawers and one of full width with bombé swelling to the front and shouldered corner pilasters ending in outward-scrolling feet. An alternative was to shape press and drawers in a serpentine outline with ornament on the projecting canted corners. Panels might be suggested by plain or carved mouldings. Even when a press, perhaps seven or eight feet tall, was fronted with two full-length doors, the interior was usually fitted with shelves, sliders and drawers.

Neo-classical treatment followed the rococo of the 1750s and 60s with panels of contrasting veneers, typical being the elliptical door panel of figured mahogany surrounded by diagonally laid satinwood. Many a press of the period with a straight-fronted line depends for its beauty mainly on good proportions and the quality of its mahogany veneers, ornament being restricted to peardrop cornice moulding, perhaps, and crossbanded panel effects, possibly a delicately pierced pediment.

In the last quarter of the century some were of satinwood, some being painted in considerable detail on a coloured ground. By then, as in Elizabethan days, there was a demand for facilities for hanging clothes instead of folding them, and wardrobes were designed in breakfront outlines (Fig. 79), the central section still being a clothes press fitted with sliders and drawers but flanked by sections for hanging. A well-made press would have its sliders fronted, perhaps, with cedar and lined with paper—marbled paper looked well—and each covered with its baize 'apron' to keep off the dust.

Spice cupboard: Usually impossible to date, a small, squarish cupboard for hanging on the wall, often richly decorated and fitted with little drawers. Doors may have stout leather hinges. Hanging candle boxes may be noted, too, shaped so that the candles can lie flat.

Wardrobe (Figs 79, 115, 116): A cupboard for hanging clothes. The very early press was thus a wardrobe, but at that time the word still indicated a room. Subsequently built-in cupboards were used or clothes were stored by folding. Hanging space in a piece of furniture was reintroduced only in the second half of the 18th century when the clothes press still predominated. Hepplewhite, who liked plain wardrobes, suggested a height of 5 feet 6 inches, width of 4 feet and depth of 22 inches.

Many 18th-century pieces that appear to be wardrobes have fitted interiors, but the breakfront design of the 1770s and later has a hanging cupboard at least to one side of the press. In some designs, from the outside, each of the three sections resembles the press, with a short door above three rows of drawers. Such a wardrobe was constructed in five pieces—cornice, plinth and three cupboard sections. Shearer in 1788 costed one at five guineas. This had clothes trays and drawers in the central section, shelves in one wing and clothes pegs in the other, the wing doors to be plain or with sham drawer fronts to match the central section. This had a plain cornice and plinth. A Gothic peardrop cornice moulding cost sixpence extra per foot. The design with the differently fronted wardrobe at one side of the press section was wholly Victorian.

Some splendid wardrobes remain from the 1800s. The elliptical veneer patterns, the urn finials above peardrop cornice moulding and the outcurved French feet linked by a cyma-shaped apron gave place to even plainer outlines superbly veneered, with rectangular panel mouldings to the doors. Some of the most attractive are slightly bowed. There was also a change from machine-shaped brass bail handles to more use of the early 19th-century knob in flat patera shape. George Smith in 1808 suggested some heavy wardrobes, including breakfronts, and with less show of drawers. At the end of the Regency period the same style of low gable pediment and rounded ante-fixae at the corners was still approved.

81. Pediments. TOP: the swan-neck broken pediment of 1750s–60s with fret; more graceful variant of 1760s onwards. BOTTOM: typical broken pediment with pedestal for bust.

By the 1820s some wardrobes were slightly Gothic in door panel shaping, and on the space-wasting panels then introduced to the sides of the doors and press drawers. The Regency bedroom might contain a cheval dressing glass or psyche, but in the 1820s the obvious sequel to this was the long mirror on the wardrobe door. Many a Victorian wardrobe was made with a plain, bold cornice, the long mirror-mounted door being flanked by two narrow sham panels and based on a deep drawer above a plain plinth. The shape of the knob handles on the big drawer may help to date the piece.

Cabinets (Figs 93, 132): Technically the most perfect pieces of case furniture ever evolved, these represent storage and display units at their most refined and personal. From their beginnings in the late 17th century under the influence of Continental fashion and craftsmen, cabinets quickly appeared

82. Pediments. TOP: chinoiserie pagoda style, 1750s; neo-classic straight lines with urn and swag ornament, 1760s on. BOTTOM: later 18th-century scrolling arch with shell centrepiece; scrolling arch with urn centrepiece.

in a notable range of design and material to meet man's new delight in china, coins, shells and other curios and at the same time to declare his appreciation of patient, exquisite craftsmanship in the range of hardwoods then arousing admiration.

English cabinet makers seldom sought to imitate the costly inlays and incrustations of early Continental cabinets. In japanning they caught something of the glitter but little of the spirit of the most splendid cabinets of imported Oriental lacquer. But it is among cabinets, especially among those of the 18th and early 19th centuries, that the collector may expect to find the finest examples of the designs and the techniques of construction and ornament attributed to the different periods in the introductory survey to this book.

Bureau cabinets are included among desk furniture: here the term cabinet is confined to pieces fitted with small drawers, shelves and cupboards, but with no provision for writing. Small cabinets of drawers were the delight of the rich in the early 17th century but widespread production began only with the late 17th century. The early shape was rectangular with flat cornice and swelling frieze above flat cabinet doors covering the whole front and opening to reveal perhaps a dozen drawers around a central small cupboard.

The fittings in a fine example were extremely attractive. The smooth running oak drawers were made of wood often less than a quarter of an inch thick, the small central cupboard, still known at the time as a till, set between rosewood pilasters and often concealing secret compartments reached by pressing a hidden spring. Such a cabinet might be mounted on a stand or on a bun-footed chest of drawers. The whole piece was most usually between 5 and 6 feet tall and between 3 and 4 feet wide —sometimes as little as 26 inches—and some 18 inches deep. Ornament was consistent throughout cabinet and stand, such as marquetry or oyster parquetry now showing particularly brilliant on the enclosed drawer fronts and the like. The flat top of the early cabinet might be adorned with Oriental porcelain, a Dutch fashion introduced by Mary II.

Cabinets in Oriental lacquer and imitations in English japanning had their own characteristic stands. Walnut cabinets of the second (Queen Anne) period include a few early glazed specimens. Others are patterned on both outer and inner sides of their doors with reserves of marquetry matched by similar ornament on the drawer fronts inside and below the cabinet and on the cornice and frieze above. Such marquetry is most usually of the late seaweed type. After about 1710 veneers of burr walnut and other highly ornamental wood were generally preferred.

In this period of arching curves and increasingly lofty rooms many of the finest cabinets from about 1700 were given extra height by raising the front cornice into a tall double arch in rounded or ogee outline (Fig. 80). The doors were arched in corresponding profile and the piece was further enhanced by false façades or arches at the sides. For emphasis appropriate to such a soaring line it was enriched with deep shadow-catching concave moulding. In such a massive piece the long doors might be mounted with mirror glass, recessed into the door and backed by a thin panel of wood in the same shape. This glass showed wide, shallow bevels and was arched, too, at the top with the particularly pleasing ogee shoulder line of this period. At its most ornate the mirror plate might be cut with a rayed star in the arch and possibly figures below, followed later by chinoiseries.

Such a massive piece, perhaps over seven feet tall, was more likely to be raised upon a chest of drawers than the current cabriole-legged stand. The latter, however, suited the slighter piece with straight cornice, chamfered at the corners, that depended for ornament upon the beauty of its perfectly matched, delicately cross- and feather-banded walnut veneers.

The whole mood changed soon for the fashionable cabinet quickly reflected current approval of the heavy style of furnishing devised by the architect William Kent. Foreign porcelain was then so avidly collected that whole closets were devoted to it and cabinets for its safe keeping were solid affairs with a broken pediment (Fig. 81) rising high over a heavily dentil-moulded cornice and supported by pilasters in the style of capital and fluted columns that accorded with the architecture of the room. Cupboards filled the lower section, with fielded panel doors.

More cabinet makers of the period, however, followed the generally accepted definition of a cabinet as a decorative storage place for curios with finely veneered doors enclosing small drawers and alcoves. This rested upon an open stand that gave the piece the air of a drawing room plaything, distinct from the library or study bookcase. The mid-century fashion in chinoiseries was met by extravagently elaborate glazed china cabinets and specimens in japanning that contrasted severe outlines with immensely rich surface ornament.

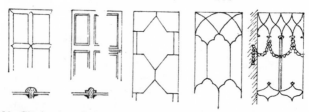

83. Glazing bars for cabinet furniture. Half-round bars with cross-banded walnut veneer, late 17th and early 18th centuries; half-round with inner fillet, found in oak, etc., late 17th and early 18th centuries and the development from this found up to about 1750, including early mahogany; three examples of post-1750 patterns in narrow mahogany glazing bars, straight, curved, and with carved detail sometimes continued on to the frame. BOTTOM: cross sections showing bar, glass and putty.

But the connoisseur's cabinet of around 1760 was still a superb exercise in carving and veneers, the doors veneered in contrasting slants of grain, the panel effects enhanced with slender carved mouldings and with enrichment of gadroons, scrolls and acanthus foliage on cornice, canted corners and harmonising frame. The cabinet maker, William Vile, is associated with some fine examples.

Some cabinets were mounted with plaques, but this ornament is associated more especially with the neo-classical work that followed when cabinets in severely simple outlines, on tapering thermed legs, depended mainly for ornament upon the surface treatment, whether inlay, marquetry or paint. Painted panels of classic figures in Kauffmann style were rivalled by the low relief white figures of Wedgwood plaques in jasper ware; for the study cabinet-bookcase there were medallions of cameo heads. Often, however, to break the angular line, the cornice was surmounted by a scrolling pediment lightened by delicate piercing and sometimes incorporating the ever-recurrent urn and swag motifs; an alternative was a spindle gallery with corner urn finials. The frieze might be carved with anthemion or pear-drop moulding.

Some of these superb pieces of cabinet making show the serpentine shaping of the 1770s in both cabinet and stand. Hepplewhite's *Guide*, 1788, illustrated 'library cases' but no cabinets, but the flowing line of cornice pediments and finials, the serpentine and bow fronts and outcurving feet of his chests and commodes may be noted in many a simple cabinet of his day.

Sheraton suggested somewhat effeminate cabinets, the most ornate with a shaped marble shelf and brass edging. But the dominant change was to more emphasis on the lower part of the case, leading to the low, compact cabinets of the Regency. These again may be said to be indistinguishable from the book-cases of the period, low rectangles on heavy feet—often gad-rooned or paw-shaped—rather than either plinth or brackets. In these cabinets the attraction is found in the fine handling of exotic woods. One notes cross bandings, marquetry or brass inlay around plainly rectangular doors filled with diamonds or interlacing curves of brass lattice backed by silk in the manner popular from 1800 to 1830. More elaborately curved lattice dates from about 1815 onwards.

With a couple of shelves above, such a piece may be classed as a chiffonier. Sometimes there was an upper stage of latticed cupboarding, but the piece was more often low enough for a mirror or picture to hang above. A frequent feature was the use of corner pilasters or free-standing pillars, sometimes in rope twist, between the gilded mouldings projecting above and below the cabinet and terminating in turned peg feet. Some of the most ornate had corner pillars of classic caryatids gilded to stand out against the zebra wood, rosewood and similar rich veneers. Some were enriched with ormolu mounts.

Inevitably Victorians turned back to the extremely ornate

work of the French cabinet makers under Louis XV and Louis XVI. Many of these cabinets are near copies of 18th-century work. Some dainty specimens may be noted in glossy early Victorian papier mâché. Mid-19th century criticism stressed the cabinet maker's reputation for 'useful, perfect quality work', but regretted, for example, the use of carving applied instead of being a part of the framing. By mid-Victorian days there was much to criticise in the Victorian-Renaissance creations enriched with inlay or marquetry of ivory, bone or coloured marbles. Some were covered with Victorian boulle. Some, cheaply assembled with run-moulded members and weakly turned knobs and spindled galleries, carried panels of painted china. Small china cabinets might be lined with velvet.

William Morris listed cabinets among 'the blossoms of the art of furniture' that he allowed could be made 'as elaborate and elegant as was possible with carving, inlay or painting'. But the current assumption that elaboration of carving was synonymous with art encouraged such individualists as W. T. Burges to choose painted ornament upon simple Gothic form.

Eastlake, in the 1860s, decried the structural weakness of the curving-legged cabinets of his day and suggested massive cabinets with heavy panelling, wide strap hinges and typical Victorian spindles. Cabinets of the 1870s, indeed, were subject to all the whims of Art Furniture with emphasis on plain outlines but somewhat fussy, niggling surface ornament. The ebonised cabinets prolific in the 1880s were prompted by art pieces of the 1870s, when an alternative finish was the light oak stained green that was originated by Ford Madox Brown, an artist of the Morris group. The most usual shape consisted of cupboards below a shelf of table height and, above that, spindle supported shelves and minor cupboards often with a central mirror and a galleried cornice. By the 1880s artistic cabinets meant spindly, supposedly Japanese forms, but already some leaders were looking ahead to smooth, sheer lines.

Buffet: In an 18th-century panelled room—from the 1690s to the 1760s—an alcove might be built into a corner, composed of tiered shelves for displaying china. This was known then as a buffet or beaufait, although the word had other earlier meanings. It is of interest here as the wealthy household's obvious forerunner of the double corner cupboard. Sheraton in his *Cabinet Dictionary* showed an ornate cabinet under this name, with open shelves supported on slender brass columns under a cornice with fringe and Gothic drapery. A bow fronted cupboard below had corner columns supporting candle branches. He suggested a pair to flank the fireplace of a breakfast room.

Breakfront cabinet (Fig. 93): Fashionable form also for bookcases and wardrobes in the fourth quarter of the 18th century. Such a cabinet had a wide central cupboard, taller than the side compartments and set slightly forward from them. In the 1790s when squarer lines were demanded, the side compartments might be given prominence with a suggestion of the current sideboard outline.

Coin: From French *encoignure*, a corner cupboard. When used in England it apparently implied the 18th-century French style of low cabinet or corner commode. Ince and Mayhew, 1759–62, showed two designs for 'ecoineurs' which they described as corner shelves. In each design a low corner cupboard with a bow front and corner bracket feet was topped by three or four receding shelves supported on curving frets in harmony with the frets in the cupboard door of remotely Gothic outlines. The authors noted that in an example made from one of their designs the shelves were backed with silvered mirror glass. This type of corner cabinet was rare in England until Victorian days, when it was popular in the style associated with other glazed cabinets and when the étagère composed entirely of open shelves also appeared in a corner version as the whatnot (Fig. 96).

Glazed cabinet (Figs 78, 83, 88): Apart from rare exceptions such as Queen Mary II's cabinets for porcelain and delft, these date from about 1700, their plain shelves suitable for displaying Oriental porcelain but doubtless often intended for books. Many stood on rebated stands; others on shelved cupboards. Early specimens are markedly plain, the simple rectangles of glass secured with brads and putty behind substantial half-round mouldings which might be veneered in cross-grain walnut or of solid wood with projecting fillets. In the 1740s the glass panel was set on waved framing, often carved with egg-and-dart borders. When the expanse of glass required glazing bars these were in heavy ovolo section.

The 1740s and 50s, however, saw developments in the use of crown glass and at the same time cabinet makers appreciated the chance to introduce strong mahogany for glazing bars that could be much lighter and thinner and highly ornamental. Thereafter some display cabinets were markedly plain, depending upon the decorative lines of the small panes. Often sides as well as front were glazed, but not so much for side viewing as to allow more light upon the contents.

In the 1750s and 60s glazed cabinets for china or books, enriched in accordance with current Gothic notions, might show glazing bars of mahogany shaped and carved in church-window outlines, some detail overlapping the glass. Chippendale freely introduced such detail in glazed bookcase design. His designs for china cases are charmingly light-hearted, for he expected them to be placed in ladies' dressing rooms, for example—the sort of setting expected of mid-18th century japanning. His designs are in the Chinese manner with such detail as pierced frets and pagoda tops, and all but one are mounted on stands. He suggested japanned softwood, but the delicate ornament has lasted better where mahogany has been used.

Later in the century light little china cabinets in the flowing

Hepplewhite style might show glazing enriched with all manner of foliated scrolling, but simple patterns of curves and polygonal shapes were more widely used. Sheraton delighted in pleats and swags of silk behind his cabinet glass. George Smith in 1808 suggested Chinese, Egyptian and Gothic motifs, but subsequently the glazing was treated as of minor importance in rooms where vast sheets of mirror glass might further confuse the furnishings.

Hanging cabinet (Fig. 78): Shallow wall cabinets were made throughout the middle years of the 18th century in architectural pedimented style. Occasionally the front opened with a falling flap in the manner of some early cabinets on stands. More usually a pair of doors revealed the drawers and compartments. An exceptionally fine one designed by Horace Walpole and made in 1743 is at the Victoria and Albert Museum. It is 5 feet high, 3 feet 8½ inches wide, the kingwood doors bearing ivory plaques and the pediment topped by carved ivory figures of Inigo Jones, Palladio and Fiammingo.

The 1750s and 60s delighted in fretted brackets and the airy grace of the hanging cabinet in Chinese taste, often japanned, with the familiar pagoda top and rococo glazing bars. The hanging design escaped the square lines of the usual stand and ended instead in wholly ornamental curving frets. Hanging cabinets might be made in pairs, most frequently glazed, but were never greatly favoured. By far the most popular was the glazed corner cupboard (q.v.).

Lacquer cabinet: Imports by the East India Company in the second half of the 17th century included cabinets and lacquer boards, in keeping with the florid furnishings of the late Stuart court. Later revivals confined them mainly to minor, frivolous rooms during vogues for 'Chinese' ornament until strident Victorian furnishings could again absorb their brilliance. More cabinets with ornament in largely Oriental style show the different, imitative European process of japanning (q.v.). Some early specimens may be ornamented in high relief, in reds and greens or in gold or silver upon a black ground—occasionally a red ground in the last years of the 17th century.

It is important to appreciate that the gorgeous late Stuart cabinets were exceptional masterpieces worthy of the period's most splendid stands and crestings in gilded, carved and gessoed magnificence. But early English japanning was to a large extent a cheap alternative to the costly new finishes of marquetry and veneer. Lady Grisell Baillie in 1715 paid ten shillings for a japanned corner cupboard. A popular treatise on the subject encouraged amateur work from 1688 and it was popular again with young ladies in the 1750s.

The characteristic Oriental cabinet or its japanned imitation is in plain rectangular outline with wide, ornately hinged doors enclosing numerous small drawers. The hand-engraved brass mounts on English work tend to be thicker than the paler zinc-alloyed brasses, sometimes gilded, found on Oriental cabinets. Ornament follows the Oriental themes but disregards the meaning of legend or symbolism and slip-shod squiggles tend to replace meticulous border detail. With the development of more cabinet furniture in European design, however, the tendency was to apply japanning to all the variously arched and pedimented styles of cabinet. Stalker and Parker in their 1688 *Treatise* referred to 'whole sets of japan work—tables, stands, frames, cabinets, boxes, etc.' These early 18th-century cabinets retain the magnificent key escutcheons, corner plates and numerous wide decorative hinges of silver or gilded brass associated with Oriental lacquer specimens, although in some early Georgian japanned cabinets one notes wholly European patterns of flowers and the japanning is noticeably less perfect in quality.

More cabinets, both Oriental and japanned, date from the 1750s and 60s, the ornament applied to the shapes currently popular including glazed and corner cabinets. The general tendency was towards lighter, gayer pieces, the massive panels of ornament being mainly restricted to low-standing drawing room commodes. On cabinets the emphasis was on delicate frets and borders, and some of the most amusing have tops in pagoda outlines supported by fretted corner brackets and with more frets filling the fronts and sides. Such fretted pattern is repeated in much of the minor ornament, with a range of brocade diapers where earlier construction would have required strappings of metal. This detail is conspicuous again in the china cabinets, for example, with many supporting spindles, characteristic of the Victorian revival.

Lacquer cabinets on stands were still important enough in 1786 to be featured on trade cards by Hodson's Looking Glass and Cabinet Warehouse, Soho. The accounts of Chippendale, Haig and Company, around 1772, refer to what was obviously minor japanned work for David Garrick, such as altering a japan cabinet, new lining in the top part with green cloth, new lock hinges and handles and japanning the cabinet, etc., for £3 6s. Oriental cabinet work continued to be imported in the 19th century—over-lavishly gilded and silvered in the opinion of P. F. Tingry in *The Painter and Varnisher's Guide*, 1804, and ill designed. Even the workmanship was less perfect than in earlier pieces.

Among European japanned cabinets it may be difficult to distinguish English work. Some heavy, swelling outlines in early 18th-century cabinets suggest Dutch work, and among details the Dutch may lack dust boards to the nailed drawers and the long cabinet doors may hang on somewhat weak pivot hinges at top and bottom. Even on cabinets less than 6 feet high the early way was often to leave the top surface untreated, a saving that would pass unnoticed when the piece stood against a wall pier between windows in a room lit at night by candles.

Stands for cabinets: These were known in the 17th and 18th centuries as frames. Most late 17th-century stands for walnut cabinets are made of walnut, too, and similarly ornamented with marquetry, etc. Broad mouldings rebated to receive the cabinet are faced by a straight or waved apron frequently containing drawers above six legs—four at the front and two at the back. These legs show the fashions of their day found on side tables. When twist turning is included, however, it is usually reduced in length by combining with baluster shaping —stronger to carry the cabinet weight. Alternatives of the period include cup-kneed trumpet and shouldered S-scroll. Low, flat stretchers are introduced in waved outline above bold bun feet.

In the second period the stand was usually cabriole legged without stretchers and often with two drawers in an apron that might be carved with a scallop shell to match the cabriole knees. The architectural style of furniture popular among the rich in the early Georgian period prompted a brief fashion for cabinets resting on cupboards. But by the 1740s the material and ornament of the stand formed a part of the intrinsic design. The vogue for Chinese cabinets in the 1750s and 60s resulted in stands with pierced Chinese frets in the straight legs and card-cut ornament to correspond in the apron, with corner brackets and occasional diagonal stretchers enriched with Chinese detail. At this time the alternative was rococo scrolling with casual suggestions of pillar and waterfall detail or slightly Gothic notions with cluster-column legs and guttae feet.

Chippendale welcomed the peculiar licence permissable in such display furniture and included in his third edition a flamboyant little rococo cabinet supported by a scrolled cabochoned stand resting on four legs shaped as male demi-figures or Atlantes. The neo-classical style that followed prompted comparatively simple stands with entirely unencumbered legs tapering on their inner sides and ornamented at most with sparse, low relief carving of paterae on the apron and husks down the legs—motifs expressed more often towards the close of the century in paint.

Some particularly decorative turned legs are noted on stands of the last years of the century when designers felt the need for ornamental detail such as a shelf for an urn supported by up-curving stretchers. By then, however, fashion was beginning to show a general preference for furniture with low-set book-shelves and cupboarding on waterleaf, paw or other short feet. Such Regency cabinets as were raised on stands were little more than small boxes for which outcurving 'bamboo' frames—usually turned and painted beechwood—were suitably slight. The stand as a separate entity did not return but may be considered to have developed instead into the Victorian étagère, jardinière and similar tiered supports contributing to the ornamental but flimsy clutter of drawing room and boudoir (*see* Part XI).

Lacquer cabinet stand: This was always European work, carved in softwood and gilded or silvered like the harmonising cresting, even when the cabinet itself came from the Orient where a low plinth was used. Late 17th-century specimens are extraordinarily ornate, the florid carving in Italian Renaissance style including massive scrolling legs shaped as demi-figures linked by deeply carved aprons showing crowns and amorini and, rather later, eagles' heads and acanthus leaves.

Before the end of the century such design gave place to typical French work with straight, tapering legs, often almost equally flamboyant with full relief carving, but with a change soon to greater use of delicate, low relief patterns in gilded gesso. On the other hand, early Georgian stands are in more slender cabriole designs, japanned or gesso-and-gilt, resembling contemporary carved side tables. By the mid-18th century the stand, like the cabinet, would be japanned, as a minor contribution to the general design, with square-cut legs and fretted corner brackets.

PART X

Desk and Bureau Furniture

In the forms we know today this furniture became established only in the last years of the first period in this review. As mentioned in considering chests, some small, lidded boxes in the 16th and early 17th centuries were specified as writing boxes: the earliest desks were writing boxes with slanted lids. The elaborate compartmented specimen owned by the Earl of Northampton in 1614—'a desque with a cobonett therein'— presumably was a Continental forerunner of the delightful fitted desks developed by English cabinet makers.

By the end of the 17th century, however, the simple oaken table box was becoming a country yeoman's piece, unimportant beside the range of handsome walnut furniture being evolved for the man of letters. This included such tall cabinet-style pieces as the fall-front scrutoire and writing cabinet, the bureau-cabinet and the bureau-tallboy. All lent themselves to the architectural furniture treatments of the day, being governed by the same principles of balance and proportion in relation to the tall, dadoed rooms they were designed to enrich. Many were narrow enough to stand against the piers of wall between the windows, but all offered expansive surfaces for the various styles of ornament then in fashion and much dominated through the 18th century from about 1715 by the various forms of broken pediment.

At the same time, for less lofty homes, the cabinet maker developed the bureau desk and the writing table. Bureau, as a term for the early writing box, derived from the colour of the rough woollen forerunner of baize—Latin *burrus*, meaning fire colour. Hence a table, cabinet, chest of drawers, etc., with

84. Bureaux and desks. TOP: two late 17th-century desks, showing (below) their different methods of opening; early 18th-century desk, with runners to support the flap. SECOND ROW: desk on stand, 1700s–40s; desk with pull-out slide, around mid-18th-century; non-committal secretary style for later 18th-century bed-sitting room. BOTTOM: typical examples of the library tables or pedestal desks important from the 1750s, these dating c. 1760s and 1780s.

this prefix implies that it is fitted for desk use. By 1803 Sheraton defined the word bureau in the current more limited sense as being applied to 'common desks with drawers under them.'

The table box-desk mounted on a stand and the bureau or

bureau-desk of Sheraton's definition continued through the period under review with interesting variants such as the straight-fronted secretaire and the massive two-pedestal library table. At the same time the writing table was developed as what is known now as the architect's table. In the late 18th century delicate neo-classical desk designs included the bonheur-du-jour for ladies and the croft for men, and minor bureau modifications may be noted under the headings of cylinder desk and tambour desk. The massive library table was supplemented by such gracious designs as the desk form known as the Carlton House table of the 1790s and Regency years— a period when the library especially lent itself to the devising of much so-called patent furniture.

Patent furniture is a subject in itself. The late 18th and early 19th centuries took a special pleasure in ingenious furniture devices. Important London makers, including George Seddon, Morgan and Sanders, Thomas Butler and the Oxenham firm specialised in it. Their desk and chest furniture ranged from the simple extra-strong units required for military and naval officers to multi-purpose pieces that could be packed closely for emigrants, and to diversions such as the harlequin tables that were illustrated by Sheraton and others.

Collectors note predictable developments of desk and bureau furniture through the 19th century as the various pieces reflected heavy classical, Gothic, revived rococo (Fig. 1) and revived Jacobean (so-called Elizabethan) moods. Late 19th-century desk furniture lent itself particularly to the massive style and heavy metal work of much Art Furniture design, but perhaps the most common early 19th-century desk pieces are the variously fitted workboxes and compendiums and the compact little davenport.

Architect's table (Fig. 86): Probably in greater demand among amateur artists, but certainly the area that can be adjusted to any required slant is larger than in the fitted writing table.

Ince and Mayhew called them merely writing and reading tables. They are found mainly in mahogany and were popular through most of the 18th century, often pleasingly utilitarian. Two main styles are to be noted. The more usual can be extended by pulling out the front apron together with the front portions of the attached front legs (revealing their enclosed strengthening pillars) and a drawer or well that extends for the whole area of the top. This has its own sliding cover so that it serves as a table area when the table top is raised to a slant. There is an adjustable strut for this at the back and often the act of raising this slope releases a spring and pushes out a narrow bead to support books or papers. A quadrant drawer swings out of the framing at the right of the well for ink bottles. Such a design may be variously elaborated, as for instance with drawers or cupboards under the table.

The other main design, which may be combined with the pull-out front, has a top that can be doubly adjusted. The table area hinges at the front and can be slanted with a strut as in the simpler version, but this rests upon a framework which is itself adjustable by means of curved metal ratchets. This hinges at the back so that when opened its front, supporting the slope of the table top, is considerably above table height, suitable for use standing up. When open in this way it offers access to the well in the table framing.

An alternative to the ratchets is another strut for the lower support. This bars access below so that the design had to be further modified with a deep pull-out bureau drawer with a fall-front and covered well. Sheraton used the double strut for his 'drawing table' and added an additional small slide, also adjustable, above for 'a model, etc. to copy from'. The weighty 19th-century piece that emerged from such designs usually rests on drawer pedestals.

A particularly elaborate variant is found among the 'patent' furniture of the early 19th century by Morgan and Sanders.

This rectangular table on the popular 'horse' legs of the period has a rising top supported on a strut. However, the upper row of what are faced to appear as drawers in the framing can be pulled out entirely, hinging at one side, and then unfolded into a slender-legged table with another strutted reading or writing slope fronted by receptacles for pens, etc. (Fig. 90).

Bonheur du jour (Fig. 85): Popular in France around 1760 and thereafter long fashionable in England. Design varied, but typically a small fitted cabinet was placed towards the

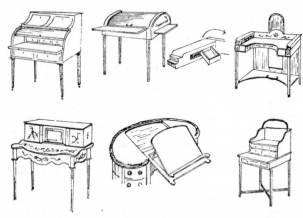

85. Late 18th-century writing tables. TOP: Sheraton cylinder desk, shown slightly open and with writing slide pulled slightly forward; tambour-top table with side and front writing slides that fit over each other when closed; specimen taken from Sheraton design with detail of one of the swing-out tills for ink etc. Sheraton says 'a lady, when writing at it, may receive the benefit of the fire and have her face screened from its scorching heat'. BOTTOM: ornamental version, often termed a bonheur du jour (Mallett); Sheraton detail for a kidney table; case of small drawers with lifting handle known as a sheveret.

back of a shallow writing box with extending flap for writing mounted on the slender, tapering legs of the period. Sometimes spindles edging the lower section to the sides of the cabinet serve as letter racks and frequently there are low galleries of brass or ormolu around the sides and back of the cabinet top. This is essentially a toy for the lady of fashion and appropriately elegant in marquetry or painted satinwood. Specimens in imitation Louis Quinze style, with rococo mounts and undulating legs, frequently date to the Victorian revival. Victorian, too, is the small central mirror which served also as a firescreen.

In the 1860s there was a revival fashion for panels painted in the neo-classical manner with figures in the style of Angelica Kauffmann or mounted with Wedgwood bas reliefs. Striped veneers such as kingwood might be mounted with insets of flower-painted porcelain in imitation of Sèvres.

Bureau bookcase (Figs 87, 90): Called a desk and bookcase by Chippendale and a secretary and bookcase by Shearer. Mirror plates in the tall cabinet furniture of the 1740s might be replaced by clear glazing, and this practice long continued for many of the tall bureau-cabinet pieces plainly shelved above for books. In the 1740s there was a fashion for the glass to be framed in stiles with waved inner edges, often with carved egg-and-dart borders. Wooden doors showed the waved outline in narrow, applied mouldings. But by about 1750 the glass could be framed in attractively light, narrow glazing bars in the period's strong mahogany. As a result, it soon developed into an ornamental feature, the glazing bar patterns reflecting pleasure in fret-cut cresting and card-cut frieze and drawer ornament around 1760.

Such pieces follow the changing fashions in glazed cabinets (q.v.) and may be found with the slant-topped bureau desk below or the fall-front fitted drawer of the secretaire. Chippendale might compose the lower section of two cupboards

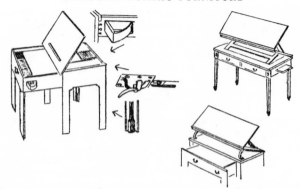

86. So-called architect's or artist's table, from second half of 18th century. LEFT: a typical specimen plainly veneered in mahogany showing the body drawer extended on part of the front legs and the slide covering it partly pushed back to reach the space or fitted compartments within, the ink till swung out at the side and the whole top of the table raised on an adjustable support, an action that releases a bookrest. Details are shown of the till; one of the springs at the back of the rising bookrest, released when the top is raised; and the strong pillars inside the plainly square-cut legs. RIGHT: two alternatives, the upper specimen with a double-folded top resting on easel support, the lower one with curved ratchets to the sides of a slide-topped drawer.

flanking a drawer-fitted kneehole, and Sheraton might back his glass with drapes and pleats of silk.

In the later 18th century this cabinet work tended to be lighter and more restful. Carving was slight and generally limited to classic motifs, sometimes overlapping the glass. Straight cornices were crested with urn finials and swags, for example. Pediments tended to be smaller. Diamond glazing dates from about 1800 and there was more use of brass grills in patterns of diamonds or overlapping curves.

The Regency continued the traditional forms, with the characteristic ornament of the period, but there was a preference for lower bookcases, to be followed by the soaring Gothic fantasies when these pieces lost their pleasing proportions.

Bureau cabinet (Figs 87, 88): The most elaborate form of desk furniture, consisting of a tall cabinet unit resting upon a sloping-fronted desk with drawers below. In some Queen Anne examples the three parts—cabinet, desk and chest of drawers—are still clearly separate units, each with its own lifting handles. Here again design follows that of other contemporary cabinets, but the interior may be extremely elaborately fitted with cyma curves to the tall divisions for ledgers or folio volumes flanking pilastered cupboard and tiny drawers. The small cupboards in cabinet and desk are treated to harmonise.

As the demand was for tall furniture to suit the current increasingly lofty rooms, an early bureau cabinet of around 1700 may show magnificent double-domed cornice and doors, topped occasionally by carved cresting at front and sides or tall vase finials (Figs 80, 81). Below there may be a shallow, cupboarded kneehole between the tiers of drawers resting on pairs of bun feet. Some splendid specimens are ornamented with japanning, others in walnut veneers and many have doors mounted with bevelled mirrors, sometimes engraved. Candleslides may be fitted below the doors, a detail outmoded by the 1740s with the fashion for handsome candlestands. Double domes were followed by many swan-neck pediments from the 1720s and ball or bun feet by corner brackets. Sometimes there is only one door, supporting a splendid piece of mirror plate: always the interior of the doors is superbly finished, since often the piece would be wide open in use.

These pieces continued to be made in mahogany through the middle of the 18th century and later, with less use of mirrors and more pleasure in rich mahogany veneers for doors that became squarer, sometimes flanked by architectural pilasters. Specimens of the 1750s and 60s may show door panelling in attractive waved outlines and fretted pediment above dentil cornice moulding. Feet are ogee brackets. In the later years of the century, however, the main fashion advances are more widely diffused among bureau bookcases.

Bureau desk (Fig. 84): In the second half of the 17th century the compartmented table desk might be combined with a stand in writing table style so that the slightly sloping desk lid, hinged at the bottom, could open out on to a pair of gate legs at the table front. A variant, now rare, and associated with Continental work, had the top folding back on itself and the top 'drawer' front falling open to form a complete writing desk unit—a forerunner of the secretaire.

The desk and stand as a combined unit, of a size and delicacy to appeal to a lady, can be traced through early Georgian days, showing the change to cabriole legs with corresponding shaped aprons and including some finely carved in early mahogany. Frequently there is a drawer in the lower section. Occasionally one is found with its early Georgian mirror-firescreen still in position at the back.

By about 1680 it was becoming more usual, however, to make the lower unit a chest of drawers with straight or shaped front, a projecting plinth mould to balance the projecting edges of the pre-1690 bureau and bun feet—soon giving way to brackets which, however, may prove to be replacements. This quickly became the single unit most sought and copied today. The desk portion acquired a steeper slope to accommodate more elaborate and delightful fittings, and no longer projected beyond the lower section. A kneehole is seldom noted in the genuine piece as it was unnecessary with the projecting flap. Drawers, oak lined at first and usually entirely of oak by the 18th century, show the same changes as in other chests of

87. Cabinet furniture containing desk fitments. TOP: late 17th-century scrutoire with fall-down front and drawer in swelling frieze (the upper portion could be on six-legged stand); Queen Anne curves with detail of desk fitment, the flap resting on runners; design c. 1750. BOTTOM: c. 1750s–60s with pierced pediment but plainer pigeon holes; Hepplewhite style, with detail of pull-out desk drawer; Sheraton, with detail of cylinder desk.

drawers. They might be topped by a writing slide so that the desk slope could serve as a book rest.

The concave curving fronts of the small drawers in the desk portion might be shaped from solid wood, flanking domed pigeon holes around a small domed cupboard with the inevitable 'secret' compartment behind its decorative pilasters. Applied mouldings on specimens around 1700 might mask a secret well for papers, but were a legacy of the two-part desk and soon discarded. Support for the open flap consisted of small oak bearers, square at first but soon matching the depth of the top drawer which replaced the early well.

The piece may be found in mahogany, a particularly fine curl veneer being chosen for the flap which has a lip-moulded edge. Inside, the fittings are beautifully finished, often with ivory or bone for the tiny handles, but lack the curving contours of earlier work. In plain oak for the provincial merchant such a desk may show the late 18th century's ideas of simple ornament with bandings of mahogany and inlay of flower or conch shell motif. Cylinder and tambour styles are associated with the late 18th century, the cylinder continuing in Victorian days.

Bureau tallboy (Fig. 65): Early Georgian variant of the bureau cabinet with the top section made as a further series of drawers, usually with a straight, moulded cornice and frequently showing the typical tallboy canted fluted corners. This is as likely to be found as a tallboy with a fitted fall-front drawer below the central moulding—a tallboy secretaire. For greater convenience there may be concave shaping to the lowest drawer. *See* also WRITING CABINET.

Carlton House table (Fig. 88): This design evolved from the writing table with a superstructure behind the writing area containing drawers and space for books or pigeon holes. Like other writing tables it has drawers in the apron framing and free-standing legs. Its distinction lies in the fact that the top is D-shaped with the sitter on the straight side and with the superstructure following the curve to flank the writing space. Emphasis to the curve is provided by concave-fronted cupboards between the tiers of small drawers and concave-lidded compartments reducing the height of the superstructure towards the front of the writing table. Early specimens of the 1780s have thermed legs; by the 1790s the legs may be turned with characteristic reeded (tassel) cappings. Sheraton illustra-

88. Regency desks, etc. TOP, two details of pediments: Smith's 'Gothic', 1808; Sheraton with anthemion motif on the corner ante-fixae. SECOND ROW: four typical outlines for bookcase glazing bars. THIRD ROW: Regency version of Carlton House table, with tassel tops to ringed legs; typical alternative of D-shaped library table. BOTTOM: six feet and two pilasters from Regency desk furniture.

ted one as a lady's drawing and writing table in 1793. This was to be made in mahogany or satinwood with a brass rim around the top part to be constructed separately. The rising desk portion in the middle was made to slide forward.

The table of the 1790s has been copied ever since. It was especially popular in later Victorian days as a slender little piece on tapering thermed legs and with the central shelving somewhat taller at the centre than the backs of the side receptacles which nevertheless retained the slanting, concave shaping. This broke with the straight horizontal backline, typical of the original, and is particularly characteristic of Victorian work.

Croft: Sold by Seddon, Sons and Shackleton from the late 18th century for 'men of method, especially when travelling, with hinges, corners, etc., convenient for the post-chaise'. Sir Ambrose Heal traced the name to the Rev. Sir Herbert Croft, Bt. It consists of a small table with D-shaped flaps. Below is a drawer fitted with partitions and lidded so that it serves as an extension of the table top for writing and below this again are small drawers and partitions enclosed by a wide door.

Cylinder desk (Figs 85, 87): A feature of some bureau cabinets of the late 18th century and into Victorian days was a rounded top to the fitted writing drawer which could be made to curve upwards and backwards into the body of the piece. At the same time the leather-covered writing surface might be drawn forward from under the pigeon holes to offer more space and perhaps to allow access to a shallow well for papers. This quadrant lid was controlled by a pair of knob handles. It was composed of segments of pine or mahogany glued horizontally and covered with a sheet of veneer.

Davenport (Fig. 89): A lady's desk, extremely convenient and compact. Early designs kept to a box-like outline with a slightly sloping lid covering a fitted well and writing area which

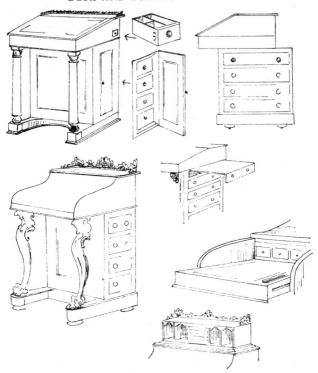

89. Davenports. TOP: early example, with pillar supports, showing also details of ink drawer and the cupboard door concealing drawers; early design, with projecting top. BOTTOM LEFT: later example, with scroll leg and scroll-shaped flap. BOTTOM RIGHT, three davenport details: an early pull-out slide with sham drawer front; pull-out front for writing with pencil wells, etc.; rising top with pigeon holes and drawers.

271

could be extended by slides drawn out from the sides, where also there might be a small drawer for ink bottles. Below, pilasters or carved brackets projected from the solid pedestal body which rested on a plinth or low feet and contained about four deep drawers opening on the right and matched by dummy drawers on the left.

Victorians made only minor changes: in particular the sloping desk lid acquired an S-curve. The writing slide could be extended, giving extra leg room, and contained its own wells for paper and ink. Simple pilasters or turned pillars at the front might be replaced by heavy S-scrolled legs, often coarsely carved. Instead of the Regency's small brass gallery a further nest of drawers and pigeon holes might be made to rise above the back of the desk in the manner of the harlequin table.

Globe writing table: Pitt's cabinet globe writing table was adapted by the firm of Morgan and Sanders, well known for 'patent' furniture, who acquired manufacturing rights of a globe table that was patented 1807. After Pitt's death in 1806 they produced what appeared to be a terrestrial globe on a carved mahogany and gilded stand about three feet high. Pressure on the quadrant finial caused the two upper quarters to slide below, revealing a circular baize-covered writing table. Further pressure raised one of the lower quarters fitted with drawers and pigeon holes. The idea may well have originated with Sheraton. Queen Charlotte bought a globe writing table in 1810.

Harlequin table: A version of the Pembroke table with only slight pretensions as a writing table, but an occasional specimen remains from the late 18th century. In this a small superstructure containing drawers and pigeon holes can be made to rise out of the table top. Sheraton, 1791–4, illustrated one with real and sham drawers in the table framing and noted the need for stronger legs to carry the added weight. Shearer, 1788, suggested also shallow wells in the table flaps and a tambour cupboard below the drawers. He priced his version, complete to the socket castors, at £3 10s. The harlequin table was raised by weights: when fitted with springs it cost an extra 1s. 6d.

George Smith, 1808, called it an appendage to the lady's boudoir. The same notion, which had originated on the Continent, was applied to some early 19th-century secretaires. What appeared to be a solid rectangle of drawers could be transformed by touching a spring into a desk with a fall front backed and flanked by tiers of small drawers and compart-· ments rising out of the sham drawers below. The flat top opened back as end flaps and a firescreen rose behind. *See* also PATENT FURNITURE.

Library table (Figs 84, 88, 90): This developed in the 1720s as a massive table usually with drawers in the apron supported on two wide pedestals of drawers flanking the user but allowing ample leg room. The typical early mahogany specimen, four or five feet wide, has pedestals resting on boldly carved feet or gadrooned plinths. Often the kneehole is flanked by carved corner pilasters. Chippendale illustrates a range of styles from ornate to plain and includes an end extension for a folding book rest, an idea elaborated by Sheraton. Decoration follows the lion, Gothic fret, neo-classical paterae and marquetry motifs characteristic of successive 18th-century moods.

Mahogany was supplemented in neo-classical work by rosewood and satinwood and the general trend through the later 18th century was towards more restrained, square outlines, avoiding the earlier flamboyance. A Shearer design of 1788 is intended for the centre of the room, being serpentine shaped on both fronts and both ends, with fluting to the outthrust corners. The serpentine shaping means that the drawers or alternative cupboards in the pedestals are concave faced.

The broad, low lines suited Regency design, sometimes incorporating bow-fronted pedestals, often corner pilasters

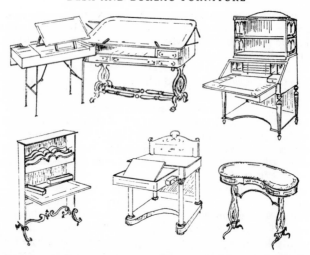

90. Writing tables. TOP: mahogany library table by Morgan & Sanders, the table top slightly raised and a subsidiary folding table erected from what appears, when closed, to be a single wide drawer (Pratt & Sons); Morgan & Sanders writing table shown by Ackermann, 1810. BOTTOM: lady's secretaire, the writing space folding up so that the piece appears to be a smooth-face cheval firescreen; 'lady's screen writing table' design in Smith's *Guide*, 1826; Regency version of kidney writing table.

carved with classic or Egyptian heads and feet in full relief. Many had massive lion paw feet. Some had brass-grilled cupboards in the pedestals and wire galleries at the table ends.

From the Regency on into Victorian days a quite different style of library table was popular, the circular top resting on a turned column with curved legs or a solid base on four paw feet. Drawers or spaces for books were provided under the top. Yet another style had a rectangular top fitted with drawers resting on end supports in 'classic' curved-X outlines, frequently on paw feet. Some had the conventionalised lyre supports on outward-jutting feet considered under the heading of sofa tables. A heavy 'cabinet writing table' is among pieces shown in an advertisement by Morgan and Sanders in *Ackermann's Repository of Arts*, 1810. This has waved legs linked by a long central stretcher. The deep pull-out front has compartments around a central writing area with a well, and is backed by a massive superstructure of drawers and pigeon holes.

Military or ship's desk: This is comparable with the familiar military chest of drawers. The design is a plain rectangular block with flush brass corner straps and sunk brass handles, including carrying handles at the ends, so that it served anyone who sought easy transport and compact storage. Customarily two units would stand on top of each other. The kneehole pedestal desk in this style is less common than the plain chest of drawers. Here the lower unit contains a shallow cupboarded kneehole between the pedestals of drawers. The upper unit may contain a fitted bureau comparable with a harlequin table fitment. The flat top opens back as end flaps and the centre part opens out as a fall-front writing area and to its back and sides is a structure of drawers and pigeon holes, sometimes backed by an adjustable firescreen.

Rent table: Popular name for a late Georgian or Victorian table with a circular, hexagonal or octagonal top deep enough to contain drawers all round the frieze. In an elaborate specimen there may be a lidded well in the table top and the central supporting column may be square instead of circular, so as to house a small cupboard.

Screen writing table (Fig. 90): Many simple designs for ladies' writing tables include adjustable firescreens (Figs 6, 85, 90) but the design so termed—and illustrated, for example, by Shearer—is basically a tall horse firescreen only a few inches deep, the upper part fitted with small drawers which are revealed when the front is let down on a quadrant to serve as a writing board. Shallow cupboards are fitted below. Sheraton used a design of this type for a 'horse dressing glass and writing table' with an adjustable mirror revealed when the fitted writing compartment was opened to a horizontal position.

Scrutoire (Fig. 87): In the later 17th century there was some demand for a form of cabinet on stand which had a falling front instead of a pair of cupboard doors. The name scrutoire may be used on the strength of Bailey's dictionary definition, 1730, as a 'kind of long cabinet with a door or lid opening downwards for conveniency of writing on'. In such a design the whole front, held by metal braces, was utilised while allowing access to large, finely fitted compartments for ledgers, etc. Typically, this piece has a drawer in the swelling frieze below the flat, boldly moulded cornice and a row of drawers in the frieze of the stand which is edged with deep moulding to harmonise. The stand follows the changes of corresponding side table work. More of these pieces are found mounted on chests of drawers.

Secretary, secretaire (Fig. 84): This appears to have been a popular name for the later 18th-century version of the scrutoire—a chest of drawers with a deep, fitted top drawer that pulls forward and has a fall front providing a sizeable writing area. These are less ponderous than the range of study-library furniture and design may include a graceful lattice superstructure for books or ornaments. Alternatively the superstructure is often composed of two small cupboards with a bookshelf between and a low upper shelf for ornaments. There may be cupboards below the fitted drawer and the piece lends itself to the simple Regency outlines, with reeded quarter columns ending in small, turned feet. This style continued well into Victoria's reign with a deep fall front, typical turnery on the corner pilasters and rounded knob handles where these have not been replaced by later fashions. In this piece, as in other desk furniture, it must be remembered that fairly accurate copying of late 18th-century work was popular with late Victorians.

Sheveret, also cheveret (Fig. 85): An obvious development of the writing table was known in the late 18th century as a sheveret. This is a small writing table with a drawer in the frieze, usually with a low shelf between its slender, tapering legs and supporting a separate superstructure—often merely a bookstand. This unit has a handle so that it can be lifted off the table top when extra space is required. The piece was frequently made in satinwood and was a simple alternative to the harlequin table.

Table desk (Fig. 92): This was the earliest desk form, usually found in oak with the carving and panelling and heavy iron mounts required by the Elizabethan and early Stuart squire or small merchant. Such a box may measure as much as three feet across, ornamented on all sides but without legs, its base a broad convex moulding intended to rest upon a table. The first advance was the change from a lifting lid hinged at the top and checked by a chain, to one hinged at the bottom that would open out and serve for writing while allowing access to the interior. This removed the need for the separately lidded box for inks to the right of the main section sometimes included in the early design. Also it prompted a wholly delightful development of the interior fittings. These were cabinet makers' work and date from the later 17th century onwards when, typically, the desk rested on substantial little bun feet.

The interior may include concave-fronted drawers flanking pigeon holes and a central domed cupboard frequently containing 'secret' compartments behind its small pilasters. Some charming specimens in the early 18th century were japanned and a comparable finish is noted in early Victorian specimens of papier mâché. The fashion for such desks continued through the 18th century, and they are found occasionally with contemporary stands. Delightful examples in satinwood veneer with panels of marquetry in neo-classical style were probably gifts sold at fashionable resorts, as were many in Regency and Victorian Tunbridge ware.

At this time, however, many were designed primarily to serve the traveller, so that they tended to become more generalised compendiums and by no means always for women's use. The *London Book of Prices* costed one at 30s in 1788, equipped for shaving as well as business, and in the early 19th century such compendiums, with layer over layer of fitted trays surrounded by bottles and boxes, were made for men, being comparable with the many superb workboxes for women.

Tambour desk (Fig. 85): Desk with rounded lid that opened by curving back into the body of the piece. This was arranged by constructing the lid of narrow laths laid beside each other horizontally and glued to stiff fabric so that the result was sufficiently flexible to be moved with its ends controlled in grooved runners. Shearer illustrated fitted tambour-topped writing tables costing £1 8s and £2 13s with many little drawers and letter holes, also a portable tambour writing box. He suggested a charge of 6d extra for making a tambour front to a cylinder fall desk—the alternative method for a rounded top —which he costed at £3 7s. This work has seldom lasted well.

Work box: Although many were writing boxes, it has seemed best to include these among chest furniture.

Work table (Figs 6, 8, 91, 131): Developed during the second half of the 18th century. The lightly constructed table might have small fly-bracket flaps and sometimes a lower shelf. Its main purpose was the drawer in the framing—occasionally a well within a hinged lid—and, frequently, below this a fabric pouch or bag hanging from a frame which could be drawn forward, allowing access to facilities for minor 'fancy work'. Sometimes a work table, fitted for writing but not for sewing, has a firescreen at the back sliding in a vertical frame so that it can protect either the face or the skirts of the user. Sheraton illustrated both forms, and delighted in ingenious notions for writing slope, ink and pen drawers and the like.

Age may be judged by the style of the leg, plainly tapering, free of stretchers in the 1780s, turned in the early 1800s and thereafter most frequently following the 'horse' outline of sofa tables and the like, the pairs of legs often being in lyre or inverted lyre outline and linked by a low shelf instead of a stretcher. Such a work table may serve also for games with a reversible top inlaid for chess.

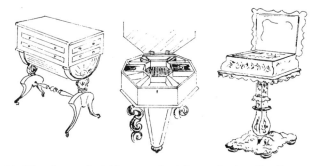

91. Victorian work tables: pouch style continuing the Regency notion of sham, illogical drawers; walnut work table showing fitted interior around central well (this has finely veneered top but poor hinges, cardboard partitions, machine-carved scroll legs); papier mâché work table in the teapoy manner.

Another shape of the period is the pillar-and-claw with a more or less circular lid to the tapering fancy work receptacle ending in dipping claw legs or a footed plinth. The top is rimmed with compartments around the well. George Smith gave one design with four hoofed legs topped by winged chimerae in the Regency manner. His most elaborate included a moveable firescreen, a pouch drawer opening at one end, a writing drawer at the front and an adjustable book rest in the top.

Both horse and pillar styles were popular with early Victorians and are found in flower-strewn papier mâché as well

as walnut. Some are as elaborate as Smith's, but the pouch is usually of wood. The opening lid may serve as the firescreen to the detriment of its veneer, and the legs inevitably tend to be pairs of turned spindles on elaborate projecting feet linked by spiky onions of ornamental turnery.

Writing cabinet: Resembling the bureau cabinet but straight fronted, the writing desk section arranged as a fall-front drawer in the manner of the secretaire. Sometimes, to ensure stability, part of the chest framework flanking the three lower drawers may be pulled forward when the writing drawer is opened in a manner seen in the architect's table. This, too, may be found in the tallboy version. (Figs 65, 87).

Writing table (Figs 85, 88, 90, 92): This began in the later 17th century with the delightful little table with a folding top that opened out onto two hinged additonal gate legs at the front (Fig. 44). Before the end of the century some were made with drawers in the front apron. Such tables show the characteristics of their period and are paralleled by similar tables with fixed tops: again there are four legs at the front, often reduced in length to support several drawers, and there may be additional drawers in the centre set back to allow knee space.

From this developed the kneehole desk and the pedestal library table. But at the same time simple tables on four free-standing legs were adapted as writing tables by introducing suitable writing drawers and superstructures. In Chippendale

92. Victorian writing tables. TOP: 'Louis XVI' with painted china insets; late 19th-century example in Hepplewhite style stamped with name of Marsh, Jones, Cribb & Co., Leeds, each drawer, leg, etc., showing six lines of contrasting woods (detail, centre, showing one of the fitted shoulder pieces containing ink, etc.). SECOND ROW: popular but poor design; fitted writing desk on stand in papier mâché; 'Louis XV' with fitted drawers. BOTTOM: with brass rail; 'commercial and diplomatic despatch writing desk' by F. Waller, 1851; by C. F. A. Voysey, 1896 (V. and A. Museum).

design the flowing French legs may support a top extending in scrolling curves to cover double drawers flanking the sitter, with a single drawer and arched apron in the centre front. Above, the writing space is backed by cupboards, pigeon holes and drawers.

This sort of design was widely popular with or without the lower drawers and was followed in the 1770s by squarer pieces with straight ,tapering legs and with an increasing ingenuity in their fittings. For the lady these might include a sliding fire-screen, and there was considerable effort to design fitted dressing tables for both men and women that would serve also as writing tables and take their place among living room furniture. By the 1780s some were made with cylindrical fall tops, others with tambour tops, some being elegant little pieces. The top might be enclosed by flaps in the dressing table manner and the fittings might include a folding book rest or writing board where one might expect a looking glass.

PART XI

Book Shelves and Racks

Early books were few and precious so were kept in boxes. In the 18th century panelled cupboards gave place to glazed cases, but only in the second half of the century did books become numerous and popular enough to oust porcelain ornaments from the open shelves that decorated the living room and become acceptable on top of minor cabinet furnishings. Collectors may delight in a range of small furniture pieces of the late 18th century onwards specifically designed to accommodate books too useful—or too trivial—to be shut away in library bookcases. These included more commodious hanging shelves; bookstands; bookshelves in association with small cabinets; bookshelves flanking the cupboards of the chiffonier; commode-style bookcases.

For music and similar matter the rack design known as a canterbury came into use, mentioned by Sheraton and persisting through Victorian days, its carved partitions comparable with the work noted on many a small book-rack of the day. For still more casual use the 19th century had the whatnot from Regency days and the more stately étagère.

Bookcase (Fig. 93): The tall glazed bookcase on a chest of drawers has been mentioned among desk, bureau and cabinet furniture (Figs 87, 88). Around 1800 some were made on a small 'dwarf' scale, with perhaps a couple of bookshelves above the usual secretaire drawer and cupboard. Here the collector may find particularly attractive presentation of such Regency detail as bandings in exotic woods; antefixae on the low cornice; corner pillars or pilasters; lion handles and other detail in gilded brass. The end-of-century interest in rather

93. Regency bookshelves, etc. TOP: chiffonier with corner pilasters and brass rail; hanging shelves with ends of brass wire; chiffonier outline elaborated into writing cabinet. SECOND ROW: 'Egyptian' pilaster commode style with pleated silk over shelving; circular design with brass grilles; Smith 'Gothic' bookstand, 1808. BOTTOM: typical plain breakfront bookcase; two Egyptian pilasters and between them Thomas Hope design for chimera leg.

284

more unconventional design is exemplified in a Sheraton octagonal library table supporting a bookcase illustrated in his *Encyclopaedia*. Open shelving of comparable design is mentioned among bookstands.

The taste of the period for low, solidly based furniture was expressed in many a wide bookcase on conventional lines, but of no more than table height: this may be regarded as one of the period's most attractive contributions. Smith noted in 1826 that it left space on the wall above for paintings. The top was often rimmed with a Gothic brass fret and the front filled with brass wire grille backed by pleated silk: Smith suggested that this would 'give repose to the eye, for nothing can distress the eye more than the sight of a countless number of volumes occupying one entire space'. He advised yellow or pink silk behind the glass of his bookcase doors in Chinese, Egyptian and Gothic styles. Around 1800 the feet might be turned stumps (Fig. 88), but a little later brass paws became more usual. Some living room bookcases were made to harmonise with Regency sofa and games tables, the two-shelf rectangular cupboard supported on trestle columns and outcurving feet linked by a central, turned stretcher.

By the 1810s and 20s bookcases tended to be more massive. There would be a heavy plinth instead of feet, suitably projecting to receive pairs of substantial pilasters or colonnettes each side of the main bookcase. Sometimes the top was a marble slab; sometimes with a small upper shelf towards the back for ornaments. In others the mood of the 1830s was expressed in greater use of carved mouldings and more wastage of space in the flanking ornament. Victorians continued this useless panelling to frame the shelves but tended to give the piece greater height. Carved enrichment included much 'Elizabethan' oak with strapwork or caryatids, bringing a reaction in the second half of the century expressed in many massive, plain bookcases, such as the forthright designs of

94. Canterbury music stands, early 19th century and Victorian. Bottom row, centre, is in papier mâché.

Eastlake and his admirers and the tall, narrow pieces of the late years of the century, many in ebonised wood.

Bookstand (Figs 93, 96): Late 18th century and onwards, composed mainly of open shelves. It might be three or four feet high and was sometimes called a moving library. This was a plain little piece, but some of the finest were in costly solid satinwood; others occasionally showed the bright glint of brass lattice at the shelf ends. Often the base was a drawer or cupboard with short, sturdy feet equipped with castors. The curved receding line of the shelf ends is attractive and characteristic, the smallest shelf at the top often rimmed with a brass gallery. Those of the Regency might be mounted on heavy gilded paws. Some were japanned, some of beechwood painted black with pictorial ornament on the cupboard panels.

Smith, in 1808, followed the current convention for wide, low furnishings by designing open bookshelves flanked by pedestal cupboards instead of putting the cupboards below the books. The horizontal line of the top could then be a little higher at the ends, as in sideboards of the day. Smith called his bookstands chiffoniers and gave them elaborate corner pilasters, ranging from Gothic columns and vase turnings to winged chimerae and Egyptian figures. Victorians continued this style, with receding shelves and base drawers, but edged the top and filled the sides with clumsy carving.

A revolving stand was patented in 1808 by Benjamin Crosby who suggested it might be 'circular, square or other convenient shape . . . with cases to receive books, as well as various other articles and things.' In this the shelves revolved around a central pillar. Remaining specimens usually consist of circular diminishing tiers of books on a tripod or claw base. The difficulty of fitting books into circular shelves was overcome by using occasional wedges backed as sham books. Victorians developed the square version, based upon four castor-footed claw legs. This might be regarded as a compromise between bookshelves and whatnot, consisting of about four shelves held by four vertical end boards ornamentally shaped or fretcut, each covering only half of one side of the stand to permit access to the books while giving them some support.

Canterbury (Figs 94, 98): A word of two meanings at the end of the 18th century. Sheraton referred to a plate and cutlery stand (*see* DINING ROOM FURNISHINGS) and to a music stand 'made with two or three hollow topped partitions, the legs with castors adapted to run in under a pianoforte'. The early design was a plain rectangle with sides and partitions of a simple open fret, the turned corner posts extending below the base to form short legs on socket castors. Sometimes a shallow drawer for sheet music was included in the base. The partition top rails were rounded and smooth, each with a slight central dip for easy withdrawal of the music. Mahogany was the usual wood but such pieces may be found, too, in rosewood and in Victorian walnut and papier mâché.

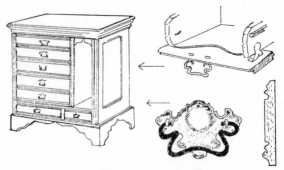

95. Music cabinet with fall-front drawers, shown in detail (right) enabling flimsy music sheets to be handled safely, the pin-hinge a patent of H. Stone & Son. Detail of the handle reverting to the earliest style of loop attachment of early 18th century; and detail of machine-shaped run moulding typical of much Victorian cabinet making, breaking away from all suggestions of panels, whether real or simulated.

Smith in 1808 suggested simple low designs with plain square-cut legs and Gothic fret-cutting for sides and partitions. Regency design included diagonal lattice between the square-cut rails, but spoiled the line by introducing the inescapable claw feet jutting out from a rectangular underframing. These usually ended in brass paws and castors. All too soon the piece became more ornate. Many had ornamentally carved partitions, including the obvious lyre motifs with brass strings. The papier mâché firm of Jennens and Bettridge showed a canterbury at the 1851 exhibition. In such ornate work the elaborate outlines of the partitions were matched by fussy, scrolling legs. Others were enriched with brass or ormolu. But later in the period lighter canterburies proved more practical.

Among the most attractive Victorian specimens are the

turners' pieces composed almost entirely of handsome little spindles. The fashion for bamboo prompted the construction of many bamboo canterburies, including some of table height and others in conventional shape even to the castors upon their slender, curving legs, their only ornament being small panels of lacquer. Occasionally at this time the term canterbury was extended to include the music stool or seat when this was fitted for storing sheet music.

Chiffonier (Fig. 63): This piece, fashionable from the 1800s, has been considered among cabinet furniture as a successor to the commode. It often included open shelves for books or ornaments above and to the sides of its cupboards. But the name was applied to several pieces of furniture. Smith used it for some open bookshelves of the kind considered above as book-stands (Fig. 93). Some bookcases of the Regency's low-topped style were flanked by cupboarding so that they could be treated ornamentally yet 'contain all the books that may be required in a sitting room without reference to the library'.

Hanging shelves (Fig. 93): A framework of shelves might be of oak in the Tudor yeoman's home, joiner made, to measure perhaps two feet square and six inches deep with a shelf across the middle, making three open shelves in all. The front edges of the framework and shelf would be trimmed with two- or three-inch facings of oak that might be carved, inlaid or painted. A few were boarded at the back. Seventeenth-century specimens tended to be wider than their height, and the top might be enriched with two round-headed arches and a corbelled cornice. Some were made to dismantle, the cross planks slotted through the side pieces and held rigid with wedges.

Some shelves for books were made entirely plain, without the facings required for breakable glass or pottery. But by the 18th century more cabinet furniture was available and open shelves became important, like brackets and other fret-cut furnishings, when the period's dense mahogany charmingly met the current demand for making a great display of porcelain ornaments.

It is interesting to note that even by the 1760s such shelves, too, were in demand for books: Chippendale in 1754 illustrated a number of 'very light, but very strong' china shelves with Chinese and Gothic frets decorating the sides and partitions and perforated galleries edging the shelves and, sometimes, pseudo-brackets below. But in his third edition of the *Director*, 1762, he added shelves for books when his competitors, Ince and Mayhew, showed pagoda-topped bracket-based pieces in the same mood as 'book and china shelves'.

For books less elaborate ornament was expected, and some of the most delightful mahogany fret-work shelves consisted merely of three or four graduated tiers of plain shelves between fret-cut sides that extended in curved outline above the top and below the bottom shelf. In some the top was galleried for porcelain and the base fitted with a row of three shallow drawers, the sides extending below as small brackets. Sometimes a backboard appeared above and below the shelves as cresting and back apron. Solid-sided hanging shelves were in fashion when Hepplewhite in his *Guide*, 1788, noted that they 'are often wanted as Bookshelves in closets or Ladies' rooms' and showed solid and fretted ends. A fashion of his day hung such shelves, tall and narrow with a drawer below, over a small side table with similar marquetry ornament. One design, suggesting the farmhouse dresser, with a scroll pediment, had some of the shelves flanked by small cupboards above a row of shallow drawers.

Sheraton in his *Dictionary* noted that 'small open hanging shelves are for books under present reading, and which a lady can move to any sitting room ... They should also find a place in the tea room or breakfast room ... in mahogany or satin-wood, banded on the edges of the shelves which are seldom

96. Whatnots, étagères. TOP, whatnots: with brass galleries (shown in detail); with elaborate gallery (shown in detail) and well turned supports; with top drawer and shaped shelves. SECOND ROW, bookstands or étagères: with diminishing shelves, third quarter of 19th century; with turned spindle supports. BOTTOM: corner whatnot (details of shaped shelves and turned foot on castor); late 19th-century piece showing Japanese influence; 1890s bamboo design.

more than two in number exclusive of top and bottom'. Generally, it seems, they were about 2 feet wide, but some were as much as 5 feet, and 9 inches deep.

Some effectively simple hanging shelves appeared around 1800. Three plain shelves were held at the corners by eight colonnettes in wood, baluster turned, or in brass, sometimes with brass cross-pieces to fill the ends of the shelves and small brass finials above and below. During the Regency this design might be elaborated with brass ornament on the shelf edges and sometimes with brass lyres filling the shelf ends. Frequently, it appears, each shelf was intended to hold twenty-four volumes of novels. Smith, in 1808, caught the mood of the period in shelves substantially based but receding so that the top shelf was no more than a narrow ledge for ornaments. Deep scrolls as shelf ends emphasised the line and appeared in reverse as brackets. He placed very similar shelves upon a design for a drawing room pier table which was supported by leopard-headed spavin legs on a plinth base.

Whatnot (Fig. 96), **étagère, omnium:** The whatnot was made from the 1790s onwards, dating in name from the first decade of the 19th century, composed of three or four tiers of square or rectangular shelving for books and bric-à-brac accessible from all sides, the shelves supported on corner columns of turned spindles. This might be as much as four feet high, the top and shelves edged with brass fret galleries. There might be ornament on two shallow drawers below the shelves, raised upon castored feet. The small peg feet of around 1800 may be noted or an early, slender version of the Regency's elbowed lion paws.

The whatnot, often made in pairs, became a standard furnishing from about 1840. A trestle variant of this period had a single support at each end with outward-jutting legs, the standards being considerably wider and heavier than the usual corner columns. A three-sided variant for a corner came into greater use from about 1855, with attractive shaping to the front line of each shelf. At first the usual wood was mahogany or rosewood, but many Victorian specimens were made in walnut, heavily scrolled and carved on the corner supports and the aproned base, with outward-turned scroll feet. Many had twist-turning for all vertical members. Among the most attractive were those with spindles throughout, elaborately turned in baluster shapings, from the pointed finials to swelling feet. Late in the century some were elaborately ornamented with fret-work; others were in bamboo.

Such pieces are often also called étagères. But the term is better reserved for a more substantial piece of furniture that originated in France and expressed the changing styles of Louis Quinze and Louis Seize. This was basically a table which had one or two upper shelves above the central area supported on carved or turned columns. In the Louis Quinze rococo style the legs were cabriole curved and mounted with ormolu; later the table, oval or D-ended, rested on tapering fluted legs and the shelves above on smaller harmonising columns.

PART XII

Dining Room Furnishings

Chairs and tables are subjects to themselves (Parts III and IV) and cupboards are considered in Part IX, but other furniture pieces associated with the dining room are sufficiently closely interlinked to require reviewing together. The collector can then trace the development of the side or serving table into the court cupboard, the low dresser and the dresser surmounted by shelving. He can see how the mid-18th century's sideboard table came to be flanked by pedestals and how this arrangement in turn became unified as the delightful late 18th-century sideboard. He can understand the subsidiary contributions of such sideboard accessories as the plate pail, butler's tray, knife box, wine cooler and cellaret to the formal dinner and equally the way servant-free informal meals were facilitated by the canterbury, dinner wagon and ubiquitous dumb waiter.

Buffet: *See* COURT CUPBOARD.

Butler's tray (Figs 51, 98): Called by Sheraton a sideboard for the butler. Specimens are known from the 1720s and they continued in use through the 19th century. Design varied in detail but the basis was a handsome tray, often more than thirty inches wide, and a folding stand on which to rest it. The tray could be carried into the room fully prepared with wines and glasses and placed where the butler could serve the company. The tray was usually rectangular, sometimes elliptical in the late 18th century, with hand holes in the galleries unless the fretted ornament served this purpose. In a plain Regency specimen the gallery was lower on the side next to the butler: Sheraton noted that 'one end should be made nearly open'. He recommended good quality Spanish mahogany for the

97. Dressers. TOP: early 18th-century dresser with corner knops, wide back boards; four outlines of the side pieces supporting the shelves. SECOND ROW: detail of top from c. 1750 with dentil moulding and cut-out frieze ornament; detail of gouge-cuts masking the joins of shelf and side vertical; more elaborate dresser with base board. BOTTOM: later 18th-century dresser with country-cabriole legs (detail of herringbone chequer inlay on drawers and cupboards).

tray bottom to withstand the stains of the glasses and liquors. His suggested dimensions were 27 to 30 inches long by 20 to 22 inches wide.

The stand was most simply composed of two pairs of X legs linked by end bars which held the strips of webbing that supported the tray. A rarer alternative was a stand with four straight legs and X-shaped stretchers, so that the folding movement was horizontal instead of vertical. There were small changes in the shaping of the stand legs, square-cut with moulded edges in the 1760s and 70s, turned and ringed with conspicuous square jointing in the late 18th century and on into the Regency and thereafter plainly rectangular. A variant came to be known as a coach table. This has X legs fixed to the wooden top which lacks a gallery and is hinged down the centre to fold flat vertically.

Canterbury: *See* PLATE STAND.

Cellaret, garde de vin, gardevin (Figs 100, 102): Differing from a wine cooler in being a lidded, locked piece of furniture for keeping wine in the dining room, the interior compartmented for bottles. It was introduced to accompany the Georgian sideboard table which lacked cupboards or pedestals, being low enough to stand underneath it: hence the term cellaret sideboard for the sideboard which included a metal-lined cupboard partitioned for bottles. Hepplewhite noted that the cellaret was usually made of mahogany hooped with brass, lacquered and lined with lead and could be of any shape. It must be realised that this furnishing, like the wine cooler, was affected by changes in bottle proportions. Until the 1760s wine bottles were six inches or more in diameter and short bodied. In the 1760s, however, they became taller, some five inches across, and during the 1770s and 80s taller still, some four inches across, reduced to about three and a half inches in the 1790s. This tended to result in taller, less squat, cellarets late in the century. Sheraton distinguished between spirit cellarets for square bottles and wine cellarets to hold six, eight or ten round-based wine bottles.

Remaining specimens show the change from the heavy commode shape of the 1750s and 60s to the taller, less expansive rectangles, squares, octagons and cylinders of neo-classic taste, attractively simple in their applied mouldings or marquetry motifs. Sometimes the design included a stand, but more often the piece was a single unit including tapering fluted legs, often on castors for pulling from under the sideboard table. Around 1800 there was inevitable use of paw feet and even the central four-claw support to a cellaret in the prevailing rectangular outline, harmonising with the pillar-and-claw dining table. Sheraton in 1803 noted the fashion for the sarcophagus form with tapering sides. This century saw various fitted designs. The upper half of the stand might be enclosed to form a receptacle for glasses and decanters or the whole stand might be enclosed, mounted on bracket feet, with a door in the front to give access to storage space.

Chiffonier (Fig. 63): Sometimes served as a small sideboard. *See* CHESTS OF DRAWERS.

Court cupboard (Fig. 79): This was essentially for display, a status symbol conveying an air of solid grandeur. As a side table or buffet it was used by servants to set out the drinking vessels which they carried to the diners as required: hence it offered the rich host an opportunity to display his finest plate on suitably handsome cupboard cloths. As it was *court* or short to take a minimum of space among the jostling servants it was given the necessary surface area by being tiered, thus becoming the more conspicuous. In royal and noble households at formal meals the number of tiers in a 'cupboard of estate' was decided by the owner's rank from the sovereign downwards—an alternative explanation for the term court applied to a cupboard which, in fact, was common enough in yeoman homes by the 17th century and continued to be made into the 18th century with a countryman simplicity. It requires no more than a brief mention here because as a fashionable piece it was largely a 16th- and 17th-century product, and typical specimens are rare outside museums. Most of those now encountered are Elizabethan-Victorian.

As explained in the survey of cupboards, the name was mistakenly applied by earlier collectors to massive enclosed cupboards. It is now accepted that the court cupboard consisted of open shelves, usually three, mounted on corner pillars. Average dimensions were about 4 feet high, 4 feet wide and 18 inches deep. Top and centre shelves often had drawers in wide friezes that offered opportunities for carving with elaborate strapwork, guilloches and gadroons, or simple geometrical inlay. The two rarely matched, and the bottom shelf or pot board was most often merely moulded at the edge. Even the pillars at the front corners did not always match, the upper pair sometimes carved as fabulous animals or given other more elaborate ornament. When the pillars were in the most familiar bulbous cup-and-cover design the lower pair were often elongated. The back supports were plain posts intended for the shadows of the wall.

In fine work the wood was oak or walnut and traces of gilding have been noted. Others were of beech painted red or green. In the later court cupboards for 17th- and 18th-century farm and villa the columns became ordinary balusters, neatly turned and ringed but not carved, and the frieze drawer fronts were given no more than perfunctory repetitive ornament. By the mid-17th century the shelves were less deep and the piece was merely a plate rack—sometimes grooved for this purpose—comparable with the shelving that transformed the farmhouse dresser in the 18th century.

Dinner wagon: In the 19th century a set of open shelves on castors continued the court cupboard's service in the dining room under the name of the running footman from the 1800s

98. Dumb waiters, trays, and stands. TOP, dumb waiters: 1810–15; 1800s with brass gallery; with turned colonettes supporting upper tables. BOTTOM: Sheraton 'dumb waiter' for cutlery, etc.; two butler's trays, the upper sometimes called a coaching table because it folds flat with central hinge; early 19th-century stand for cutlery and plates in a style also found with four vertical legs.

and, more familiarly, dinner wagon to Victorians. This resembled a Victorian whatnot with rectangular trays, usually supported at each end by a single wide standard on the customary jutting feet of trestle furniture. The trays might be galleried but were often left plain on one or all sides for ease of un-loading. (Fig. 98).

Dresser (Figs 97, 101): Like the nobleman's court cupboard, this was a side table primarily intended to display the family's finest table equipment, whether silver, pewter, tin or earthenware. It came into wide use as Tudor families took to dining in a parlour, away from the throng of retainers in the hall, and by the 17th century it might be as much as seven feet long and two feet deep, a table still without any superstructure but often fitted with a row of drawers. At the front it was supported by either three or five shapely turned legs, stretcher-linked and at the back by flat corner posts. Glowing nut brown wain-scot oak was used, or elm or fruitwood, with little ornament save the attractive grain.

Collectors note the changing styles of moulding around the drawers, such as the most conspicuous applied border and panel moulds in a variety of geometrical shapes mitred at the corners and projecting beyond the drawer face. Sunk panels succeeded this style, but tended to be poorly finished as the piece lost any direct association with the furniture of high fashion. Fielded panels are noted on 18th-century specimens or coarse bandings of walnut or mahogany.

Swash turned legs are noted occasionally on a late 17th-century dresser, but far more on subsequent reproductions. As an interesting variant one may find the joiner's substitute for such costly turning, with waved or baluster outlines cut from flat boards (Fig. 49). The table top of the early dresser was finished on front and sides with bold moulding, matched beneath the row of drawers. But around 1700 a deep wavy-edged apron might be introduced beneath the drawers as a slight concession to prevailing fashion.

The first step towards greater elaboration came around 1690 with a low back board behind the dresser top, occasionally fronted with a row of small drawers. Crossbandings of walnut might be introduced, but the dresser retained its homely style to suit the prospering middle-class home. When a rack of shelves was hung above it this was intended for the English delftware that remotely imitated costly Chinese porcelain in the early 18th century. Such a rack in its original state usually lacked backboards.

From this arrangement the country furniture maker evolved the tall, shelved dresser for the yeoman home, occasionally incorporating such fashion details as cabriole shaping and shell carving to the front legs—now customarily two—and retained long after high fashion had forgotten them. The main feature, however, was the superstructure which in a dresser of good quality included ornamental shaping not only to the cornice frieze but also to the front edges of the side uprights and to the apron below the row of drawers in the lower section. Sometimes two small cupboards flanked the lower shelves, their doors arched, with fielded panels, perhaps, and small central inlay motifs.

A variant of this dresser design introduced a pair of cupboards to fill the space below the drawers. This was popular in North Wales, but the term Welsh dresser dates to no earlier than late Victorian days. The style has as little direct regional association as has Yorkshire with the 19th-century dresser dominated by the round face of a clock high in the shelving.

Dumb waiter (Fig. 98): Variant of the circular pillar-and-claw table, with two or three tiers of trays in diminishing sizes above the table top. Its height ranged from about 40 to 60 inches, with 24 to 30 inches for the diameter of the lowest tray. Easily moved on castors, it was widely used through the 18th and 19th centuries for side table service at informal suppers, after-dinner drinking and especially for the elegant little refreshments known as desserts, offered in great abundance at informal party gatherings. Frances, Lady Colepeper, mentioned one in her will in 1738 and they figure in records of the 1750s, being welcomed by those who distrusted their gossip-carrying servants and preferred their meals unattended. But as late as the 1770s press comment indicated that this English invention was only then becoming acceptable in France.

As with other pillar-and-claw furniture there is a marked distinction between the dumb waiter produced expensively by the cabinet maker and the simpler turner's work. In the costly early specimen of fine mahogany the baluster units below and between the tiers were elaborately carved, perfectly fitting together to enable the trays to revolve smoothly without rocking. The top tray rested upon the top of the spindle, being thickened on the underside by a wooden flange. More carving ornamented the knees of the claw legs and in some instances low carved rims or vertical lattice galleries ringed the tray tops. But for the most part the specimens that remain are turners' work.

Turners were advertising dumb waiters by the 1750s. Each tray was shaped from a single piece of mahogany or less desirably of two pieces almost invisibly joined, thick enough not to warp and slightly dished in the course of the lathe shaping so that the edge formed a low rim. Occasionally, like the claw table, the edge was rounded into scallops and these might be dished for individual vessels. The surface was laboriously polished to a hard surface known as teaboardy. Stem sections were in vase form, the upper part often fluted and the lower swelling gadrooned. In a well-made specimen the whole stem tapered gracefully in harmony with the diminishing sizes of the upper trays, and by the mid-1770s it might lack even the distraction of surface ornament. Leg outline lost the early bold curves. A thick sole of wood under each pad foot, of opposing grain, made it possible to attach a castor. Until the 1770s these were composed of leather discs.

The less vigorous designs approved by the late 18th century often included dipping claw legs in place of the earlier arching

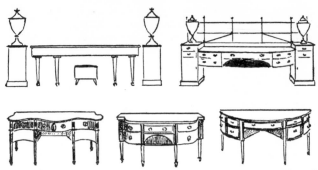

99. Sideboards. TOP: mid-18th century method, with a sideboard table flanked by pedestals; the full sideboard—illustrated, for example, by Shearer in 1788. BOTTOM, simpler pieces evolved during 1775–1800: with serpentine front; with subsequent bolder shaping and cupboard with tambour front; late half-round style, veneered in contrasting woods.

S-line; some were reeded and reeding appeared, too, on some vertical tray rims. Sometimes the central tray was fitted beneath with hinged candleslides. From about 1800 the trays might be flat surfaced, too thin to be shaped with rims. Brass socket swivel castors projected from the ends of the claw legs, fixed without the aid of screws. Cast fluting or reeding on horizontal brass sockets directly over the swivelling wheels dates from about 1805.

Two-tier dumb waiters date mainly from the 1780s onwards and were little more than three feet high. As with the three-tier variety of this period the upper tray occasionally contained a turned finial for tightening the stem units. But by the 1790s other innovations were being devised for what had become almost entirely a dining room accessory. Sheraton gave a two-tier specimen four dipping legs. He equipped the lower tray

303

with drawers for cutlery and galleried its surface for plates, decanters and the like. On the upper tier he suggested a low gallery to guard the wine glasses. Reference is made among social tables (Part IV) to his three-tier dumb waiter for dessert plates, wine glasses and candelabrum.

The four-claw leg prompted Regency development of rectangular trays around an octagonal stem on a reeded pillar. Such trays were more easily fitted with drawers and candlestands; the top one sometimes folded with hinged flaps, and folding flaps on wing brackets became usual as furniture makers faced a wartime shortage of large-girth mahogany. Smith suggested pedestal bases for massive two-tier specimens with Gothic detail in 1808.

An unattractive variant dating to the early 19th century dispensed with the central pillar. In this design a pillar-and-claw table with a revolving top supported three colonnettes as legs to a second tier and this in turn might be topped by a similar construction. Sometimes the colonettes were of cast brass matching brass galleries on the trays. From about 1820 there might be four colonnettes for each tray and all the trays of equal size.

Knife box (Fig. 102): Decorative receptacle for the silver flatware and cutlery used in the dining room—the forerunner of the flat box known to late Victorians as a canteen. Valuable tableware was washed in the dining room for each course and never risked loss in the kitchen quarters. The boxes were compartmented to hold them handle or bowl upwards and the owner could tell at a glance if any were missing. Randle Holme illustrated such a case in 1649 with a flat, forward-sloping lid and canted front corners at a time when it might be of walnut or covered with leather or shagreen or japanned and gilded.

Shagreen was customary in the early 18th century when the case would be lined with velvet. In about 1760 John Folgham offered shagreen and mahogany knife cases, and his trade card showed a case with two dozen knives, pistol handled, and a dozen each of forks and spoons, the spoons in the rounded front of the case. Folgham was a specialist case maker, the work being too specialised for the 'regular cabinet shops' as mentioned by Sheraton. The shaping of the deal case and the application of decorative veneers on so small a scale was delicate work, the shape customarily including a rounded or serpentine front and sloping top. Cock beading on box and lid rims masked the joining of veneer and carcase wood and the tiers of interior partitions had to be lined with velvet or baize, sometimes with a panel of cedar between the baize and the wood of the lid for protection against moth or tarnishing damp. Silver mountings were frequent until the 1770s and were not wholly replaced by brass until the 19th century.

Such cases were made in pairs and sets of three through the second half of the 18th century and in sets of four towards 1800. They were at their most ornate in the neo-classical fashions of the 1760s onwards, in satinwood ornamented with marquetry or delicately painted, but many more were of mahogany. The interior was simplified by introducing a panel of polished wood pierced with apertures in the shapes required to hold the different articles in place, sometimes with each aperture edged with chequer stringing. The lid interior might show a fan or star motif in inlay or marquetry, while the sloping outer surface might carry the owner's coat of arms. Stringing became popular on the outside of the case late in the century and cross banding around the front panel and the lid. Early in the 19th century the bold front curve of the case was narrowed and flattened, either with a convex pilaster each side or with narrow concave corners. Other knife cases were of japanned wood with chinoiserie scenes.

The vase shape associated with the sideboard pedestal of the 1760s reflected the fashion for the classical urn shapes. Sophie von la Roche in 1786 noted with approval in London 'three vases to hold spoons, knives and forks. These pieces are extremely tasteful in ornamenting a dining room'. The design usually had a round stem on a square plinth which might have a bracket foot at each corner. Because it was difficult to hinge the circular lid, the dome cover of the vase case was supported on an extending shaft rising from the centre of the body. The cutlery was placed concentrically in a circular rack fitting into the rim of the vase.

In the 19th century the knife box, like the wine cooler, tended to be a four-sided sarcophagus shape (Fig. 100), tapering downwards like the pedestal below and frequently raised on four feet of gilded brass under the canted corners. By then it was usual to fix the box to the pedestal. Sideboard design might also include alternative uses for its pedestal urns (q.v.).

Omnium: *See* DINNER WAGON.

Plate pail and voiding pail (Fig. 102): Straight-sided bucket shape with bail handle for ease of carrying between remote kitchens and the dining room; usually made in pairs. The plate pail may be distinguished at a glance by its opening from top to bottom, essential for lifting the plates out of the vessel. The sides were often perforated, which allowed for keeping the plates warm near the fire at informal meals. At their most ornate around the mid-18th century such perforations might be Chinese or Gothic tracery frets, but more were pierced with plain vertical pales. The bail handle was often attached to a brass rim-he p. The voiding pail was a sturdier vessel, comparable and often confused with the plate pail but lacking the side slit. Such pails had several uses. They served for removing crumbs, etc., between courses. They could supply the water for washing glasses and cutlery during the meal. They could be used as wine coolers. For all such purposes an essential was a metal lining, often missing in specimens found today which, typically, are of plain, handsome mahogany bound with several bands of brass to harmonise with the late Georgian wine cooler.

Plate stand (Fig. 98): Associated with the second half of the 18th century. Like a dumb waiter the piece obviated the need for servants at informal suppers, for example. It might consist of no more than a stool-like piece with a spindled gallery around its top with spaces for lifting off the plates—a legged plate pail. Alternatively it might have a compartmented top part round-ended for plates and part rectangular with divisions' for cutlery, etc. It was essentially mounted on castors, but the leg arrangement varied from the pillar-and-claw to four unconnected legs, straight or splayed.

Sheraton devised an elaborate design and applied the name canterbury to it, as well as to the more familiar music stand (Part XI), both being mobile stands partitioned for easy access. In its dining room sense he described it as a supper tray 'with a circular end and three partitions crosswise to hold knives, forks and plates, at that end, which is made circular on purpose'. Sometimes, as in the music canterbury, there was a raised division between sections with a hand hole for lifting.

Running footman: *See* DINNER WAGON.

Sideboard (Figs 99, 100, 101): This was evolved in the 1770s, though the Gillow firm called it new as late as 1779. Shearer, in 1788, was the first to illustrate a specimen with the side table and its flanking pedestals joined to form a single expansive unit. He fitted one pedestal with a wine drawer and the other with racks and a heater for warming the dinner plates, costing his design at £13. It was somewhat ungainly, but was bettered by Sheraton who arranged tall knife vases on the pedestals to flank an ornamental brass rod intended for supporting large dishes.

More interesting today, however, are the designs illustrated by both Shearer and Hepplewhite of what Shearer called a

cellaret sideboard, a term continued through Victorian days
(Figs 99, 100). This was intended especially for rooms too small
for the pedestal arrangement. It consisted of a side table, usually with two pairs of front legs in the current side table manner,
but with the spaces between them partly filled by cupboards

flanking the centre, where there might be a single drawer in the table frieze. With one cupboard fitted for wine bottles this cellaret sideboard could also accommodate a wine cistern or cooler standing under the table centre. Arched brackets or fan-shaped spandrels usually rounded the angles of this central hollow. Sometimes the space was partly filled by a tambour cupboard such as Sheraton approved. Whatever the purpose of the cupboards they were fronted both sides to match, sometimes as sham drawers.

The small, minimal version of the cellaret sideboard consisted merely of a couple of squarish cupboards with a shallow drawer between them below the table top and raised on tapering fluted legs (Fig. 99). This dated mainly from the late 1780s onwards. Far more are comparatively recent, lacking the imaginative detail of early experimental work. Both Shearer and Hepplewhite suggested a number of shapes for the top, all tending to cut the projecting corners and suit a small room—bow, serpentine, semi-circular, 'with ovalo corners' and in more complex outlines such as 'an elliptic middle with an ogee on each side' and 'hollow middle and astragal on each side'. Hepplewhite suggested a length of $5\frac{1}{2}$ to 7 feet, depth of 28 to 32 inches and height of 3 feet.

Sheraton delighted in inventive designs with tambour fronts to the pedestals, perhaps, or sham drawer fronts as cupboard doors to conceal fitments for plates and bottles. In an *Encyclopaedia* design he introduced tiers of circular shelves above the

100. Sideboards. TOP: Sheraton design of cellaret sideboard with revolving doors to front compartments, appearing as sham drawers; Sheraton with Egyptian pilasters to the massive sections. SECOND ROW: with cupboard door masking zinc-lined drawer for washing up water; typical Regency (V. and A. Museum). **Wine coolers and cellarets.** THIRD ROW: Hope design, 1807; Smith design, 1808; finely turned specimen. BOTTOM: a Morgan & Sanders piece, displayed 1809; heavy classic style from Ackermann's *Repository*; simpler cooler with gadrooned rim and lion feet.

rounded projecting ends and urn knife cases within them, fitting the whole front of the central area with silk-draped cupboarding. When a pot cupboard was included this might be opened from the back by pressing a hidden catch so as to render it inconspicuous. Smith kept his sideboards low and massive and, like Sheraton, saw advantage in setting the edge of the table portion a little back from the fronts of the end pedestals, for the convenience of the butler. Some designs of this period were deeply concave and fitted into recesses to suit the popular circular dining table.

Regency design produced many heavy paw-footed pedestal sideboards, and post-Regency years a change from marquetry to carving for ornamental detail. Marble and slate were used for the top and plinth, but for the top mahogany proved less hazardous to the vast array of dishes. But perhaps the most interesting detail of the 1820s was the rise and development of the central backboard as an increasingly important decorative feature at a time when 'sideboard dishes' were in vogue. One has only to note the Regency and post-Regency approval of the ornate 'pier commode' with marble top and plinth and a towering mirror above to understand the development of the Victorian sideboard.

Splendidly veneered woods and restrained neo-classical carving made many post-Regency pieces lastingly pleasing despite massive proportions, but soon the outline became obscured by deeply carved ornament. At first from the 1830s the ornament was called 'Elizabethan' with strapwork and other more or less Jacobean detail, but soon a few master carvers were favouring rich clients with elaborate pictorial and story-telling masterpieces. The so-called Warwick school of wood carvers produced a wide range of naturalistic carving in the 1850s. Perhaps the most famous of these elaborate pieces was the sideboard peopled with carved figures from Scott's *Kenilworth*. More usual subjects included the 'appropri-

101. Nineteenth-century sideboards. TOP: from Loudon's *Encyclopaedia*, 1833; two cellarets around 1850; massive 'Gothic' of 1851 with ten supporting pillars (detail shown) but little storage space. SECOND ROW: typical mid-century style with naturalistic flower carving and cupboards flanked by open shelves; individualistic dresser design by Eastlake in 1869 edition of his *Hints on Household Taste* with (below) a detail of the construction in the early joiner's manner. BOTTOM LEFT: this piece by B. J. Talbert won a grand prix at Paris 1867, the ornament including carvings, mouldings, metal strapwork (detail shown), spindles, characteristics of the period's 'art work', defying cut-price commercial imitation (V. and A. Museum). BOTTOM RIGHT: late 19th-century rosewood veneer with marquetry of ivory, etc., showing grotesques, foliated scrolls, arched cupboard brackets and turned spindle ornament.

311

ate' mythological figures of Ceres and Bacchus and their attendants, together with fruits, dead game, etc., much of the work being mediocre.

It is rare to find an early Victorian sideboard in the former six-leg style: the massive Graeco-Roman pedestal ends had become normal, often rounded—more especially from the 1840s—so that the pedestal cupboarding was quadrant-shaped. Solid panelling with carved enrichment might back the space in the centre below the table top which housed the wine cooler.

Mirrors were beginning to be included in sideboards design by the 1840s where previously they had hung on the wall above. A three-piece mirror followed the divisions of the sideboard, square topped at the ends and rising higher in the centre in the 1840s, but with more rounded arching tops by the 1850s, the central section rising higher still. The sideboard topped by a single vast sheet of mirror plate came in during the 1850s but was more usual later. Then the whole piece was often a series of curves—a bowed mirror to the back, bowed front to the table top, quadrant pedestal cupboarding and rounded corners even to central cupboards where earlier designs left space for the wine cooler. Eastlake decried its 'indescribable curves', the cupboard doors bent inwards, the drawer fronts bent outwards, the angles rounded off, tasteless mouldings glued on, the whole surface glistening with varnish —'eminently uninteresting'. Instead he suggested a structure somewhat like a Welsh dresser with open shelves above and cupboards below, flanking a central opening for the wine cooler (Fig. 101).

By the 1870s and 80s, however, perhaps the most customary style was the tall oak sideboard with heavily projecting mouldings to a complexity of upper shelves and colonnaded compartments. This might be deeply carved, still with considerable Jacobean pretensions to its wide frieze and ornate

312

pilasters and rested on a heavy plinth base. However, many simpler versions survive, some associated with the art movement, some with light Japanese-inspired design. Some resembled drawing room cabinets with baluster-turned colonnettes supporting tiny arcaded shelves backed by mirror glass, with grotesques among foliage in ivory or bone inlay. From the end of the century a return to 'period' made Jacobean ornament again the most acceptable for dining.

Sideboard pedestal (Figs 99, 102): A pair to flank the sideboard table became fashionable around 1760, harmonising with the current neo-classical style. They were usually the same height as the sideboard table—about 28 to 32 inches and 16 to 18 inches square in section. When distances were long between dining room and kitchens they served as plate warmers and cellarets, and might be topped by lead-lined waste receptacles for iced water or cutlery rinsing water which the butler obtained from the urns above.

The pedestal fitted with a rack for warming plates required a lining of tin to avoid damage from the heater in an iron frame or stand fixed to the bottom. The other pedestal might be compartmented for twelve bottles laid on their sides. For example, George Smith noted that one of his pedestals served as a plate warmer and the other 'should have a tray capable of holding six to eight bottles which turns on a centre, also a drawer under, containing water to wash glasses during dinner'.

Pedestals and urns were most often veneered to match the sideboard table: thus they might be of satinwood, rosewood or mahogany in the later 18th century, but most usually of mahogany in the 19th century. The piece was generally square on plan—some were round—the base a substantial plinth. Top moulding and frieze might be treated with neo-classical carving, marquetry, applied swags and other detail, and often the angles were chamfered, the splay inlaid or fluted. The front might be decorated with moulding to suggest a round or elliptical panel, but some of the most ornate, dating from the 1770s, were enriched all over with neo-classical ornament in marquetry. Where a visible handle or key would spoil the design, the door—perhaps at the side—might be opened by pressing an ornamental detail such as a patera.

Sideboard table (Figs 46, 99): The forerunner of the fitted sideboard. During the first period of this review diners were served from court cupboards and dressers set out with displays of plate and from sideboards which, heavily draped with cloth, were basically plain tables. By early Georgian days the mahogany sideboard was an important architectural feature. Yet it was still primarily a table, massive like other side tables of its day (q.v.) Legs might be heavy scrolls or richly gilded, elaborate cabrioles, and from the 1720s the top was often of marble or scagliola, still lacking so much as a drawer. Some splendid specimens remain, the mahogany richly carved on frieze, pendants and cabriole legs.

Ince and Mayhew acknowledged current approval of a massive style but Chippendale was at pains to give one of his designs 'an aery look'. The third edition of his *Director* showed a change from his earlier Chinese notions to a pleasant confusion of rococo and the new classic style.

Probably inspired by Robert Adam, the fashion of about the 1770s was to flank such a sideboard table by urn-topped pedestals. Such a table in the side-table fashion of its day would often have a pair of legs towards each end of the front and perhaps delicate pendant carving below the swag-carved or fluted frieze. At the back of the table top a brass rail might be introduced, unifying the group of knife boxes, serving vessels, etc., placed upon it.

By the 1770s, as explained above, cabinet makers were already producing delightful versions of the fitted or cellaret sideboard (q.v.). This was a convenience for a room too small for the flanking pedestals. Shearer, in 1788, was probably the first to suggest building the pedestals into the structure. Perhaps it is more surprising, however, to find that the earlier unaccommodating side table continued in demand, being fully illustrated by Hepplewhite. Sheraton noted that 'in spacious dining rooms the sideboards are often made without drawers of any sort, having simply a rail a little ornamented, and pedestals with vases at each end, which produce a grand effect'. He noted too that another alternative was a sideboard 'without either drawer or pedestal; but they have generally a wine-cooper to stand under them, hooped with brass, partitioned and lined with lead, for wine bottles'.

As late as 1804 in his *Encyclopaedia* Sheraton illustrated an arrangement of table and separate pedestals, and designs in much the same mood, with bronzed plaster figures on the pedestals holding lights, were shown by Smith. In one, semi-circular so that it could not harmonise with flanking pedestals, Smith placed a wine cooler on the marble plinth that supported its Egyptian monopodia legs. He permitted three drawers 'for holding naperies, etc'. It is easy to understand that a purist such as Hope would choose an arrangement of table and wine cistern.

The early 19th century saw a liking for an elaborate brass rail or gallery at the back, and this was soon followed by a more substantial back as part of the wooden structure. Thus in 1826 Smith illustrated a typical seven-foot table with a solid back rising above the flat top in an arch carved with trophies. The four reeded, tapering front legs ended on a solid plinth recessed at the centre to receive a plinth-based sarcophagus wine cooler. The design was supported by a pair of plinth-mounted circular pedestals.

Sideboard urn (Figs 99, 102): Usually recorded as a pair of vases. Fashionable ornament for the pedestals flanking sideboard tables from the 1760s. Hepplewhite suggested a height of 2 feet 3 inches. They had two main purposes, as noted by

Sheraton. 'The vases are used for water for the use of the butler and sometimes as knife cases. They are sometimes made of copper japanned, but generally of mahogany.' Those that remain are usually of the same wood veneer as their pedestals. This may mean that the urn plinth appears to be part of the pedestal and it comes as a surprise to find it fitted with a tap for obtaining the water from the urn above. *See* KNIFE BOX.

Wine cooler, wine cistern (Figs 100, 101, 102): Open vessel for ice and water to keep wine bottles cool in the hot, candle-lit dining room, the ice being obtained through much of the summer from the storage ice house frequently built into a north-facing hillside of the country house estate. Such vessels were used from Tudor to Victorian days. Silver was long preferred, but the early Georgian copied silver cisterns in more effective marble and granite, and these in turn were copied in mahogany cut from the solid balk, with a projecting rim and a slab of marble set into the base. On the outside the bowl might be enriched with gadroons, or rococo carving, and sometimes it rested on a low oval foot separately turned and carved to harmonise. More often the bowl was placed on a stand with four massive cabriole legs to bear the considerable weight.

Chippendale gave four cistern designs in his *Director*: 'the ornaments should be of brass'. Of one design, a shell upheld by Bacchantes, he noted that it should be 'made of wood or marble, and cut out of the solid. The others may be made in parts, joined with brass work'. Usually at this time the parts consisted of separate sections for the sides and rounded ends, shaped to receive an inserted base. Sometimes a carved encircling rib was placed around the centre to mask further joining. Massive swing handles at the ends were double

---

102. Sideboard equipment. TOP: metal-lined wine cistern on stand, 1730s–40s; wine waiter partitioned for bottles, 1760; cellaret, 1770s on. SECOND ROW: Hepplewhite design and his diagram of its compartmented interior; cooper cistern, later 18th century, brass-bound with tap for emptying, sometimes on stand; brass-bound bucket for dinner plates. BOTTOM, for cutlery: box on stand partitioned for knives and forks; case of c. 1770s open to show holes for knives and forks and slits for spoons with (below) an end-of-century Sheraton knife-box design; two sideboard 'vases' serving as knife boxes, showing method of opening preferable to a hinge on a round outline; alternative use (Hepplewhite) for a sideboard urn as a water vessel complete with base tap.

gilded and lacquered and meant that the heavy, lead-lined cistern could be lifted from its stand. As pointed out in considering the later wine bottle holder known as a cellaret, the cistern had to be massive until the 1760s to contain the wide bottles of the day.

Through the rest of the century the need was for ever deeper cisterns, to immerse at least half of the taller, narrower bottle. Hence the fashionable use of the brass-bound oval mahogany cistern in the style the joiners had long been making in oak for taverns, assembly halls, etc., which continued in production into Victorian days, being an important detail in the brewhouse. The staved cistern in mahogany had a plain, rounded rim, sometimes with applied beading, and was broadly hooped top and bottom with the hammered brass known as latten. Rolled brass, thinner and less tough-textured, might be used from the 1770s and invariably from the 1790s, which meant that a central band of brass, ornamentally shaped, might be introduced as well. At each end was a massive lion mask and ring handle, and the piece might be lifted onto a mahogany stand.

Neo-classical versions of the staved cistern included wide bands of mahogany top and bottom, strengthened, perhaps, with underlying bands of steel and enriched with inlay and low relief carving. The base might rest directly upon four tapering legs. Late in the 18th century a tap was introduced low in the side for draining the vessel. In one attractive design two of the staves were extended above the rim to serve as lifting handles to a vessel often given a pronounced taper. But the vertical-sided cistern with lion mask handles continued far into the 19th century. When a stand was used it showed current approval of heavy tapering legs, reeded or faceted on the swell, or the projecting four-claw design.

Regency and early Victorian fashion produced many rectangular cisterns, tapering like the sideboard pedestals and mounted on paw feet. Examples with fixed linings of zinc are later in date than the late 1820s when rolled zinc came into production. But the collector has to recognise that by the 19th century other craftsmen were finding wonderful opportunities here to contribute to the pompous glitter of the fashionable dinner table. Vase-shaped wine coolers, each accommodating a single bottle, were arrayed along the table, some of silver, but probably far more of Sheffield plate and others again in the magnificent ceramics of the period.

Wine waiter (Fig. 102): Comparable with the canterbury but partitioned for bottles. This somewhat stool-like piece had its four legs mounted on castors and its frame supporting a low, decorative gallery with cross partitions and a central raised hand-hole. Thus it could be brought into the room in advance of an informal meal and circulated without requiring the presence of a servant. In an elaborate version there might be a cupboard below for locking away bottles until required.

PART XIII

Screens

In 1547 Henry VIII had 'four screens of purple taffeta fringed with purple silk standing upon feet of timber gilt silvered and painted'. But such details could apply to any of the entirely different styles of screen that were evolved before the end of the first period under review: the vertical panel, or several panels hinged together; the trestle shape that the 18th century knew as a horse firescreen and the 19th century as a cheval; the pole screen that followed the developments of other pillar-and-claw furniture through the 18th century and in the 19th produced variants in pedestal and banner.

Adjustable screens were built into various writing-table and work-table furnishings in the late 18th century (Fig. 6). The 19th has left us not only delightful hand screens in such materials as papier mâché, but table screens for lamp and candle in bead-fringed embroidery and the swivel attachment in green silk that was fixed to the chair arm or even to the window-sill as a sun-shield. Even the medieval screen of woven wicker was recalled by Victorians in the screen that could be attached to the back of a chair to shield the head of an over-heated diner. **Banner screen** (Figs 104, 105): A Regency fashion from about 1812 that continued popular through mid-Victorian days. The banner was a piece of velvet, damask or other rich stuff that hung, unframed, from a carved cross-bar, being weighted at the bottom by tassels. This cross-bar could be moved on a pole in the same manner as the usual pole screen's framed panel. Similarly a cheval screen might be modified into a banner style. Smith approved such screens in carved or gilded wood for the drawing room and in mahogany inlaid with ivory.

Candlescreen: In use from the mid-18th century onwards, about 12 to 18 inches high and often comparable with a full size specimen of either a pole or a horse screen. In the pole screen version the screen was much wider than its depth to give maximum shelter to the flame, and in both the screen panel was adjustable. Some were in plain wood, usually mahogany, but the banner variant of Victorian days may be found in beadwork on a brass support, the beads being heavy enough to ensure a good hang.

Cheval screen: *See* HORSE SCREEN.

Folding screen: *See* PANEL SCREEN.

Horse or cheval screen (Figs 103, 104, 130): The familiar shape with the screen flanked by uprights or standards, each mounted on a pair of out-jutting feet, sometimes linked by a central

103. Horse or cheval firescreens. TOP: beginning of 18th century; Queen Anne; early Georgian; Chippendale design with dolphin feet. BOTTOM: Chippendale design with pillar sides; c. 1770; Hepplewhite design 1788; Sheraton *Drawing Book* design.

stretcher. Bailey's dictionary, 1730, defined a horse as 'a piece of wood jointed across two other perpendicular ones'. The French word cheval was used in England from about 1815

onwards. It may be argued that many of these screens were unsuited to use near the immense Georgian fire, but probably these served more often to mask the empty hearth in summer when grate, fender and fire-irons of burnished steel were oiled and laid away, the chimney closed and the space filled with ornaments or dummy board figures.

The screen panel might be movable, sliding up and down within the standards to shield the user's face or legs as required. As with other furnishings of the late 17th and early 18th centuries the screen framing was richly ornamented with a carved and pierced cresting and often also a harmonising base rail apron. The feet were massive little scrolls projecting almost horizontally, and in an ornate gilded specimen the standards too, might be carved.

Many more through the first half of the 18th century were in walnut or mahogany, changing from the Queen Anne style of rounded arch to the squarer early Georgian line, with somewhat projecting, rounded corners or ears flanking a cupid's bow cresting—the line familiar in early Georgian mirror and chair back. This would be about 4 feet 6 inches high and 3 feet wide. Pictorial embroidery for such a screen might be worked in fine tent stitch or bolder cross stitch (Fig. 130): alternatives included tapestry, water colour painting and printed paper.

Chippendale recommended burnished gilding for the wood of his horse firescreens. It is interesting to note that his designs, plate 158, were engraved in 1761 for the third edition

104. Firescreens, very important in a period when women's clothes were flimsy and their complexions of paramount concern. TOP: Sheraton *Encyclopaedia* design, 1805; draped style, c. 1810; Hope design, 1807; Smith design, 1808. SECOND ROW: Sheraton folding footstool firescreen; Ackermann *Repository* design, 1815; Smith drawing room cheval screen, 1808. THIRD ROW: firescreen feet of c. 1810–15 including (right) profile of foot to cheval screen above. BOTTOM: four hand screens.

of his *Director*, indicating that they were only then in the height of fashion, the irregular cartouches floridly carved and pierced. Only one was restricted to the straight sides required for a movable panel. The piece lent itself particularly well to the reversed scrolls and asymmetrical extravagance of rococo ornament, made possible by the use of mahogany, often with every part of the framing following curved lines. Mahogany was expensive, however, and screens became somewhat smaller, about 3 feet 6 inches high and less ornately crested.

Through the second half of the century, too, the tendency, as in folding screens, was towards lighter design, the panel itself smaller in proportion than before. Ornament was restricted to small neo-classical motifs surmounting moulded framing with low relief fluting, beading, etc. The panel was most often elliptical, and this line dominated the top and base framing. A cross stretcher linked the standards where they divided into scrolling, slender legs, the scroll feet usually given small shoe-piece projections to ensure steadiness. Hepplewhite, for example, showed this detail in a sliding screen which, when fully raised, was a considerable hazard.

Panel ornament might still be home embroidery at a period when more ambitious furnishings were mainly left to professionals, and the counterweights that controlled the movement were hidden within harmonising tassels. Embroidery might be of wool or silk in colours, or in silk and hair in black to suggest a fine print. The most usual compromise, however, consisted of embroidery on silk largely augmented by water colour paint. Faces, skies, etc., were painted, but laborious satin stitch and french knots filled in such popular pastoral details as flowering tree stump and the inevitable sheep. Some screens of the 1780s were mounted with filigree effects in the amateur craft known as rolled paper work (*see* Part II).

In his lyre screen Sheraton suggested 'an entirely new plan' with the screen itself in the horse shape but mounted on a bowed tripod stand, the support consisting of a single short rod so that screen and standards could swivel. It also could be raised and lowered within its standards which were topped by pulleys and hung with tassels to conceal the counterweights. His more conventional horse screen was 'suspended by little springs fixed in the dovetail grooves of the standards'. He suggested about 3 feet 6 inches for height and 18 to 19 inches width.

Early 19th-century developments included the cheval screen with three panels, the central screen being flanked by hinged or sliding extensions (Fig. 104). When glass attracted public attention in the 1840s some cheval screens contained panels of wide-bevelled plate glass, but the collector is more likely to be misled by another fashion of this period, the screen in walnut, carved and crested in the Georgian manner and supporting brilliantly coloured embroidery or tapestry.

Overwhelmingly ornamental papier mâché screens were made, and tip-up tables that served as screens (Fig. 131), the supports sometimes harking back to amorini groups of the late 17th century but more often somewhat incoherent scrolls. Spiers and Son of Oxford sold such screens, painted with local views (Fig. 42). Even what the Victorians regarded as Elizabethan furniture included cheval screens, with pillars and feet in the late 17th-century manner, although with the twist turnings arranged symmetrically. But the mid-century saw more enterprising alternatives known as multiformia. These included a specimen by Thomas Nicoll, shown at the 1851 exhibition, which could be converted into a stand for lights or music, a chess table or a coffee table.

Panel screen: Early records indicate that these ranged from silk embroidery in gilded wood frames to leather, painted cloth and woven wicker. Late in the 17th century lacquer boards for screens were among the important imports of the East India Company, some screens being composed of as many as a

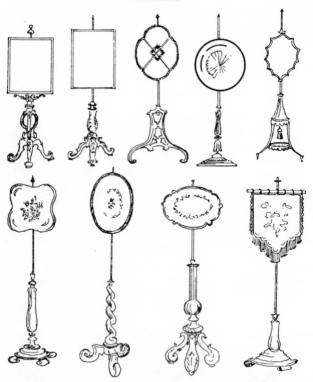

105. Pole firescreens. TOP: 1750s–60s, related to Chippendale design; standard 18th-century outline often found in reproductions, sometimes with the later, more sagging feet; Ince & Mayhew design, 1762; Hepplewhite design, 1788; Sheraton design, 1790s, the tassel concealing a counterweight: BOTTOM: four 19th-century developments. The banner screen (right) has free-hanging embroidery.

dozen panels, and these continued popular through much of the 18th century.

Through the middle years of the century smaller folding screens included handy two-piece frames about 3 feet to 3 feet 6 inches high, centrally hinged, a matching pair of squarish panels being mounted on fairly plain straight legs. Some had carved cresting and apron, or corner brackets, but they relied mainly on the panel ornament, which was usually of embroidery or woven tapestry, but might be a pair of mezzotints, water colour paintings on paper or silk or papers printed with Oriental themes such as were sold for the purpose by the paper warehouses. Chippendale suggested simple rococo and Chinese designs, much less elaborate than his horse screens. Panel screens were important through the 19th century and are often found loaded with amateur ornament which can sometimes be dated. Some were sold with glazed compartments to receive the owner's photographs or other decoration.

Pole screen (Figs 104, 105): Pillar-and-claw tables and candlestands indicate the style of work to be expected among pole screens, beginning with ornate, carved and gilded examples around 1700. A few remain in walnut from the first half of the 18th century, but far more are of later mahogany, when the screen might be an imposing little furnishing some five feet tall. The baluster-turned pillar on arching claw legs with ball-and-claw feet supported a massive screen on its slender pole. The screen was adjusted by a wing screw which tightened a brass ring to grip the pole at any required position.

Chippendale occasionally topped his pole with tiny bells instead of the conventional ivory turning or pineapple, and suggested a scrolling asymmetrical frame about 16 by 18 inches, but more frames that remain are plain rectangles some 20 to 27 inches wide or show slight carved cresting. The pole base consists of the grouped scrolls common to the well-carved claw furniture of the period, or simple turner's work.

Patterns of the 1760s and 70s included some by Ince and Mayhew constructed entirely of open scroll units to support the pole, and others of the period had cluster columns for the pole base, with attractive play of convex and concave shaping and ornamental outlines to the panels. Widely projecting claws were essential, the scroll feet elaborated into 'heels' or blocks. It was fashionable to have such screens in pairs flanking the fireplace with harmonising panels.

In neo-classical style the pole, topped with an ivory urn finial, was only slightly widened into a vase based upon a triangular plinth above paw-footed scrolls. The screen panel itself tended to be smaller and in harmony with chair back outline—most often a shield (vase to its designers) or an ellipse. Before the end of the century some rested on solid circular pedestals suitably weighted, while an alternative was the tall tripod of plain concave thermed legs inlaid with lines of contrasting wood. Many were of mahogany, others of satinwood or rosewood, but more were of japanned and painted beech to match other furnishings. Some were carved and gilded.

Hepplewhite showed round, elliptical and rectangular frames and suggested that they might be 'ornamented variously with maps, Chinese figures, needlework, etc'. By then the fine all-over embroidery of tent stitch on linen canvas was no longer popular, but the slighter embroidery on silk or satin included somewhat unimaginative embroidered maps in back or running stitch. Other panels were quickly ornamented with chenille, ribbon and the gauze known as aerophane and, as Sheraton noted, the work required protecting by glazing, with a straining board at the back lest warping in the heat cracked the glass. Often the back was cheaply 'lined with India paper'.

Sometimes an ellipse or circle was filled with pleated silk finished with a central patera. Smith in 1808 suggested flutes of the silk known as lutestring, with tassels to match. Sheraton's designs, like Shearer's before him, indented and elaborated the outline of the tiny screen panel and he gave a pronounced dip to the claw legs, raised on small peg feet. He also introduced a hollow pole and a pulley and cord arrangement for raising the panel, the counterweight concealed in a tassel between the legs (Fig. 104).

Pole screens were popular in the early 19th century. The solid base became a deeper, more substantial pedestal, sometimes as a concave-sided triangle with a scroll or paw foot at each corner. Smith introduced Egyptian motifs on the pedestal and substantial collared poles (Fig. 104). His panels included oblong and circular shapes and the hexagonal shield of antiquity first introduced by Hope, who gave his pole finial and base the shaping of lance point and handle. Smith suggested a range of woods—mahogany, rosewood, satinwood and ornate finishes of gold or bronze or japan. Even before 1820 styles were becoming somewhat fussy, however, with pendant knobs and other unnecessary detail. *Ackermann's Repository* illustrated a number with elaborately shaped panels. In the Trafalgar mood that lasted through much of the Regency, the S-scroll tripod claw might become a trio of dolphins, a usual alternative being a round or triangular pedestal with a plinth below.

Through Victorian days the same range of panel shapes continued on footed plinth or tripod. Painting in oil colours became a popular alternative to embroidery. The painting might be on copper plate or light, glossy papier mâché in a gilded frame of four, six or eight sides. Soon the whole screen was of papier mâché with massive-looking complexities of scroll supports enriched with gilding and bright colours. Another early Victorian delight was the pole screen elaborately carved, especially the meticulous carving then considered comparable with the work of Grinling Gibbons. This is now known as the Warwick style, originating from a small group of firms between 1848 and 1860 whose more elaborate contributions have amazed and confused the tyro collector ever since.

PART XIV

Beds, Cots and Cradles

The term standing bed generally implies the whole arrangement of wood and draperies: that is bedstock, bed furniture, pillars and tester. For many centuries this was the most important furnishing item in the house, involved in all important occasions and regarded as a status symbol. With the curtains drawn back it suggested the grandeur of a throne; closed, it offered warmth and privacy in whatever many-purpose room it might occupy.

In the medieval bed, cords from the ceiling supported the tester and the draperies that hung from it on all sides of the bed. But in the 16th century wood began to become important in the bed's structure. Eventually the standing bed consisted of a bedstock with solid panelling above the head end and two detached pillars on pedestals at the foot: these together supported a flat wooden tester with carved frieze.

The same features of pillar and panel shape and carving are familiar in other Elizabethan and early Stuart furniture, but one must realise the probability of Victorian adaption or invention. Paint and gilding enhanced the carving. Walnut was an alternative to oak, sometimes with ornamental inlay—for example, on the underside of the carved and panelled tester. But much of the bed's glory was to be found in its rich textile 'furniture' and its corner ornaments of coloured plumes in settings of spangles and gilded lace.

Many that have not survived, it appears, continued the older tradition with tester and celour of splendid fabric and for a time in each century the bed-head panelling was reduced in height, being topped by draped fabric. During the late 17th century, in the state bed dominating the wealthy household, fabric might entirely cover the wood framework, including the

106. Beds, Elizabethan to Queen Anne. TOP: late 16th-century bed, with wooden tester, carved headboard, bulbous columns with wide bases to mask the legs supporting the bedstock; details of carving and central inlay on head-board panel and cup-and-cover column swell; bed of mid-17th century or later with (below) detail of bedstock rail grooved for ropes, a feature often overlooked in replacements. BOTTOM: bed c. 1700s, the wood entirely masked by fabric and with corner plumes contributing to a height sometimes as much as 15 feet; angel or half-tester variant, c. 1710s.

107. Beds, early Georgian to 1760s. TOP: architectural style of 1740s; two bedposts of 1730s–50s and one of 1760s; bed of c. 1750s with gadrooned cresting, often no headboard. SECOND ROW: two Chippendale designs, 'Chinese' and 'Gothic' flanking a detail of a carved headboard from a bed in the *Dictionary of Arts*, 1755. BOTTOM: standing bed without footposts from the *Dictionary of Arts*; 'A single headed Couch or field Bed' by Ince & Mayhew, 1762; two contrasting cornices, 1730s–40s and 1760s.

tester cornice and frieze and the immensely tall posts that rose directly from the bedstock. Such woodwork was then of less enduring beech or other easily worked wood. The outmoded oak style was soon no more than a good quality workaday bed, with plain panelling and unambitious pillars.

Late in the century height was still further increased in the state bed to suit increasingly lofty rooms, the fabric-covered tester topped by an extravagantly carved cornice, fabric-covered and fringed.

The 18th century saw plainer but no less massive framework for these enormously tall and costly state beds, and fringe was soon abandoned. Some were angel or half-tester beds, but the general preference was still for the standing bed with panelling and foot posts to support a valance-draped tester which contained a complexity of cords and pulleys so that the occupant, with little effort, could wholly enclose himself in a private draught-free sanctuary within the lofty chamber.

For the great majority of these standing beds the 18th century preferred simple cornice and free-hanging draperies, and soon welcomed the clear-cut virility of early Georgian mahogany. Such a bed had a panelled head board and gracefully turned pillars, eight feet or more in height, supporting a panelled tester, often with the cornice gadrooned. The bed-posts were usually turned in three sections—the uppermost pillar, the central vase-shaped section and the square pedestal. The early tough Spanish mahogany was abandoned in favour of the more amenable baywood which became available in the second half of the century. Baywood might be stained to suggest the harder wood.

In the middle of the century there was a typical change to rococo and Chinese motifs, again with a preference for a low, shapely head-board topped by curtaining. These were followed by serpentine outlines for the tester, supported by slender, fluted pillars. Some followed the Adam dome design, and to-

108. Late 18th-century beds. TOP: Garrick's bed at the Victoria and Albert Museum, made by the Chippendale firm from designs by Robert Adam, 1775; bed-pillar designs, two Hepplewhite, one Sheraton; late 18th-century bed in serpentine outline. BOTTOM: Hepplewhite design; two designs for bed or window cornices; Sheraton design for a sofa bed showing his favourite dome outline.

wards the end of the century there was a liking for arched cornices with urns or vases, perhaps, at the corners instead of the long-favoured plumes. The low, undulating head board was often of satinwood but might be stuffed fabric, and as yet there was no foot board.

Early 19th-century designers made some attempt to follow classical example and there was welcome reduction in the amount of drapery, noted as 'a chastened style' in *Ackermann's Repository* in 1816. There was conspicuous approval, however, for deep net trimmings bordered with long tassels on draperies of muslin or chintz, for example, instead of silk. Southey in 1807 noted that 'the damask curtains which were used in the last generation have given place to linens . . . full enough to hang in folds; by day they are gathered round the bed posts, which are light pillars of mahogany supporting a framework covered with the same furniture as the curtains . . .'

Posts tended to lose their graceful proportions, becoming more heavily fluted or reeded, sometimes with cable twist, and a deep foot board came into some use with draped bases below. One recurrent fashion was the 'French style' of 'Grecian' couch to stand sideways to the wall with a curtained canopy secured to the wall above. Sometimes the couch was gondola shaped, standing on a dais or in a mirrored alcove. Other Regency beds were produced on long established lines with merely minor detail to indicate their period, such as antefixae on the cornice, collared pillars, paw feet. At the same time couch or sofa beds, undraped, were widely used from around 1800 onwards, with high scrolling head and foot boards, and in the 1830s and 40s there was renewed approval for the curtain arm projecting from the wall to spread a canopy of expensive draperies.

Among the more conservative, however, the tendency was to follow late 18th-century styles through the 19th century, with a range of four-posters, tents, domes and coronets of draped fabric. The impressively tall tent line like a heavy chandelier was fashionable in the 1820s and Smith in 1826 illustrated a 'French dome bed'. Half-testers gradually tended to replace the fully curtained four-poster, but it was late in the century before this disappeared completely.

109. Early 19th-century beds. TOP: Sheraton, including three bed posts. SECOND ROW: beds from Smith's *Household Furniture* including (right) 'a French bed'. BOTTOM: Egyptian post from bed foot; bed post continuing 18th-century line; 1820 bed with corner pilasters and brass mounts; chair bed by Morgan & Sanders shown in trade card of 1806.

336

The expected wood was mahogany, but from the 1820s brass was a very occasional alternative and in 1833 Loudon noted iron beds in fashion in London, 'sometimes even for the best beds'. By the 1850s brass taper tubing had become an important bed material, while many more beds were to be found with wrought iron joints and drawn sheet iron angle rails. Manufacturers boasted of the beds' rigid joints. Couch beds with canopies and even four-posters were made, with fluted tapering pillars. Some were folding designs. Even the famous papier mâché bed of 1850, now at the Victoria and Albert Museum, was composed largely of japanned metal.

The heavy elaborations of scrolling ornament associated with post-Regency and early Victorian furnishing were introduced, also Gothic filigree (Fig. 11). Eastlake, in 1868, deplored the poor design of metal beds with the intersections masked by bits of ornament resembling 'a friendly association of garden slugs'. But he still approved the use of air-restricting draperies, hung from the ceiling, at a period when many more beds were entirely uncurtained, with simple rails at head and foot. It was long before manufacturers ceased to japan the iron to resemble oak or bamboo.

Early iron beds had springy steel laths to replace the wooden bed's laths or cords, but mattresses fitted with coil springs revolutionised bed comfort after their patenting by Samuel Pratt in 1828. Later in the century feather over-mattresses were largely ousted by fillings of springy hair. Throughout the second half of the century metal beds were made in countless numbers, and by the end of it manufacturers were finding it hard to reinstate the wooden bed.

Bedstock, bedstead (Fig. 106): In medieval days a deep box shape, but by Elizabethan times a solid framework supported on four heavy legs, those at the head being extended to contain the bedhead panelling. The frame might be strengthened with lateral bed staves, but a usual basis for the vast quantities of

110. Victorian beds. TOP: four-poster advertised by Heal & Son, 1851; details showing alternative form of tester and a metal bed-head undraped; the metal tent bed with its furnishings. SECOND ROW: two half-tester designs of 1851 by Heal & Son, and between them a typical scroll design for iron bedsteads, 1860s–70s. BOTTOM: bed head of iron rods with applied flowers, 1851; carving with buttoned padding, 1851; japanned iron with brass rods, 1890s.

mattresses and bedding was a crossing of cords accommodated by holes and channels in the wooden framing.

Canopy bed (Figs 108, 109): French couch bed or sofa bed introduced around 1800, the curtain draperies supported by a wall fixture.

Celour: Early term that may be variously interpreted from old references to have indicated either, as is now accepted, the bed-head, or the tester (q.v.).

Field bed (Fig. 107): Term in use from the 16th to the 19th century. Also known as slope bed. Randle Holme noted it as a bed made 'higher with an head' to fit under a canted roof, and a century later Ince and Mayhew showed a design for a single-headed couch or field bed, 'the tester being to take off and conceal'd in the Recess, under the Seat'. The slanting top meant that the side draperies could not be drawn as curtains but had to be looped up. The bed was more lightly constructed than the four-poster, the entire arching framework designed for quick dismantling and packing. It was long essential for the fastidious traveller.

Four-post bed (Figs 106, 108–110): Differentiated from a standing bed in 18th-century trade cards by having a low head board so that pillars to match those at the bed foot were required to support the tester.

Furniture, bed-furniture: This was the term always used to cover all the draperies essential to the standing bed. From innumerable fascinating inventories of bed furniture a Hampton Court record is interesting, made in 1659 on the Protector's death. This describes a 'bedstead with a sackcloth bottom, the furniture of rich incarnardine velvett imbroidered very rich with gold and silver conteyning, Three Courtines, Fower cantoines, deep Vallons and bases, fower capps of the same velvett and imbroidered suitable for the same bed. The ceeler and head cloth of the said bed is of rich cloth of gold with inward vallons, cases for the posts and lynings of the curtains and cantoines all of the same.' To protect the velvet the bed had also 'three large courtines of scarlet bazes being a case about the bed'.

This record is typical in including not only a variable number of curtains but valances above them with cantons or cantonnières to link these at the corners and with bases as lower valances below the bed frame. The caps were corner finials: dyed plumes were fashionable in these from the 16th century until well into the 18th, when urn or vase shapes might be used.

All parts of the furniture offered opportunities for embroidery—heraldic, pictorial, story telling, or Oriental in the spreading, soaring tree-of-life style. Pictorial work was favoured for the valances which were often taut and easily viewed, and for day-time pillow beres or cases. Appliqué work and quilting may be noted. Blankets and coverlets of wool, silk and fur and sheets of linen or cheaper harden were used, with mattresses and bolsters and less frequent pillows. Mattress fillings ranged through down, feathers, flock and straw, under mattresses often being quilted. Rich families might also have summer furniture for the bed, as well as mourning furniture.

Half-head bed: Generally assumed to mean the bed with a low panelled bed-head, as noted in Elizabethan and later records.

Half-tester bed, angel bed (Figs 106, 107, 110): From the end of the 17th century. The tester extending from the bed-head over most of the bed, so that it could still enclose the bed with curtains, but lacking foot posts. In the 19th century, when it was popular, it more usually extended over only the upper half of the bed. It was advertised in Georgian days as a royal bed.

Press bed: From the late 17th century, a bed that could be folded away so that it appeared to be a cupboard. Typically the tester let down to serve as the cupboard door and there were drawers below for bedding. The name is also applied to the farmhouse and cottage bed boarded on three sides.

Stump bed: The simple style of cheap bed used by the great majority, consisting of a wooden framework on four short turned legs. If it had a head-board it became a stump-end bedstead.

Tent bed: (Fig. 109): Simple version of the field bed with four posts and domed or arched canopy covered with tester cloth. Thus it looked like a tent when the curtains were drawn. Popular through much of the 18th and 19th centuries, and sometimes known as a sparver bed.

Tester: Now applied to the canopy or ceiling over a bed. There seems to be reason to think that this and the celour were confused in early records, and the mistake has been perpetuated by more recent acceptance of this interpretation.

Truckle bed, trundle bed: From medieval days and still in use through much of the 18th century. A low bedstock on wheels, usually for a servant or child. It could be pushed under the standing bedstead during the day and at night too, for a good quality bedstead was of considerable height above the floor as slight protection from mice.

Turn-up bed (Fig. 109): Georgian term for chair or sofa that could be converted into a bed. Several of these dual-purpose designs were patented around the end of the 18th century.

Children's beds: For centuries babies were swaddled and half smothered in attempts to protect them from the dusty, dirty world around them. Cot, cradle and crib were made large enough to accommodate thick mattresses and voluminous coverings and were furnishings of enormous importance and pride to the mother receiving congratulatory visitors at her bedside, celebrating the birth with cakes and caudle. Each had its own specific purpose, but the same trends may be distinguished in the three forms and may help in dating what are now in any case comparatively rare antiques.

Oak was used in the 16th and 17th centuries (originally, one assumes, widely supplemented by beech, elm, fruitwoods, etc.) with lesser late 17th- and early 18th-century approval for soft woods closely covered with braid-edged velvet or leather. Mahogany is noted in combination with cane through the later 18th century and into the 19th century, when the cheaper alternative was a soft wood, painted and grained to resemble oak.

Wrought iron with cast brass ornament was welcomed as a hygienic substitute in the 19th century (Fig. 11). And always, of course, for the simple baby basket or bassinet cradle, wicker or osier was in wide but impermanent use. This, though never a collector's item, is to be noted in the ceramic miniatures of around 1800 that conveyed small congratulatory gifts to the mother. Some of these record the practice of covering the rough surface with draught-excluding quilting (Fig. 112). Victorians concealed all vestige of the framework in many layers of goffered frills.

111. Cradles and cot in traditional styles difficult to date: cradle associated especially with 16th-17th centuries, with handles for rocking, often oak; hooded type of cradle associated with 17th to early 18th centuries; early 19th-century cot, a cane version of the suspended cot.

In design and construction the collector notes the advance from the medieval hammered-up lidless box through the phases common to 16th-, 17th- and 18th-century joiners' work with subtle changes in carved detail, panel shaping, run moulding, etc. The base might be boarded but as often, like a bed, composed of cords, or sometimes of horizontal laths.

Changes in the outline of cradle and cot hoods may be some guide in dating. These included the rare wagon-tilt of the Tudor days, the flattish tops of the 17th century, the delightful ogee arch found in association with fielded panels in a Queen Anne specimen, the late 18th-century rounded arch and the Regency Gothic point. Similarly, the crib might show changing outlines to its hood or dome of drapery comparable with the styles of contemporary beds.

Cot (Figs 111, 112): By derivation this was a hammock-style of slung bed fitting the child's body and thus came to imply the swinging form as distinct from the rocked cradle. The usual design from medieval days consisted of a box shape slung between end trestles linked by a central stretcher. As indicated above, this was deep enough for two or three mattresses and often hooded by the 17th century. It lent itself to particularly attractive shaping, suggesting the lines of a boat and, indeed, Queen Victoria's children had a perfect boat cot. Ornamental detail usually included carved or turned finials to the end posts—sometimes crosses—originally often painted or gilded.

During the 18th century strong mahogany was introduced for the cot framework. This was rendered lighter and more practical by panels of cane, and the cot became immensely popular during the late years of the century when 'horse' furniture was in vogue.

An alternative then was a cot with sides composed of turned spindles. This led to some confusion in naming: Sheraton in his *Dictionary* called his spindled cot a swinging bed crib. His

112. Cots, cradle and crib. TOP: cot, early 19th century; Sheraton cot design, 1803, rocked by clockwork; foot of 'Gothic' cot design by Smith. BOTTOM: typical example of everyday, shortlived wicker cradles, this specimen being an earthenware ornament of the 1800s showing the wicker lined with fabric; part of a 'classic' cot shown by Henry Moses, 1823; country chair-maker's crib.

design had a dome canopy, but a simpler and more usual alternative was to extend a horizontal bar from the post at the head of the cot and drape fabric over this as a draught-shield: Sheraton referred to it as a wagon top. His main concern, however, was with a clock-spring device to keep the cot in motion. George Smith suggested oak as an alternative to mahogany for his heavy Gothic version. At the other extreme, clean simple cots are found in 19th-century japanned iron, some with folding X legs.

Cradle (Figs 111, 112): Made with a box-shaped bed like the cot, but mounted on cross bearers shaped as rockers instead of swinging. By the late 16th century the side panels might be higher round the child's head and in the 17th century a complete hood became popular. In the cradle it was easy to arrange for this to open backwards on hinges for safe access to the child: sometimes, too, a cupboard was included behind the hood. Tall corner finials made it possible for the mother to rock the child from her bed, and there might be wooden pins inserted horizontally down the sides, either to secure the covers or to carry webbing to support the bedding and its occupant well above the stone floor.

Such cradles were treasured heirlooms, and some in 17th-century oak remain, carved with initials and date, and probably once enriched with paint and gilding. More rarely a specimen is noted with velvet glued to its rounded hood and plain body in the manner of late 17th-century beds. Others again were given sides and hood supports of turned spindles.

Apart from such obvious details ·as early 18th-century fielded panels, it may be difficult to date a late cradle simply made with boarded sides and hood: they were still in production in the 19th century, often grained to suggest oak.

Crib (Fig. 112): The manger or feeding stall design, the box part constructed with vertical spindles and mounted on four corner legs. This was for the toddler and might on occasion be a miniature of the four-poster bed. It is interesting to note that Catherine Naish, joiner, in 1766 supplied George III with a split wicker cradle and, in the same year, met another commission—for a 'couch bed' with pillars. This had turned banisters along the sides 'to keep the Prince from falling out'.

PART XV

Bedroom Furnishings

In the Tudor and Stuart house a bed might be found in any—often almost every—room from garret to pantry. The standing bed, for those who could afford its wealth of textiles and weight of carved joinery, offered adequate draught-proof privacy, but few of the bed chamber amenities associated with a civilised ritual of dressing. Ladies of fashion had to make do with dressing coffers which were little more than fitted boxes or miniature cabinets.

Only in the later 17th century was there much thought for furnishing minor apartments or closets specifically for their personal enjoyment and even then they were intended for the admiring scrutiny of visitors who would be alert to minor fashions of the day too bizarre and fleeting to be expressed in more important state rooms. Typically japanned work, with a wealth of chinoiserie motifs, was a recurrent delight.

Simple dressing tables in oak of the mid-17th century are now rarities. The method then was to place the table against a wall with a small mirror upon it or hung on the wall, flanked by a pair of candlestands. This meant that the accompanying seat presented its back to the room: hence the popularity of dressing stools and back stools (q.v.) with elegant back legs. From this there developed in the early 18th century the dressing table enhanced by a dressing glass mounted upon a fitted stand—which might be a separate entity throughout the period (*see* below).

By the mid-18th century the looking glass might be placed upon a handsome dressing commode well suited to the japanned chinoiserie of the fashionable dressing room. This

113. Dressing tables. TOP: late 17th century; early 18th century, late 18th century, with fitted drawer containing mirror, etc. BOTTOM, folding styles: known from 1730s and popular from c. 1760s; serpentine commode adapted as dressing table, 1770s–80s (V. and A. Museum). Both would be acceptable in a living room.

required little additional complexity to become the most elaborate style of what was then called a dressing table or a toilet table, with the mirror supported between additional small drawers in equally flamboyant contours. Collectors today seldom realise the enormous importance of draperies to these pieces throughout the period under review, stressed by every contemporary picture of a beauty at her toilette.

At the same time the 18th-century cabinet maker sought to meet the needs of those who preferred to forget the tiresome details of shaving, wig dressing and the rest while putting their apartments to personal daytime use. The chest of drawers

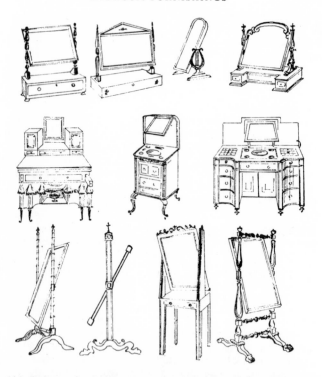

114. Bedroom furnishings. TOP: dressing glasses, that on the right showing change to wider supports in Smith design, 1826. SECOND ROW: Sheraton dressing tables and wash basin stand, early 1800s. BOTTOM, Regency cheval glasses then sometimes known as psyches: with ring turning and reeded foot; Smith design, 1808; with drawer fitment and mirror cresting; design development of more ponderous turning and lion feet.

(q.v.) often included a top drawer lavishly fitted with what the period's designers called 'the apparatus'. This is considered under its common names of bureau dressing table and commode dressing table and dressing drawer. But the most fascinating piece was the folding dressing table which also was advertised merely as a dressing table by the Georgian. It was greatly developed late in the 18th century under such names as the Rudd's table.

The Regency contributed mainly new names to established furnishings but witnessed popularity for newly available long dressing glasses. Meanwhile, from early Georgian days, the need for washing and shaving facilities had been met in a range of increasingly complicated wash basin stands which even to-day—and with no possible logic or justification—are often called wig stands. Once the latter, totally different, domed articles became redundant they were seldom considered worth keeping, but wash basin stands are to be found in 18th-century mahogany as well as 19th-century iron. The more expansive wash stand was a 19th-century development associated with the Victorians' wish for a bedroom suite of harmonising furniture and today valued mainly for the well-finished marble slab.

Dressing table (Figs 113–6): It is probably simplest to accept this as the comprehensive term for the unit as understood to-day before giving separate consideration to the variants now less familiar but in their day quite as important and accepted under the same name. A rich table cloth would be spread for the array of toilet accessories, and records note the continuation of this practice when oak gives place to the late 17th-century walnut veneers, exquisite marquetry and occasional gilded gesso on tables in the current side table outlines (q.v.). Some charming specimens of around 1700 show the frieze containing the fitted drawer in a curving silhouettte with a round kneehole flanked by two smaller drawers.

115. Regency bedroom furnishings. TOP: Morgan & Sanders 'toilette dressing case', 1810, intended also for travelling; from Smith design of 1805 (V. and A. Museum). SECOND ROW: chest of drawers (details of its ring handle and turned foot); wardrobe. BOTTOM: bedroom chair simulating bamboo; bed steps; Morgan & Sanders bedroom cupboard with sham drawers pulling out as table surface (General Trading Co.).

The 18th-century ways of draping what were called petticoats around the table's legs are illustrated in such familiar paintings as Hogarth's *Marriage à la Mode* (1745) and Zoffany's portrait of Queen Charlotte with her toddler sons (1767). Even the simple deal dressing table would have its petticoat of tammy cloth and gauze cover with a gauze scarf for the mirror. This was easily explained: on hot summer days until as late as the Victorian era the housemaid might be expected even to drape the picture frames in gauze and cover the chandeliers with muslin bags in her endless fight against dust and flies.

By the mid-18th century the toilet table could be an extremely handsome piece. Chippendale suggested a commode outline for the lower part and cuboards or drawers or merely elaborations of scrolls to flank the draped mirror above. Ince and Mayhew illustrated magnificently draped 'toilettas' with oval and escutcheon shaped mirrors such as one 'intended for Japan or burnish'd Gold'.

The fashion for these elaborate toilet tables continued through the rest of the century, introducing the familiar serpentine commode lines and some fine inlay and marquetry. Towards 1800 it became more usual to include washing facilities in the dressing table unit. Sheraton's most elaborate design, which he called a cabinet dressing table, included not only cupboards almost to the top of the elliptical mirror and additional wing mirrors to the sides which could be adjusted to view any part of the head, but also a wash basin in a deep drawer below a writing slide in the lower half of the massive piece. Even for the gentleman, Sheraton suggested a massive dressing table with swags of fabric around the mirror in his *Encyclopaedia*, and very similar heavy styles were fashionable in the 1820s.

Later Regency dressing tables tended to lose their petticoat swags and tassels, however, and indeed in another design Sheraton himself was willing to accept drapes merely painted on the framing. The athenienne or trestle shape was introduced, sometimes in lyre outlines, to support a heavy rectangular top, often with drawers. This held a swing toilet glass, sometimes also with lyre supports. The ingenious fitted compartments might be limited to shallow trays in the table top. Sometimes there were no fittings at all, but this brief trend can be exaggerated. Even George Smith in some designs included folding mirrors, wash basins, etc., despite the austerely square outlines, such as one inappropriately Gothic.

The sideboard style was prominent with a low shelf below the drawers that flanked the kneehole and a suitable low rectangular mirror to correspond with its wide square lines and the hair styles of its users. The tendency was to make the top larger and more impressive, with less regard for concealed ingenuity, and to place a separate glass upon it with its own cheval or drawer-fitted box support. Accepting the current revival of rococo whimsy, many an early Victorian dressing table was no more than a walnut table, lacking drawers but elegantly serpentine on spindly legs (Fig. 116).

Some were in papier mâché and a desirable set consisted of table, chair and footstool. Others continued the athenienne style of the Regency with lyre-shaped end supports or the classic curule line of opposing curves linked by a stretcher running the length of the table. Sometimes such a table had a pull-out fabric bag underneath like a pouch work table, and always there would be a cover—often two layers of different fabrics. A flat slab of china with flower painting was one early Victorian idea, and some elaborate painted cabinet dressing tables were made. Mid-Victorian comment applauded the widespread use of painted bedroom furniture which could be kept clean merely by dusting, and cheap woods were often grained.

It must be realised, however, that by mid-Victorian days the factories were catering for a vastly wider range of quality and price in bedroom furnishing. The utilitarian dressing

116. Victorian bedroom furniture. TOP: dressing glass flanked by dressing tables by Trollope and in papier mâché by Clay, all 1851. SECOND ROW: dressing glass and wash-basin stand of 1880s. BOTTOM: three-compartment wardrobe, two doors mirrored (details of dentil moulding and handle and lockplate), late Victorian; chest of drawers, late, of poor design that wastes all the space behind the heavy pilasters (details of pilaster scroll and turned handle).

table might have a rectangular top with a low gallery and a knob-handled drawer above an open shelf. But in the best bedroom a vast wardrobe with mirror-fronted hanging compartments, drawers and hat cupboards would be matched by a mirror-backed, shelved and cupboarded wash stand, an elaborate towel rail and a dressing table of commensurate vastness. Detail varied, but the 1880s still approved the tall rectangular mirror topped by a purposeless spindled gallery and flanked by small drawers on spindle legs with large drawers in the table below flanking a shallow drawer and open shelf.

Athenienne: *See* DRESSING TABLE above.

Dressing drawer: Shearer illustrated fittings for toilet use under the name of furniture drawers. Such a drawer could be incorporated into many a graceful little table through the middle and late years of the 18th century. This followed the fashion for concealing the table's purpose but lacked the elaboration of the bureau or commode dressing table. Some are noted in Chinese style and more in serpentine outlines with French legs associated with the 1780s. This may be considered as a variant of the folding dressing table but more completely hid its purpose.

Dressing table bureau; dressing chest; commode dressing table (Figs 113, 115): This style of furniture was introduced in walnut in early Georgian days for furnishing the 'bed-sitting-room' of 18th-century luxury. Typically, from the mid-century onwards, it was serpentine-fronted in the manner of the commode with a deep top drawer, sometimes with sham detail to suggest that it was a row of three drawers. Below, the central cupboard was often set back from the flanking tiers of drawers so that the user could sit at it when closed as a bureau. When required, he could pull open the drawer to reveal, first, a baize-covered slide to write on and, under this, a range of fitted compartments partly covered by a mirror, 'coming forward with folding hinges' as described by Chippendale.

An elaboration of this arrangement was his dressing chest and bookcase, the latter fronted with mirror glass. Ince and Mayhew distinguished between the bureau dressing table with straight-sided cupboard pedestals and central drawers and the commode dressing table in scrolling serpentine outlines. Instead of the drawer, the method of opening consisted of a rising top with a quadrant to hold it vertical, the dressing glass being attached to the lower face. Shearer suggested a 'gentleman's dressing table' with a rising top of this kind and a tambour cupboard as well as drawers. A serpentine front increased the cost from £3 to £4, and its veneering from 2s 6d to 4s 6d.

Some particularly attractive specimens date to this period, around the 1780s, following the flowing, simple lines either of the chest of drawers on French feet or of the small kneehole sideboard of the period. Sheraton suggested a shallow writing drawer instead of the customary slide above the fitted drawer. In his more elaborate dressing commode the lifting top could be made to slide down behind, and he introduced flanking drawers containing fittings for writing and for washing. Some of these late 18th-century pieces were superbly veneered in light woods such as satinwood with ornamen t in marquetry or paint.

Dressing table, folding (Figs 113, 115): Another contrast to the gaily effeminate toilet table was offered from around the 1750s by the compact little cabinet with a flat top divided in the centre and hinged to open back as shallow trays flanking the apparatus. This too, was a dressing table to its designers. Frequently the mirror folded forward and flat, being raised by a spring catch. At its simplest the piece appeared to be a writing table with a deep ornamental frieze.

Shearer illustrated an elaborate example, calling it a dressing stand (Fig. 120). This he suggested should close to a top of twenty inches square and run on castors. It presented a bland front of sham drawers concealing at the top the usual

117. Dressing glasses. TOP: hanging glass with nearly flat frame and cresting marquetry ornament, late 17th century; glass in raised embroidery sometimes banded with tortoiseshell, mainly c. 1660s; two of around 1700, that on right above a dressing box, black japanned. SECOND ROW: c. 1720s, walnut with gilt fillet around glass, flat cresting and stretcher; dressing box from a glass of c. 1710; glass with fret-cut cresting and concave drawer, c. 1760s. BOTTOM: horse glass of c. 1790 flanked by dressing glasses with boxes. The vase shape (right) is also often found on a serpentine-fronted box (left) and the oval glass on a bow fronted box.

356

collection of fittings and mirror under the folding trays, and below this a fitted wash hand basin. Water bottles and a cistern for the used water were concealed at the back. When the table was cupboarded it might conceal the mirror at the back, raised by a weight and pulley device.

Rudd's table: Illustrated, for example, by Shearer who costed it at £2 18s. A variant of the bureau dressing table but with a row of three deep, fitted drawers. The central drawer had a writing slide; the flanking drawers, each with a swivel mirror, could be swung out on quadrants so that they could be used in combination for viewing back or profile.

Sheraton devised what he claimed was a cheaper arrangement of a Rudd's table with only the two mirrors pivoting. He suggested that they were often made in satinwood and banded, sometimes in mahogany.

Shaving table (Fig. 114): Eighteenth-century term for the compact form of enclosed wash basin stand complete with mirror and candlerest.

Cheval glass: *See* HORSE DRESSING GLASS.

Dressing glass, toilet glass (Figs 114, 117, 118): Collectors of old embroideries delight in the occasional small toilet mirror framed in raised work (known to Victorians as stump work), usually made by a girl in her early teens around the 1660s. This is now as costly a rarity as the embroidery-mounted toilet or work cabinet (q.v.) which it doubtless accompanied as forerunner of more spacious furniture for the toilette.

The late 17th-century looking glass, only a little larger and in a rectangular or crested frame, might hang over the simple dressing table. But from the beginning of the 18th century the glass was developed into a delightful little piece of furniture in the current arching crested outline with ogee curves to the upper corners of the wide, shallowly bevelled glass. This was held by swivel screws between finial-headed uprights mounted on a nest of small drawers. It might be placed upon the dressing

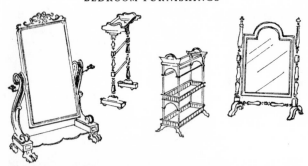

118. Victorian bedroom furniture. long mirror, early, and dressing glass flanking towel rails of 1840s and 1880s.

table or upon a small light stand, perhaps with an additional drawer, veneered or japanned to match.

The nest of drawers is comparable with the most dainty fittings of the period's ornamental detail. Some in walnut were exquisitely finished, sometimes with merely a single drawer shaped in elaborate outline and mounted on small bun feet. Other glasses were plainly supported by hinged back struts, but by early Georgian days a more usual alternative was the pair of uprights on trestle feet with a shaped cross stretcher.

By the 1730s both glass and frame might be plainly rectangular without the arched cresting. Some lavishly carved and gilded mirrors are associated with the Chinese vogue of the mid-18th century, but far more were plainly framed in mahogany and in japanned soft wood for men's use or for draping with chintz or other gay fabric.

More dressing glasses remain in the style of the later 18th century when the box stand was seldom more than a single row of drawers, made of mahogany, perhaps, or satinwood with delicate bandings. Sometimes simple classic motifs were

119. Wash basin stands, 18th century: 1750s–60s; two of the 1780s–90s; folding type that hides its purpose; 1790s; Sheraton design with cistern and tap to lead-lined drawer.

introduced on the drawers. At this time two shapes were especially approved; a shield shape for the glass, then known as a vase shape, on a serpentine-fronted box; and an ellipse for the glass, usually on a bow-fronted box. At the end of the century, when high hair styles were abandoned, there was a return to low, square lines with a wide rectangular glass on a rectangular box. In the elliptical and vase-shaped glasses the uprights followed the frame outline with a particularly attractive outward curve at the bottom before broadening a little into vertical stumps for attaching to the box—a familiar chair back line.

This style of support required a square-cut tapering section, often moulded and sometimes inlaid with small details in ivory and topped by tiny urn finials. But in the rectangular glass the supports could be ornamentally turned in the fashion of the day, sometimes being taller than the glass and always left square for the swivel. At the base they were broad, square-cut wedges that could be pegged securely into the stand. Tall ivory or bone finials were matched by the ivory knobs, keyhole escutcheon and bun feet associated with the 1800s.

It is interesting to note how soon the glass began to return to a vertical emphasis, though the tall side uprights were continued and elaborated into trestles with wide scroll bases, for instance, in Smith's 1826 designs. A Regency idea in keeping with this liking for substantial supports was the mirror, rounded now at the top, resting on two squat little lyres. A bombé front was in fashion by then with two drawers and four small feet and the trestle uprights extended the whole depth of the box or stand from front to back, their edges reeded.

Victorians recalled various past mirror outlines and included an ellipse with a U-shaped support on a central swivelling base, but the rectangle with arched top was among the most favoured, with a variety of turned supports including, inevitably, the barley sugar twist.

Horse dressing glass (Figs 114, 117, 118): Eighteenth-century term (compare horse firescreen, etc.) for what became a cheval glass in the 19th century and occasionally a psyche during the Regency. A long glass on trestle feet introduced in the last quarter of the 18th century when glassmakers improved their methods of producing sheet glass. Usually the glass, rectangular for cheapness and in a simple moulded frame, could be tilted to any angle, using swivel screws and its height adjusted by using cast lead counter-weights. Shearer suggested a size of 22 inches by 34 inches for the glass which with beaded corners cost a guinea. But many were considerably larger. A Sheraton design included a nest of drawers at one side, sensibly including a pincushion. In another design that appears to have been made in some numbers he included a writing fitment. He noted that they were mounted on concealed castors and often imitated bronzed metal with gilded ornaments.

In Regency specimens the supporting pillars might have carved heads or consist of caryatids, but more were plainly turned and fluted or reeded. As with the toilet glass, a later specimen might have an arched top to the glass. An occasional 'studio glass' may be noted later, but in the bedroom the cheval glass became unnecessary when wardrobes were fitted with mirrored doors.

Psyche: *See* HORSE DRESSING GLASS.

Lavabo: *See* WASH BASIN STAND.

Wash basin stand, basin stand (Fig. 119): Like the dressing table the wash basin stand could be a straightforward, obvious little bedroom furnishing openly meeting minimal requirements with all the elegance of carving or japan work, or it could masquerade as a small cabinet in a dual-purpose room when the temptation was to elaborate it with a wealth of extra apparatus. The obvious piece, from around the mid-18th century, was the tripod stand. This is the piece now curiously often called a wig stand.

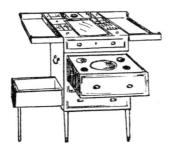

120. Design for a dressing table by Thomas Shearer from his *London Book of Prices*: 'a gentleman's and lady's dressing stand with folding tops 20 ins square. . . . The other drawers are shams, in the back part of the stand is a cistern which receives water from the basin drawer'. Of the 'Particulars of the Inside Work' he says: 'a glass hung to a sliding piece, three powder boxes, a lift-out to hold four razors, hone and oil bottle, a ditto for combs, and partition'd off for tooth brushes, a shallow ditto for tweezers, knives, etc., 2 places for essence bottles, and 2 ivory boxes, at the back part are partitions for 2 water bottles which go down in a place for a tumbler, and a place at each side for rolls of pomatum . . . £2 6s'.

An open ring of wood—later a circular hole in a flat wooden tray—supported the basin and its tiny water bottle, and rested on three open scrolls linked by a triangular shelf. This shelf with a couple of small drawers, often lead-foil lined, was for the domed wash-ball holder—presumably the origin of the wig stand myth. Below again, three further scrolls were linked by a small triangular shelf, slightly dished to receive the water bottle when the basin was in use and resting upon three scrolling claw legs. This basic design was illustrated, for example, by Chippendale in the third edition of the *Director*.

In the later years of the century it acquired more flowing, less vigorous lines. It was more usually given four legs and a square top with clipped corners or serpentine edge and an apron to hide the under-side of the basin. Legs from top to floor were smooth, slender French curves, but the basic design changed little. It was known as a lavabo to the Regency.

At the same time, parallelling the development of the concealed dressing table for the many-purpose room, designs were evolved for washing and shaving tables resembling other cabinet furniture, which, as Sheraton suggested, could 'stand in a genteel room without giving offence to the eyes' (Fig. 114). Hepplewhite and Shearer, as might be expected, recorded the current delight in well-equipped little designs, and at the end of the century Sheraton contributed to their elaboration.

The piece remained small, the top about thirty-one inches high and often as little as fourteen inches square, with a central hole for the basin and smaller holes to the sides for wash-ball and sponge dishes, but tended to acquire cupboarding almost down to floor level. A tambour-fronted cupboard was frequent between basin and box-drawer. As with the folding dressing table the top might open out as trays or upwards as a splash-back. A mirror was essential, either attached to the back or fitting down behind the basin and raised by counterweights. When the piece lacked side trays a candlestand was provided in the framework. In one end-of-century design the lid included side wings so that when open it served as a splash-board on three sides. But a frequent alternative was the tall corner stand hidden by cupboard doors or draperies. Sheraton suggested a design with a tapped cistern for the water.

The fully concealed stand with lifting top and capacious cupboard for the water ewer was still in use in Victorian days. Loudon in 1833 noted that the piece was then commonly placed in a library closet or gentleman's study. It is interesting to note sometimes on an end-of-century bedroom basin stand that the low shelf is no longer dished for the small water bottle. Jugs became important in the ceramic world at this time and the long-necked water bottle was replaced by a larger ewer.

Wash stand (Fig. 116): In the early 19th century the concealed wash basin was often an important feature of the bedroom dressing table. But on the wash basin stand both basin and ewer outgrew their graceful little support and prompted the 1820s to develop the marble-topped washstand en suite with the dressing table and wardrobe. A version of the tripod per-sisted far into Victorian days in the basin stand of painted iron.

PART XVI

Long Case Clocks

Clocks are for the specialist. The furniture collector welcomes the long case clock for its rich contribution of colour and ornamental detail, but for dating he must depend upon the outward evidence of case and dial. The accompanying illustrations indicate important points to note. Usually the maker's name can be read on the dial—in late work often merely the name of the man who put together the factory-made parts of the simple mechanism. Many thousands of British clockmakers with their dates of working have been listed in, e.g., G. H. Baillie's *Watchmakers and Clockmakers of the World.*

Figs 121–125 show chronologically the general changes in shape and proportions of the case and important hood and dial details. The arched dial, introduced about 1720, at first often contained the maker's name. Moving moon faces appeared from the 1730s, recording the phases of the moon. Moving figures such as the popular rocking ship date from the 1740s onwards. Alternatives in the arch include a seconds dial and hand or a pointer to regulate the striking of the clock.

Other details for the collector to note include: the large arabic figures for the minutes used in the 1730s; decorative formal motifs to mark the half hours between the hour numerals, seldom included after the 1740s; the increasing use from the 1750s of a dial consisting of a single metal plate without a separate hour ring; the cast brass dial plate introduced around 1775, when a frequent alternative was the creamy white enamelled copper plate, introduced in the 1740s and becoming fully white by the 1780s; a common substitute of white-painted iron or wood from the 1790s.

121. Early long case clocks, in order of date; slender style of late 17th century with gable pediment; square top without pilasters, side hood windows and bob glass in body door, often rich with marquetry; late 17th-century clock with curved cresting, twist-turned pilasters attached to lift-off hood; late 17th-century clock with 'cushion' hood, half-column pilasters at front and quarter-columns at rear; early Georgian example for taller rooms.

It is important to remember that many clocks made throughout the 18th century were extremely simple. When the dial is square and of brass it is easy to ante-date such work despite the large size of the dial, and the frequent use of mahogany to ornament the oak case.

122. Long case clocks, 18th century. Rounded arch with harmonising top and body door, panelled plinth base, from 1720s; fret-cut pediment, body pilasters, clipped corner base panel, c. 1740s on; 'pagoda' pediment c. 1750s–60s; broken pediment, short body with shaped door, bracket feet; swan-neck pediment, shaped back to hood (see Fig. 125) and 'Gothic' body door, second half of century.

123 (*below left*). **Long case clocks, later 18th century**: carved ornament under swan-neck, body pillars, ornate base; pear-drop moulding under hood, whole design becoming squat; smooth surfaced with marquetry, towards 1800; plain style of c. 1800, serpentine pediment, no columns, base with projecting panels.

124. Long case clock details. TOP: typical late 17th-century hood which had to be lifted off to reach clock face, showing twist-turned pilasters and half-pilasters (quarter-columns) at back, carved cresting, convex moulding at base; three details of dial's corner spandrels, the early winged head, more complex developments and asymmetrical scrolls of towards mid-18th century and below them typical strike-silent indicator and early and later date apertures. BOTTOM, hands: late 17th century; early 18th century; very delicate, especially around 1770s; heavier, towards end of century.

PART XVII

The Crafts Involved in Making Furniture

Basically, household furniture as we know it in England to-day was evolved by the joiner and turner. Primitive furniture, such as chests, could consist of riven planks, crudely trimmed with saw and adze and held together with clout-headed nails. This work was well within the scope of the carpenter whose timber-framed buildings would necessarily include much built-in seating, shelving and cupboarding. But stronger methods of neat, small-scale construction were needed for the stresses of movable seat furniture and prompted the development of the basic mortise-and-tenon method of joining end grain into side grain, the tongue or tenon driven into its matching hollow and secured by pinning through both pieces of wood with a headless wooden dowel pin (Fig. 127). When the holes were slightly out of line the pin would pull the tenon extra tightly into the hole, a process known as draw-boring.

Soon the joiner's work included all chairs, bedsteads, tables, forms, chests, cabinets, cupboards and presses, defined in 1632 by the Carpenters' Company as 'pannelled, duftalled, pynned or glued'.

On the other hand the turner depended basically upon work that could be shaped on his primitive pole lathe, using fairly unexacting local woods such as ash, elm, beech and fruit woods. He, too, could produce useful, plain furniture such as stools and tables and everyday chairs, boring holes in blocks of wood to insert the shaped tips of lathe-moulded legs and back rails: the leg was often tenoned right through the seat and fixed with a foxtail wedge. Heating shrank the dowelled

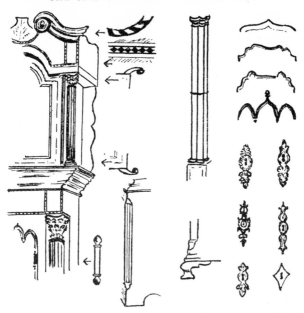

125. Long case clocks, late 18th-century details. LEFT: part of hood, mahogany veneer with loop ornaments of marquetry stringing (detail at top), and panel effects with marquetry diamond bands. Below this are shown details of hood door hinges and a body door hinge. CENTRE: cluster-column pillar such as flank the body door and (below) two alternatives for the chamfered base, one reeded, one with cabriole bracket foot. RIGHT: four typical tops to body doors and (below) six key escutcheons to such doors including the simple diamond of the 1800s.

end so that it could be fixed the more tightly into its hole. Some of his methods have never been bettered, such as for the Windsor type of chair. He retained his independence when

369

126. Japanning applied to wall or coaching clocks, the only other time-pieces which are collected as furniture. LEFT: c. 1740s, the early clock style with narrow body black-japanned and painted with chinoiseries. CENTRE: c. 1760s. RIGHT: c. 1780s, banjo style, also found in mahogany case. Frequently the face was black with gilded hands and figures. Because such clocks did not strike, there was only one winding hole for the eight-day movement. The weight fell behind both face and body so the smaller face necessitated a longer body. The minute hand has a long compensatory tail.

such crafts as chairmaking became specialist branches of joinery with the co-operation of upholsterer, carver and gilder and soon merely part of the whole craft of cabinet making.

By Tudor days home makers were distinguishing between the stools made by the turner and the superior joint-stool with its seat frame, legs and stretcher all secured to each other by mortise-and-tenon joints. The joiner was responsible for the Elizabethan and Stuart extending table known as a draw table (Fig. 46) and the same style of jointing was employed for making the case furniture of the period—chests, Bible boxes, table desks, coffers and panelled chairs and settles.

By the method generally accepted from the Continent in the later 15th century the joiner formed his framework of cross rails, vertical stiles and intervening muntins suitably grooved to enclose flat panels of wood without nails or glue. Such panels, even of temperamental oak, could respond to atmospheric changes and remain serviceable for centuries. An early chest frequently contained a small till, but by the 17th century there was a general demand for fitted furniture. A chest might include a couple of wide drawers at the bottom—the 17th-century mule chest—and the massive hall or parlour cupboard introduced the refinement of small compartments in its upper portion. Drawers were grooved to run on bearers projecting from the framing, and primitive through dovetails were evolved for joining their corners.

Such developments inevitably compelled craftsmen to specialise, and by the end of the 17th century—which for most of us is no more than the beginning of the collectors' period—furniture craftsmen included not only joiners and turners continuing traditional methods in oak, walnut and other mainly native woods, but also a great number of men with more specialised skills, using costly foreign woods for their patient, exquisite craftsmanship.

As some indication of their scope, it may be recalled that an 18th-century cabinet, with every refinement of drawer and pigeon hole and secret hiding place, might be finished with veneer or marquetry, with tortoiseshell or rolled paper filigree, inlay, carving, lacquer, japanning or paint. Many were mounted with mirror glass and the mirror frame carver and gilder became immensely important. Some rested on stands covered in gilded composition known as gesso; all required metal handles and hinges of comparable charm in brass or ormolu. By the second half of the 18th century a furniture-making firm of any size and importance usually covered the whole range of crafts and advertised as cabinet maker and

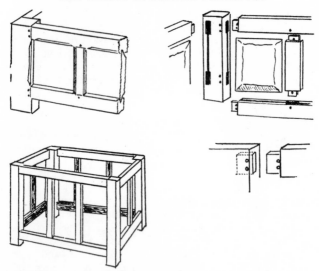

127. Joiner's work in chest construction, showing panels held by corner stiles, muntins and cross rails. The mortise and tenon joints linking these are held by square-cut dowel pins driven into round holes right through the carcase. TOP LEFT: outside corner of chest, the panel framing edged with scratch mouldings (top and left), run moulding (right), splay (bottom) in architect's manner. TOP RIGHT: the inside, taken to pieces to show loose panel adze-trimmed round its inner edges. BOTTOM LEFT: basic carcase for a chest. BOTTOM right: detail of mortise and tenon joint—end-grain into side-grain.

upholsterer. Below, alphabetically, are brief summaries of a few of the more important crafts and processes involved.
Cane (Figs 19, 29, 111, etc.): obtained from the variety of palm known as rattans grown in the Malay Peninsula. It was introduced to give light, resilient seating and back panels to chairs

soon after 1660, being split and interwoven at first in coarse mesh, but soon more finely. It was thus an alternative to the webbing and horsehair that formed the basis of the upholsterer's chair. It returned to favour to some extent with each renewal of fashion interest in Oriental ornament.

Native English substitutes included rushes for seating and osiers for basketry—country work in contrast to the specialist London cane work.

Carving (Figs 12, 14, 45, 52, 103, etc.): Primitive chisel-and-gouge chip carving is noted on some medieval chests (Fig. 58). More elaborate carving, in high relief and usually somewhat crude, was popular for costly work through Elizabethan and Stuart days in oak and solid walnut (Fig. 106). In the late 17th century even the country joiner might shape his planks in elaborate baluster and wave outlines to avoid calling upon the turner for small table legs and the like (Fig. 49).

Mirror frames and stands for cabinets were carved in soft woods and gilded from the late 17th century onwards and carving was an important preliminary to much of the ornament covered in gilded gesso (Figs 4, 5). Early Georgian Spanish mahogany blunted the carver's tools but rewarded him with brilliant and enduring relief work such as chair arms and feet (Figs 22, 23).

In this early mahogany, pierced work was possible on chair splats and the like (Fig. 24), but later in the 18th century when inferior bay wood might be used, the frets of pediments (Fig. 81), for example, were cut through three thin layers of the wood glued together at different angles of grain. The silversmith's cut-card work was often produced by gluing such frets against a smooth ground of the same wood—easier than producing a perfectly smooth background behind solid carving (Fig. 23): the alternative for an inferior craftsman was to matt the background. On examination an elaborate ribband-back chair in the style of Chippendale may be found to consist of pieces separately carved at suitable angles of grain and glued to a shaped and fretted base.

Later 18th-century and Regency styles made comparatively little use of the carver, and in Victorian days machine carving produced much second-rate, shallow work, particularly among later Victorian makers who continued conservatively with long-accepted design. By the 1850s saw piercing also could be achieved with machinery, pioneered by Prosser and Hadley. In the second half of the century amateurs were encouraged to make use of the various aids to carving patented in the 1840s, and there was demand for such works as *The Amateur's Practical Guide to Fretwork*. Treadle machines did the rough work which was finished by hand. Today, however, the collector may be more easily confused by the amateur work, typically in blackened oak, associated with the 1890s and the first years of this century, often incorporating mottoes and similar elements.

Cofferer's work: This has caused some confusion, as simple chests were often inventoried as coffers. The term is best reserved for the traveller's trussing coffers, with rounded tops and coverings of nailed-on ox hide or strong fabric to throw off the rain and keep out dust (Fig. 60). From these the cofferers—basically leather workers—came to be responsible for the specialised craft of making furniture, such as chairs and stools, wholly covered with leather or fabric secured by brass, dome-topped nails. Such fabrics as the 18th-century's popular horse-hair with a linen warp lacked resilience and could only be secured by nailing (Fig. 26).

Gesso (Figs 52, 67): To the furniture collector this is associated especially with fine quality gilded tables, cabinet stands, sometimes chairs and stools, particularly those in the costly architectural manner of the early 18th century. The surface might be smooth pine wood but as an alternative 'roughed out' carving might be glued on as a basis. This was covered with thin layers of a paste made of powdered chalk and size to build up a low relief pattern using tools, stamps and brushes. Finally this was water gilded. Characteristically the pattern is composed of intertwining arabesques against a matted ground.

Gilding and silvering: associated with the flamboyant furniture of post-1660, such as stands for Oriental cabinets. Silvering under time-weathered varnish may now be mistaken for gilding. Mirror frames were magnificently carved and gilded through much of the 18th century and even on mahogany furniture there was some·gilding of ornamental detail.

In the second half of the 18th century much drawing room furniture was gilded all over. For gilding that could be burnished the process was known as water gilding; for inferior work—and generally in the late 18th century—a cheaper fat oil gilding was used, based on boiled linseed oil mixed with chrome. Oil gilding did not require an elaborate base of gesso and was more damp resistant, but it lacked the brilliance of burnishing and could not be 'double gilded'. In both, the method was to cause filmy thin gold leaf, the product of prolonged gold-beating, to adhere to the prepared surface by applying a suitable mordant or gilder's size. R. W. Symonds drew attention to the fact that the final layers of water gilding or burnish size were of different tones at different periods—brown around the turn of the 17th and 18th centuries, reddish brown in early Georgian days, lighter red around the mid-18th century and thereafter old rose or mauve pink.

Brass mounts on furniture might be fire gilded. For this process the gold was applied in a mercury amalgam. Heat evaporated the mercury, leaving the gold strongly adhering to the metal. This was, however, a dangerous hazard to the gilder's health. Ormolu was a term used in England in the second half of the 18th century for gilded furniture mounts cast in the brassy alloy bronze. This was introduced by Matthew

Boulton and in 1762 the *English Gazette* declared that Birmingham ormolu was highly esteemed in Europe. Ormolu might replace gilded brass on top quality furniture for handles and key escutcheons and ornamental, veneer-protecting corner and foot mounts in the French manner.

Inlay: This 'set work' is less elaborate than marquetry and the two terms should be differentiated. In inlay the face of the solid wood is ornamented by cutting small cavities about an eighth of an inch deep and filling them with contrasting woods such as dark and light oak and holly. The ornament is associated with oak and walnut furniture of Elizabethan and early Stuart days, at first in simple geometrical patterns and at its most elaborate in flower and vase designs. Ivory inlay might be backed with holly for greater whiteness, as noted by John Houghton. Some furniture with a Spanish-Moorish flavour shows pearl and ivory inlay: these pieces date mainly from early post-Restoration years, inspired perhaps by the ornate, gold-mounted caskets incrusted with ivory or pearl from the Portuguese colony of Goa which Charles II presented to his favourites.

There was a little metal stringing early in the 18th century, but brass inlay is associated with the end of the century and the Regency period (Fig. 13) when a banding plane was devised to cut ornamental lines from sheet brass and also grooves to receive them in cabinet furniture in a single operation. This won an award from the Society of Arts in 1818. The same year Robert Clayton patented a way of making brassy inlays by using a metal alloy fusible at a low temperature that could be poured into incisions cut or punched in the wood.

Boulle or buhl was a form of marquetry produced with thin tortoiseshell and brass cut together in elaborate patterns. The work took its name from a Frenchman, André Charles Boulle (1642–1732). English work dates mainly from 1815 onwards.

Japanning (Figs 126, 131): Charles II's court returned from

128. Veneer ornaments of 18th-century furniture. TOP: parquetry with pieces of veneer arranged in balanced pattern, the oyster pattern shown consisting of four pieces of laburnum wood; marquetry of early colourful 'Dutch' style; detail of foliated arabesque marquetry which may also include fantastic birds, usually in a few light and dark tones; detail of subsequent more intricate seaweed marquetry in two tones. BOTTOM: Adamesque scroll and anthemion from 1760s; urn with ribbons and husks from 1760s; shell, flower and fan mainly found in satinwood, shaded by being burnt with hot sand, late 18th century.

exile with a delight in flamboyant furnishings. There was an obvious welcome for the East India Company's imports of Oriental lacquer and it was inevitable that the gorgeous colours and imaginative designs should be copied by inferior processes in England. In 1664 a hundred pieces of Oriental lacquer reached England; in 1706–10 imports included 224 cabinets and 818 lacquer boards, as well as other items. The lacquer boards were used then and later for panelling ladies' boudoirs or closets or were cut up and made into furniture with 'the finest hodg-podg and medley of Men and Trees turned topsy-turvy' as observed by Stalker. In 1750 records show that three

ships alone brought Oriental furniture to the value of £30,000
—a large sum at that time.

It must be stressed that the Oriental lacquer process differed
entirely from European japanning: it depended upon the
gum of a small Chinese tree, *rhus vernicifera*, that had to be
used as soon as tapped, involving repeated applications under
warm, humid conditions, sometimes over a basis of silk or
paper covered with a clay paste. An alternative source was a
lac produced by an Indian insect, *coccus lucca*. Each layer was
smoothed with a succession of polishing powders to produce
results that were lighter, harder, more durable and less liable
to peel than later Oriental work or European substitutes.
English japanning tends to lack the smooth brilliance, and
design is tame and contrived, but the effect at its best may be
very splendid. Even Oriental ornament was made specifically
for the European market, but in the japanners' imitations the
Oriental themes lost all meaning and might mingle Chinese and
Japanese motifs.

The English work was known as japanning as distinct
from the 'right Japan' or 'right Indian' products of the Orient.
A popular *Treatise of Japanning* was brought out by Stalker
and Parker in 1688 and some work remains from Queen Anne
and early Georgian days. Interest revived around the mid-18th
century, in the Regency, yet again on early Victorian papier
mâché and still later with the craze for Japanese furnishings.

The *Treatise* gave 'above an hundred distinct patterns of
Japan work, for Tables, Stands, Frames, Cabinets, Boxes,
etc'. as well as recipes for the coloured backgrounds and the
metal dusts in the decoration. At first even the raised lacquer
known as Bantam work was attempted, itself a Dutch-
Javanese imitation of the Oriental incised lacquer. A gesso-like
basis of whiting and size was built up on a softwood foundation, coloured, polished, cut with a graving tool and suitably
gilded, but this was 'almost obsolete' by 1688. More usually a

few details of the ornament were raised a little with blobs of gesso paste, perhaps thickened with fine sawdust, but this tended to flake. Oak proved an unsuitable basis for such work, the best woods being lime and pear. A large area such as a cabinet door might be veneered first on both sides.

The japanning process was defined by Robert Dossie, 1758, as 'covering bodies by grounds of opaque colours in varnish; which may be either afterwards decorated by painting or gilding or left in a plain state'. The basis for this highly decorative japanning was a varnish composed of spirits of wine and a resinous gum lac: Stalker and Parker recommended seed-lac because shell-lac lasted badly. Shell-lac—resinous secretion of the scale insect—made the spirits of wine viscid enough to hold the colours suspended but was too brown for the now rare blue and cream toned grounds.

Dossie noted as an improvement the reduction of slow hand polishing expected of early japanners and the substitution of five or six coats of strong seed-lac varnish dried by slow stoving and finished with rubbings of rotten stone and oil. It was possible thus to produce strong, dark backgrounds including the black and red mottling popular as counterfeit tortoise-shell. Dossie foresaw, however, 'a consummate degree of perfection' for the art in the newer method of dissolving gum copal in oil of turpentine. He noted that by then the early undercoating was omitted, understandable in a process that always lent itself to enthusiastic amateur dabbling.

Gilt effects were particularly popular as the coats of varnish protected the brilliance of such copper gilt powders of the day as 'German gold'. Modern japanning that has been 'aged' may sometimes be recognised by coarse cracks intended to suggest the fine crazing of the antique. Colour fading can be judged by removing a metal mount.

The japanning process became important again on 19th-century papier mâché as the basic surface could be polished

129. Tunbridge ware. TOP: early forms popular in Regency, the vandykes or long triangles probably inspired by the marking of the backgammon board; typical star from small box lid; popular flat cube pattern, the three-dimensional effect enhanced by the direction of the grain in the diamond shapes of different woods. SECOND ROW: simple and, later, more complicated borders, that on right showing the basis of small squares that composed the mosaic form. BOTTOM: the Victorian mosaic form showing the general effect in a 'framed picture' of Battle Abbey; typical souvenir obelisk thermometer, flower border.

to a lacquer-like gloss and the varnishes could be fixed by prolonged oven heating without risk of warp or shrinkage. For such work the superb final gloss was achieved by long hours of polishing with the bare hand.

By the later 18th century a cheap form of oil varnishing called japanning was widely applied as a finish to soft wood furniture but was sometimes so poor that it could hardly be distinguished from varnishing over common oil paint. There was, for example, an enormous demand for cheap little japanned rout chairs with rush seats, lent out by cabinet makers for parties and entertainments. By the end of the 18th century there were 'japanned chair manufactories' producing also sofas, occasional tables and bed cornices. Here too old furniture could be re-japanned. Much was darkened with lamp black—some with more costly ivory black—but such colours as blue, green and yellow were also used; many painted to resemble satinwood, rosewood or bamboo, others finished with bronze or burnished gold enrichments. By 1800 more than 60 furniture japanners were at work in London. Victorians delighted in vast quantities in straw colour and much was grained to suggest bird's eye maple. The highly skilled craft of japanning metals is largely outside the scope of this book.

Marble: Rich homes in early Georgian days were furnished with handsome, marble-topped console tables and side tables, the marbles usually imported and given great consideration by their selectors (Fig. 52). These were serviceable in dining room and hall where walnut veneers and gesso might be spoilt in use. The slabs became thinner late in the 18th century when artificial scagliola was a popular alternative: both suited the smooth horizontal lines of Regency furnishing and the archeological enthusiasts drew attention to remnants of furniture from the Roman occupation in oiled and polished shale.

Improvements in marble-cutting machinery, steam driven, prompted price reductions and a consequent use of the material on early Victorian dining room and bedroom furniture. English supplies such as the black marble of Derbyshire were in use as early as the 16th century and in the 18th-century neoclassical mood there was a vogue for Derbyshire's spectacular and unique fluorspar known as blue-john. But it was more especially in the 19th century, when blue-john was becoming scarce, that Derbyshire marble workers developed the mosaics for covering the tops of console and pedestal tables and smaller ornaments.

At first these were merely veneers of marble scraps naturally coloured and variously lined and speckled and cemented on haphazardly. These were followed by geometrical and flower patterns reminiscent of Italian work, and around the mid-19th century such mosaics were made in several parts of Britain, including Yorkshire, Devon, Cornwall and Ireland. But collectors look for Derbyshire's distinctive inlay work with hollows cut in the local soft black marble and filled with contrasting pieces. Regency geometrical devices were followed by realistic birds, butterflies and flowers in the restless early Victorian mood, all polished to a uniform silky glow. Sometimes a whole table is composed of marble but the work is found also as panels inset in chests, cupboard doors, etc. Patterns were commissioned from industrial designers such as R. Redgrave and occasionally a piece is found inconspicuously signed.

An early substitute for costly imported marble was scagliola, composed of plaster of Paris and glue and suitably tinted and given its peculiar quality by the addition of small pieces of marble, alabaster, etc. Highly polished slabs were used for side tables as well as for home decoration. It was famous in Italy in the 17th century and made in England from about the 1760s, and widely used at the end of the century, made by the London firm of Vincent Bellman.

In Victorian days, however, another substitute eventually defeated even the makers of elaborate marble inlays. This price-cutting material, shown at the 1851 exhibition, was painted slate. It was claimed to be stronger than stone, lighter than marble, non-absorbent and immensely tough and compact. A japanning process using prolonged heat rendered the coloured ornament durable and such specialists as G. E.

Magnus of Pimlico offered a wide range of cheap home furnishings, whereas a superb table of marble inlay by S. Birley of Ashford, Derbyshire, cost as much as £240.

Marquetry (Figs 64, 65, 102, 128 etc.): In contrast to inlays set into the solid wood this craft consists of producing patterns of different wood tones entirely in the veneer applied over the surface of a furniture carcase. In the most advanced work, patterns and background might be cut together from woods of contrasting tone to achieve elaborate and meticulously matched interlacings for gluing to the furniture surface. Slight slanting of the saw ensured that the pattern and its 'background' would fit closely into each other.

Some early specimens of the late 17th century are found in the Dutch style of naturalistic flower and bird groups in coloured woods, ivory or bone, presented in shaped reserves, but these soon gave way to leafy scrolls and arabesques in a few tones and the ultimate intricacies of seaweed or endive style worked out in box or holly wood against the walnut ground. Sometimes only walnut was used, suitably bleached and darkened.

The vogue soon lost importance in the 18th century but the neo-classical delight in smooth veneered surfaces from the 1760s created a new demand. Marquetry took its place with paint and inlay in presenting vases, swags and other popular neo-classic motifs on table tops and cabinet furniture in holly, satinwood, harewood and various exotic woods and stained substitutes.

Much dyeing and tinting of woods is associated with the 19th century, such as knotty burr birch dyed to suggest rosewood. At the 1851 exhibition the boast of one firm was that marquetry panels in a satinwood bedroom suite were not 'artificially dyed according to modern practice'. This too was a boast of the Tunbridge ware men who depended almost entirely upon local Kentish and Sussex trees and shrubs with natural contrasts of colour and grain when composing their small-scale marquetry patterns (*see* Paint and stain).

Regency Tunbridge ware shows geometrical designs, such as 'three dimensional' diamonds and long vandyke triangles. These were followed by mosaics composed wholly of tiny squares, occasionally as many as sixty to the inch presenting pictorial views and flower borders for mounting on veneered furniture and small wood wares (Fig. 129).

stained with oxide of iron. Early Victorians 'freshened' and stained many woods with alkanet, barberry root or gamboge according to the tone required. Mahogany was stained with bichromate of potash. Ebony was enriched with a mixture in which gall nuts had been boiled and in which steel filings had been steeped. Birch wood was widely stained and its knotty root fibres tinted with cochineal. This cheap wood was much used for chairs, coloured to imitate rosewood or mahogany.

Papier mâché (Figs 42, 91, 92, 131): made an important contribution to the furniture makers' minor crafts in the first half of the 19th century. Henry Clay's paper ware was patented in 1772 and expensive painted trays, panels for tea caddies, etc., were produced. His successors from 1816 were the well-known firm of Jennens and Bettridge, who continued to use high quality paper ware for most of their work. Cheaper pressed paper ware first appeared under the name of papier mâché only in the 1830s, evolved by Richard Brindley. This was heavier, less perfect in texture, more brittle and liable to damage. Clay's method consisted of building up successive layers of suitable paper saturated in paste and laid over a mould, dried, layer by layer under heat, until it was hard enough for carving or filing. It was then coloured and given the further slow treatment of repeated stovings to fix the layers of opaque japan varnish that were finished by hand polishing.

Brindley developed a method of shaping his wet sheets or pulp between dies. Repetitive ornamental mouldings were easily formed by casting the pulpy material in moulds. In 1850 egg-and-tongue moulding cost 2d or 3d a foot, a Tudor rose 8d, a console table leg 25s, a table with three lion legs £6. Today's collector looks for stools, firescreens, table desks, work tables, or an occasional wildly curving chair. The material, like iron, was used basically as a substitute for wood, but unaffected by the heat of the japanner's stove, so that it was peculiarly well suited to this slow process.

Ornament on early work is in oil paints with gold borders. The popular bronze powders in many shades, often used for increasingly elaborate Oriental scenes, date mainly from the 1820s onwards, being patented in 1812. But fadeless black backgrounds, composed of a tar varnish mixed with lamp black, date only from the 1830s. Pearl ornament encrusted upon the japan was patented in 1825, being imitated in thicker, coarser shell. Acid was used for shaping the shell from 1840.

Flower and fern ornament is associated especially with the 1830s onwards, but was becoming somewhat blowsy by the 1850s. Peacock designs are associated with Fred Newman from about 1840; sea shell designs were popular from about 1845. What has come to be known as the Wolverhampton style of ornament introduced bronze powders to achieve such effects as sun's rays through the stained-glass windows of romantic ruined buildings among groups of sombre trees. Inevitably, too, there was considerable imitation of other materials, in the 1850s, including blue-john, malachite, agate, even veneers of walnut for hard-worked trays.

Collectors look especially for the work of such important manufacturers as Jennens and Bettridge, occasionally impressed with their name. Views of Oxford may be found painted on papier mâché blanks from Birmingham by the Oxford firm of Spiers and Sons. Irish views turn up occasionally, issued by S. Fraser. Picture trays are favourites with collectors.

Pen work (Fig. 132): A distinctive form of japanned furniture ornament for decorating table tops, cabinet doors, etc. Sheraton defined the work as 'in imitation of etching but made more pleasing by working in Indian ink'. The furniture was first japanned black, then hand-painted with all-over designs in white japan—now yellowed—and finally given more lively definition by line work drawn in Indian ink with a quill pen and fine brushes. In some instances the ground was entirely white japan with the design carried out in fine black lines.

Finally the surface was glazed with transparent varnish. Early examples were decorated with much leaf and scroll work and incorporating motifs from ancient Rome and Egypt. Somewhat later the motifs might be derived from the Chinese.

Sheraton suggested several of the main designs fashionable in pen work from 1795. Such patterns were prepared by professional designers following a recognised trade of the period and drawn with lead pencil on heavy paper. Penwork artists then copied them upon the japanned surface. Writing masters, then numerous in London, were employed for this work.

Poker work: The Victorian firm known as the Burnwood Carving Company specialised in relief ornament, but the craft is associated especially with early Victorian amateurs using hot skewers to engrave formal designs and pictorial scenes on small table tops and the like. The charred wood was removed by rubbing with sand. One specialist, Brigg, devised a way of charring only the surface of the wood to achieve, for example, effects of more costly wood graining that would be more lasting than paint, but this was ousted in 1854 by the use of acid applied with wood blocks.

Turnery (Figs 18, 19, 30, 49, 53, 57, 88, 100 etc.): Turnery in Britain dates back to prehistoric days. As indicated earlier, the turner's most important tool was his lathe that revolved a piece of wood—cleft rather than sawn for strength—against the cutting tools that shaped its outline. With pole-lathe or bow-lathe he used a foot treadle. This revolved the wood in one direction and at the same time tautened the pull on a springy wooden pole or bow. When he stopped treadling, the tension caused the wood to be revolved in the opposite direction. The alternative was the throw lathe powered by a boy turning a large wheel. In the 18th century the craft became a hobby in rich families making ornaments in amber, ivory, etc.

The turner made chairs, stools, tables and the like and contributed legs and spindles for many purposes as well as the massive screws for presses, etc. But to the collector his work is especially important because the outlines of turned members, such as chair and table legs on fashionable work, are some indication of date. Straight stick legs with minor incisions were followed by the Flemish inspired bulbous cup-and-cover

swellings of the Elizabethans, enhanced by carving. The early 17th century produced somewhat crudely proportioned baluster or vase outlines. A double head-to-head baluster with a central knop was an ornamental outline of this period noted, for example, in illuminated lettering such as the headings of important James I and Charles I documents.

The mid-17th century is associated with repetitive ball or bead turning and the more ornamental variant suggests a series of reels; also alternating balls and reels. Then came the later 17th century's most flowing, well-proportioned baluster line at a time when Continental influences compelled English turners to master swash turning—the familiar barley sugar twist. In this the English work tends to be more open than the Continental. It is noted in single and double twist; and required a change in technique to cut obliquely to the axis, and the outline had to be finished by hand filing or rasping. The last years of the century saw turned legs with various forms of swelling at knee height, including an inverted cup outline and the trumpet leg.

Through much of the 18th century turnery was limited to the shapely tops and pillars of claw tables, as the early dense mahogany was heavy on the turner's tools. When better cutting steel was available late in the century turned legs became fashionable again. Simple tapers were alternatives to shallow twists in slanting ribbon lines. A tight rope or cable

131. Papier mâché. TOP: three chairs and between them a small writing desk and a footstool. The lack of grain made it possible to shape the material at angles impossible in wood but specimens are rarely found in perfect condition. Ornament includes paint, gilding and thin wisps of pearly shell laid upon the surface and surrounded by japanning. SECOND ROW: three worktables shown at the Great Exhibition, 1851, when the cheaper, more brittle pressed work was replacing the sturdier smoother paperware developed by Henry Clay. BOTTOM: folding table; vase stand; occasional table; teapoy.

twist was much in evidence around 1805, possibly inspired by the naval exploits during this time.

Heavy turnery in the early 19th century became particularly conspicuous in the so-called Greek leg. Subsequent turned detail is confused, but the collector quickly comes to recognise Victorian turned spindles, their shaping consisting of little more than surface incisions. The lack of coherence in turned detail is summed up by Eastlake in the third quarter of the 19th century in a reference to 'gouty table legs looking like inverted cups and saucers piled upon an attic baluster'.

Upholders' work: In considering old records it is important to realise the importance that came to be attached to the upholder or upholsterer. In the *London Tradesman*, 1747, the upholder is defined as 'originally a species of Taylor, but by degrees he crept over his head, and set up as a Connoisseur in every article that belongs to a House. He employs journeymen in his own proper calling, cabinet makers, glass grinders, looking-glass framers, carvers for chairs, Testers and Posts for Beds, the Woolen Draper, the mercer, the Linen Draper and several species of Smiths, and a vast army of tradesmen and other mechanic branches'. Such important firms as Ince and Mayhew and the various Chippendale partnerships usually specified that they were cabinet makers and upholsterers. The fact that a Society of Cabinet-makers and Upholsterers began to publish trade catalogues in the later 18th century indicates how the various furniture crafts had become interdependent.

Upholstery (Figs 8, 10, 31, 69, 74, 104, 108, 109 etc.): Inevitably little remains that belongs much earlier than the 19th century. Particularly enduring turkey work may be noted, dating from the 17th century and the first half of the 18th. This was then in commercial manufacture as a covering for stools and chairs such as those used at guild meetings and as an alternative to leather, serge, kersies, etc. in everyday merchants' homes, in contrast to such luxury furnishings as velvets and silks. Turkey work was a professional rather than an amateur skill, with a pile woven by a carpet making technique or knotted onto a canvas ground. Typical patterns show formalised flowers.

In the 1680s the woollen manufacturers supplying upholsterers complained that the current popularity for French walnut chairs with fillings of Indian cane had put 50,000 in the woollen trades out of work.

Eighteenth-century records, especially those by women, such as Celia Fiennes around 1700, Lady Grisell Baillie, Mrs. Lybbe Powys and Mrs. Delany, indicate the splendour of upholstered furniture, often matching the room or bed hangings. William Linnell, about 1740, priced some chairs at £2 each for the frame, and £2 7s for the basic upholstery work without the covering.

It is important to note that rebated chair rails to take upholstered seats that could be lifted out for renovation were introduced at the end of the 17th century. Nevertheless Thomas Chippendale, for example, specified that his chairs looked best 'stuffed over the rails but are most commonly done with brass nails in one or two rows and sometimes the nails are done to imitate fretwork. They are usually covered with the same stuff as the window curtains'. Close nailing was essential for most leather and hair cloths lacking elasticity.

In the 17th century fringes dominated upholstered seats and the many details of bed draperies. In the first half of the century the silken threads usually hung straight and loose, but through the second half of the century and onwards they were twisted and tufted in costly elaboration. Books of fringe patterns were popular, for much of this was amateur work by the ladies of the house and by house servants who could thus be kept occupied through long candle-lit evenings. However, the fashion disappeared in early Georgian days.

For amateur embroiderers through late Stuart and early

Georgian days there were endless opportunities for lavish furnishings. These were stitched in coloured crewels on curtains of linen and cotton twill and there were bed covers worked in silks, in satin-stitch, chain-stitch and the like, often over squared or meander quilting. All this owed much to the fashionable Indian chintzes to some extent prohibited but never, it seems, very adequately kept out of the country. For seat furniture the embroiderer worked patterns of massed flower heads, frequently against mustardy yellow grounds, using the particularly strong, close tent-stitch or the speedier cross-stitch (Fig. 130).

In Georgian days, however, home embroidery was largely forgotten in favour of more diverting hobbies such as shell work and ornamental turnery, and little remains beyond the occasional firescreen with minimal satin-stitch embroidery such as a shepherdess and her French-knotted sheep. For furniture upholstery there was an abundance of damasks, printed chintzes and the tapestries approved by Chippendale. In 1761, for example, the firm of Vile and Cobb quoted for a mahogany sofa 'stuft and quilted in Linnen and covered with damask and finish'd with Burnish nails' for eight guineas.

Small springs had been introduced in the early Georgian exercising 'horse' chair, but the overstuffed chair depended for its comfort upon horsehair on a basis of criss-cross webbing, strengthened by a narrow bar of wood down the centre of the back and another from back to front of the seat. An essential detail on the chair seat was a roll of horsehair around the front edge, fixed separately from the main stuffing.

Silks were expected in rooms then fashionably hung with silks or paper instead of panelling, but upholsterers frequently quoted also for cases of linen or serge that would protect them during everyday use. Early in this period there was a liking for silk and satins with medallion patterns and stripes, followed by more plain fabrics. Sheraton revelled in voluminous draperies for his French-fashion beds and put 'French printed silks' on the backs of some chairs.

During the Regency cabinet furniture often showed pleated silk behind the neat brass grills of cupboard doors 'strained in straight puckers' as approved by Sheraton. Tassels and fringes had returned to some extent near the end of the century. Delicate netting as a furniture trimming suited the wispy dress of Regency days and is prominent in the groups of laconic Grecian-dressed ladies intriguingly portrayed by Moses. Like women's costume, such trimmings became more massive and elaborate as the 19th century advanced.

Most of the old fabrics on antiques today date to the 19th century, when the range was spectacularly wide. In printed cottons alone the annual supply rose from 32 million yards in 1800 to 347 million yards in 1830. Contemporary comment draws attention to such details as the paisley shawl draped over the ottoman, the table cover of mohair, or even hand stencilled to reproduce the grain of mahogany or rosewood.

The early 19th century's liking for pale tones in plain materials soon gave place to bright and then darker colours, the heavy Victorian tones of the 60s in velvets and worsted damasks, endlessly patterned and hung with all manner of braids and fringes. To some extent the developing use of the Jacquard loom was responsible for the many cotton-and-worsted and silk-and-worsted damasks which vastly supplemented the rich folks' furnishings of velvets and fine silks from Spital-fields and Macclesfield. Patterns ranged from traditional flower formalities to 'Elizabethan' strapwork and rococo scrolling cartouches. Until well into the 1850s romantic historical scenes were printed, too, and sentimental groups of the royal family: even imitations of the Berlin wool cross-stitch needlework. Profusions of huge naturalistic flowers dominated the mid-century, and in the second half of this period stripes were combined with every kind of pattern. But delicate ferns were also in favour during these years.

Texture-loving early Victorians delighted in smothering, all-embracing fabrics on the substantial seat furniture that met their need for stability and security. It is easy to understand their affection for silk plush, their respect for horsehair. In Victorian days the latter acquired a new elasticity when the linen warp of the late 18th century was replaced by more pliant American cotton.

Lace was important for windows and mirror furnishings as the Heathcote patent for machine-made net expired in 1823 and Nottingham seized eagerly upon the new trade. This was a period that produced great quantities of superb white embroidery and met the demand for home furnishings with commercially developed tambour-stitchery on machine-made net. But by as early as 1840 every kind of 'lace' pattern could be produced by machine. By 1871 nearly 30,000 English women were employed in the trade of machine-made lace.

More enduring furnishings included many by little-talented amateurs using exactly squared canvas that made it possible to reproduce patterns printed on squared paper, in quickly worked cross-stitch. Silks and beads were early alternatives, but the characteristic Berlin work is in merino wools, softer than the traditional English home needlewoman's crewels. Patterns and suitable meshed canvas were available in Germany by about 1820, and in this country the fashion took root about ten years later.

By 1840 some 14,000 pattern designs had been published for English needlewomen, mainly taken from English and French prints. The gaudy dyes of later Berlin wool work followed the discovery of aniline purple in 1856. This all-pervading Berlin work is found on workboxes, stools, even chairs, and framed as wall pictures such as the popular Landseer *Hawking Party* or *Mary Queen of Scots Mourning over the Dying Douglas. A Useful and Modern Work on Cheval*

132. Penwork ornament, a late Regency speciality. LEFT: typical cabinet, its top, front and edge of sides smothered in penwork, white on black. CENTRE: typical flower detail suggesting line embroidery at a time when print-like stitchery was in vogue. RIGHT: typical alternative with semi-classic motifs simply outlines showing great use of foliated scrolls and mythological creatures.

and Pole Screens, Ottomans, Chairs and Settees, for Mounting Berlin Needlework, by Henry Wood, published in 1845, indicates the current enthusiasm. By then some patterns were being printed by lithography directly upon the canvas.

The mid-19th century saw some revival of furnishing embroidery in satin-stitch and chain-stitch, however: here too, from about 1830, lithography brought down the cost of printing the patterns directly upon the fabric. Patchwork in silks and velvets was popular for small furnishings, and crochet was worked, and even hand lace. Even the least talented amateur could stitch machine-made braid in scrolling designs upon table covers, etc. Crochet antimacassars were in use under that name in the 1850s, but according to Lady Marian Alford were replaced by the 1880s with 'linen veils worked in crewels', reflecting the current craft movement atmosphere.

The Morris family produced elaborate figure embroideries and simpler flowers worked in worsteds upon serge, and the late years of the period are conspicuous for considerable revival of skilled needlecraft.

Coiled springs for upholstered seats were patented in 1828 by Samuel Pratt, but only gradually came into wide use, fixed to strong fabric or webbing further strengthened by cane or whalebone.

Veneer (Figs 61, 62 etc.): A covering of wood frequently less than an eighth of an inch thick covering the furniture carcase, obscuring constructional detail and offering opportunities to display the fine grain and colour of expensive timbers and those unsuited to structural stresses. The method achieved effects of great charm with the tangled knotty growths of delicate fibres known as burr wood: walnut burr is especially familiar in early 18th century work.

Tiger walnut has dark wavy stripes. 'Fiddleback' is familiar as a finely rippled grain. Among other grain patterns the plume or flame was obtained from the crotch of a side branch and the oyster was sliced transversely from a branch or small tree trunk to show the annual growth rings.

Hard, brittle ebony was an early favourite in the 17th century, applied over yellow deal. Veneers became conspicuous in the beautiful walnut cabinet furniture of the late 17th century and far into early Georgian days. In good work successive veneers cut from a single piece of finely grained wood would be applied to make almost exactly symmetrical patterns. In walnut these would be bordered with strips of cross-grain veneer without interrupting the level surface, to achieve panel effects with carefully mitred corners.

Early Spanish mahogany, superb for carving and lacking much grain pattern, put veneers out of fashion, but they were extremely important from the 1770s with the later Cuban mahogany veneered upon Honduras mahogany (bay wood)—cheaper but of huge girth—or still cheaper but knotty red pine. Veneers are widely found in satinwood and in decorative bandings of many exotic woods throughout the later 18th century and onwards. They contributed conspicuously to furniture of all qualities through the 19th century, although in Dickensian days the element of sham earned them disrepute.

The veneer was attached to the carcase with hot glue of varying composition. It long proved difficult to produce commercial glues that would keep in store, and a bone glue was patented as late as the end of the 18th century. The veneer might be soaked in hot size to make it pliant, but, even so, great skill was required when, as on 18th-century bombé commodes from the middle of the century, the surface might curve in two directions at once.

The most important detail was to ensure an even basis of glue. This could be spread on the carcase beforehand and re-softened when, with the veneer in position, the surface was heated with a wooden caul that completely covered it and was screwed tightly down. This caul, being slightly convex, pressed the glue outwards to all parts of the veneer panel. The same method could be used for applying panels of marquetry.

To achieve a balance of tension on a large panel it was necessary to veneer it upon both sides with the veneer grain running in a different direction from that of the base. The old method was to cut veneers with the saw six or seven to the inch, with great loss through sawdust. In 1806 Brunel patented a horizontal compound knife and eventually it became customary to use power-driven knives, avoiding the waste of sawdust but ill-suited to some fibrous growths. One method is to cut the veneer spirally from the log in one continuous sheet.

Many uses of veneer can only be explained when it is realised that materials represented the cabinet maker's main costs and labour was comparatively cheap—around three shillings for a cabinet maker's twelve-hour day in the 1780s. With materials of high quality it might prove cheaper even to veneer the four sides of a table leg than to cut it from costly solid wood.

PART XVIII

Woods Used by the Furniture Maker

Acacia (now known as *robinia*): whitish yellow tones with brown veinings, very hard. Used for bandings, inlays, occasionally for construction.

Alder: brown fading to pinkish tones with good knotty figure; strong for turnery. Country furniture in the 18th century.

Amboyna: warm light brown, much like walnut but with somewhat more curls in the grain. Veneers and bandings in 18th century.

Apple: pale or warm buff tone. Country furniture, especially in 18th century.

Ash: light brown with yellowish streaks and sometimes knotty markings; tough, springy, hard. Country furniture including chairs and the seats of Windsor chairs.

Bamboo (Fig. 96 etc.) (giant Indian reed with jointed stems): creamy yellow. Sometimes painted. Furniture in the Chinese taste and especially in late 18th and 19th centuries. Much imitated in turned beech painted cane colour.

Baywood: *see* MAHOGANY.

Beech: whitish-pink to pale brown with a flecked satiny grain. Subject to worm but endlessly used from 17th century onwards for country furniture, stained imitations of walnut and for painted and black-stained work. It was much used for the black bentwood furniture introduced from Austria in the mid-19th century. Also usual for out-of-sight work such as seat rails on upholstered furniture; could be close-nailed without splitting.

Bentwood (Figs 32, 33): developed from the second half of the 19th century, cheap woods being bent under pressure with heat and moisture. Usually stained black.

Birch: whitish with pinkish or yellowish tones and wavy grain. Substitute for satinwood in solid and veneer; also country furniture.

Bog oak: black because obtained from peat bogs. Used for inlay; also for small cabinet work by early Victorians.

Box: pale yellow to light brown, silky, hard. Much used for the light tones in marquetry and inlay, including stringing.

Brazil wood: reddish in tone with dark markings, rich when polished; hard, somewhat like Cuban mahogany. One of the woods of the Regency.

Burr wood: extremely dense, fibrous swellings started by injury or other interruption of normal development, especially in walnut, yew and elm. The rich, irregular patterns were much favoured for early 18th-century veneers.

Calamander wood: *see* COROMANDEL.

Cedar: warm light brown. Dry, aromatic, insect-repellent. Used especially from later 18th century for drawer and casket linings and cabinet fittings.

Cherry: reddish, close textured and could be stained to suggest mahogany. Country furniture, especially turnery.

Chestnut, horse and Spanish or sweet: both light brown but the latter whiter, less yellow. Both substitutes for satinwood, solid and veneer, in later 18th century.

Coromandel: like dark rosewood with some lighter striping. Bandings, etc., in late 18th century and Regency. This name and calamander given indiscriminately to several similar woods.

Cypress: reddish, very hard, close grained. Occasionally used for chests, etc. Houghton, 1727, stated: 'nothing outlasts it, or can be more beautiful, especially than the roots of the wilder sort, incomparable for its *crisped undulations*'.

Deal: term used for planks of softwood, mainly pine, such as were imported in great quantities from the Baltic coast; hence a general term for coniferous wood (*see* PINE.)

Dogwood: contrasting yellow and red tones of sapwood and heartwood; hard, but small girth. Some early inlay.

Ebony: black, very heavy, brittle but smooth. Early inlays. It has been suggested that the wood prompted cabinet makers to develop the technique of veneer.

Elm: brown, durable and tough but subject to worm. Recommended by John Houghton for extremes of dry and wet. Used for thick Windsor chair seats. The wych elm has a particularly attractive grain and polishes well.

Fustic: yellow. Used for inlay as well as for dye making, but was noted by Sheraton as turning a 'dead brownish hue'.

Grenobles wood: high quality French walnut.

Harewood: 19th-century term for the later 18th century's silverwood. This was English sycamore stained greenish-grey with oxide of iron.

Holly: white, slightly flecked, hard. Recommended by Evelyn (1664) as 'the whitest of all hard woods'. Used for inlay and marquetry, sometimes stained black.

Kingwood or violet wood: deep purple, close-grained, hard; bandings and inlays.

Laburnum (Fig. 128): yellowish with light brown streaks. Transverse cuttings from branches used for oyster parquetry.

Larch: yellowish white to reddish brown. Well-grown, it may resemble pine and is sometimes found as carcase wood, but warps badly.

Lignum vitae: contrasting brown and black; one of few imported woods before 1650 and long retained medicinal reputation. Immensely strong for machinery and turned work; used a little for veneers.

Lime: pale yellowish or whitish, soft, close-grained and excellent for fine undercut carving in mirror frames, etc.

Mahogany: originally the warm brown woods of the genus

swietenia and two other similar genera obtained from the West Indies—Hispaniola, Puerto Rico, Cuba and Jamaica—and from Honduras in Central America. Eventually a great number of fairly similar woods have come to be classed as mahogany. The Hispaniola or Spanish variety which first became a considerable import in the 1730s, is dark, with slight grain, hard, of huge girth and excellent for expert carving. The Cuban variety was welcomed around the mid-18th century as easier to work, with a rich but lighter hue and often showing a fine grain of ripple or curl. Honduras mahogany was widely imported in the second half of the century, often called baywood. This faded to a lighter tone, was light in weight with an open grain, but still of huge girth. Eighteenth-century mahogany was never 'red'.

Maple: this is *acer campestre*, as distinct from the *acer pseudo-platanus*, which in England is known as sycamore. Pale brown, fine grained; not big enough for more than small turnings, etc. The Victorian's bird's eye maple (golden, with fine lustre and small dark spots) is one of the characteristic grainings of the American sugar maple.

Mulberry: yellowish brown with dark streaks, heavy, tough. Sometimes used for veneers.

Oak: whitish to brown, heavy and hard. English oak was probably used for important early furniture, but Henry VIII ordered its preservation and in Elizabethan and Stuart days European oak was largely imported as clapboard and wainscot —whiter and more easily worked. Early joiners used riven wood and so obtained the fine 'silver grain' with an extremely hard surface (*see* Part II: MEDULLARY RAYS).

Olive: greenish-yellow with dark markings, hard. Parquetry veneer and cross-grain mouldings.

Padouk: purplish-red to brown, hard and heavy. Most often found in it is the furniture made for Europeans in the Dutch and Portuguese East Indies.

Partridge wood: brown and red mingled to suggest plumage. A little used for veneers.

Pear: pinkish tones with fine, smooth grain. Carvings and country furniture. Stained black and polished to suggest ebony.

Pencil cedar: brownish-red, soft, somewhat brittle. Used for bureau fittings, small drawers, etc.

Pine, Scots pine: yellowish to reddish, soft, easy to work, smooth surfaced. Abundant through northern Europe where cold conditions resulted in closer grain for carcase work. In pale tones, is known as yellow deal; red, as red deal or pine. Came into use largely after 1660 with new demand for carcase wood.

Plane: white, close grained. Sheraton refers to its use instead of beech for painted furniture. The sycamore is sometimes called Scottish plane.

Plum: deep reddish heartwood surrounded by yellowish tones. Country furniture and some inlay.

Poplar: whitish with yellow or grey tinge, close textured. Inlays, sometimes stained.

Robinia: *see* ACACIA.

Rosewood: dark brownish-purplish, with still darker figure, heavy, dense. Sometimes in solid, but mainly veneer. Kingwood is of same genus and the two are often confused.

Satinwood: golden tones with wonderful sheen. Obtained from West Indies and East Indies during second half of 18th century. The West Indies wood shows somewhat richer grain, the East Indies being paler with dark streaks but, according to Sheraton, 'runs narrow and is used only for cross bandings'. Satinwood was popular again around 1860–85.

Silverwood: *see* HAREWOOD.

Snakewood: deep reddish-brown, marked with dark spots and rings, hard. A veneer in late 18th century and the Regency.

Spruce: a kind of fir, white, soft, used for joinery. The term spruce found in early documents has been thought to be a corruption from Prussia, and hence a term for goods shipped from the Baltic ports, especially spruce chests.

Sycamore (in England a species of maple or false-plane): white when young, yellowing with age, some with rippled grain. Close grain, but not difficult to cut and used for turnery and veneers. Also stained, as silverwood or harewood.

Teak: brown, oily, heavy but durable for garden and ship furniture, etc.

Tulip wood: yellowish to red with stripes, hard, heavy. Related to rosewood and kingwood. Used for bandings, etc.

Wainscot: by early 17th century this was the accepted term for the planks used in furniture making and panelling imported from the Baltic and Low Countries and generally implies oak. Smaller sizes of split oak were known as clapboard.

Walnut: two species used for furniture—*juglans regia* and *juglans nigra*. *J. regia* of England, France, Italy: light brown or golden tones with fine markings. Used for furniture of high quality from 16th century and immensely popular after 1660 in solid and veneers, including burr walnut. Scarce after 1709 and unobtainable from France after 1720. Houghton, 1700, noted that the best came from Virginia, polished with its own oil to 'look black and sleek'. Walnut furniture was used through most of the 18th century.

Willow: white to pinkish, soft, but tough and light. Often dyed black as ebony substitute.

Wych elm: *see* ELM.

Yew: reddish-brown, hard, elastic. Solid wood for country furniture; its springy strength made it popular for Windsor chairs. As veneer and for parquetry and in burr veneer when it resembled amboyna (q.v.).

Zebrawood: light and dark stripes, strong. Cross bandings, etc.

Bibliography

Histories and Surveys

Aaronson, Joseph	*The Encyclopaedia of Furniture.* 3rd edition revised. London, 1966.
Boger, L. A.	*The Complete Guide to Furniture Styles.* London, 1961.
Gloag, John	*A Social History of Furniture Design from BC 1300 to AD 1960.* London, 1966.
	A Shorter Dictionary of Furniture. London, 1952.
Hayward, H.	*World Furniture.* Edited by H. Hayward. London, 1965.
Ramsey, L. G. G.	*Connoisseur Guide to Furniture.* Edited by L. G. G. Ramsey. London, 1961.
Reeves, D.	*Furniture: an Explanatory History.* London, 1948.
Schmitz, Dr. H.	*The Encyclopaedia of Furniture.* Revised edition. London, 1926.

English Furniture – General

Bracket, Oliver	*English Furniture Illustrated.* Revised edition. London, 1950.
Edwards, Ralph and P. Macquoid	*The Dictionary of English Furniture.* Revised edition. London, 1954.
Edwards, Ralph	*The Shorter Dictionary of English Furniture.* London, 1964.
Fastnedge, Ralph	*English Furniture Styles, 1500 to 1830.* London, 1955.
Gloag, John	*English Furniture with some furniture of other countries in the Irwin Untermyer Collection.* Introduction by John Gloag. London, 1958.
	English Furniture. Revised edition. London, 1965.
	The English Tradition in Design. London, 1959.
Gordon, H.	*Old English Furniture: A Simple Guide.* London, 1948.
Heal, Sir Ambrose	*The London Furniture Makers.* London, 1953.
Hughes, Therle	*Old English Furniture.* Revised edition. London, 1963.
Joy, E. T.	*The Country Life Book of English Furniture.* London, 1964.
	English Furniture. London, 1962.

BIBLIOGRAPHY

Macquoid, P.   *A History of English Furniture.* 4 vols. London, 1904.
Rogers, C.   *English Furniture.* Revised edition. London, 1950.
Symonds, R. W.   *Masterpieces of English Furniture and Clocks.* London, 1940.
                        The Present State of Old English Furniture. London, 1921.
Wolsey, S. W. and   *English Furniture: The Specialist Craftsman.*
R. W. P. Luff   London, 1962.

English Furniture – Period Studies

Aslin, Elizabeth   *19th Century English Furniture.* London, 1962.
Cescinsky, H. and   *Early English Furniture and Woodwork,* London,
E. R. Gribble   1922.
Cescinsky, H.   *English Furniture of the 18th Century.* 3 vols. London, 1909–11
Clouston, R. S.   *English Furniture and Furniture Makers of the 18th Century.* London, 1906.
Coleridge, Anthony   *Furniture Making in 17th and 18th Century England.* London, 1955.
                        Chippendale Furniture. London, 1968.
Fastnedge, Ralph   *Sheraton Furniture.* London, 1962.
                        Regency Furniture. Revised edition. London, 1965.
Harris, E.   *The Furniture of Robert Adam.* London, 1963.
Hayward, H.   *Thomas Johnson and English Rococo.* London, 1964.
Jourdain, Margaret   *Georgian Cabinet Makers.* 3rd revised edition.
and Ralph Edwards   London, 1962.
Jourdain, Margaret   *English Furniture of the Georgian Period.* London,
and F. Rose   1953.
Jourdain, Margaret   *Regency Furniture.* Revised and enlarged edition. London, 1965.
Lenygon, F.   *Furniture in England, 1600–1760.* London, 1920.
Musgrave, Clifford   *Adam and Hepplewhite and Other Neo-Classical Furniture.* London, 1966.
                        Regency Furniture. London, 1962.
Nickerson, David   *English Furniture of the 18th Century.* London, 1963.
Reade, Brian   *Regency Antiques.* London, 1953.
Roe, F. Gordon   *Victorian Furniture.* London, 1952.
Symonds, R. W. and   *Victorian Furniture.* London, 1963.
B. B. Whineray
Symonds, R. W.   *English Furniture from Charles II to George II.* London, 1929.

BIBLIOGRAPHY

Tipping, H. A.   *English Furniture of the Cabriole Period*. London, 1922.

Victoria and Albert   *Catalogue of English Furniture and Woodwork:*
Museum   *I. Gothic and Early Tudor; II. Late Tudor and Early Stuart; III. Late Stuart to Queen Anne; IV. Georgian.* 4 vols. London, 1929–31.

Specialised Studies

Edwardes, Ernest L.   *The Grandfather Clock*. Altrincham, 1952.
Gloag, John   *The Englishman's Chair*. London, 1964.
Hayward, John   *Tables in the Victoria and Albert Museum.* London, 1961.
    Chests of Drawers and Commodes in the Victoria and Albert Museum. London, 1960.
Hughes, Bernard and   *Small Antique Furniture*. London, 1958.
   Therle Hughes
Hughes, Therle   *Cottage Antiques*. London, 1967.
Joy, E. T.   *The Country Life Book of Clocks*. London, 1967.
    The Country Life Book of Chairs. London, 1967.
Ormsbee, Thomas   *The Windsor Chair*. London, 1962.
Roe, F. Gordon   *Old Oak Furniture*. London, 1905.
    English Cottage Furniture. London, 1949.
Symonds, R. W.   *Veneered Walnut Furniture*. London, 1946.
    Old English Walnut and Lacquer Furniture. London, 1923.
Toller, Jane   *Antique Miniature Furniture*. London, 1966.

Reviews of Original Designs

Edwards, Ralph   *The Universal System of Household Furniture by Ince and Mayhew, 1762.* Reprint with preface by Ralph Edwards. London, 1960.
    Sheraton Furniture Designs from the Cabinet-Maker's and Upholsterer's Drawing Book 1791–4. Preface by Ralph Edwards. London, 1949.
Fastnedge, Ralph   *Shearer Furniture Designs from the Cabinet-Maker's London Book of Prices 1788.* Preface by Ralph Fastnedge. London, 1962.
Harris, John   *Regency Furniture Design from Contemporary Source Books 1803–26* London, 1961.
Symonds, R. W.   *The Ornamental Designs of Chippendale from The Gentleman and Cabinet-Maker's Director 1762.* With a preface by R. W. Symonds. London, 1949.
    Chippendale Furniture Designs, from The Gentleman and Cabinet-Maker's Director, 1762. With a preface by R. W. Symonds.

Index

Numerals in bold type refer to figure numbers

411